# Sustainability Policy

## Hastening the Transition to a Cleaner Economy

**STEVEN COHEN**
**WILLIAM EIMICKE**
**ALISON MILLER**

A Wiley Brand

*To Donna, Gabriella, Ariel, Karen, Annemarie, Balsam, Carol, and Gary*

# Contents

# Preface: The Role of Government in the Transition to a Sustainable Economy

## The Need for Governmental Sustainability Policy

It's a great paradox that at the moment the United States needs government the most, we don't seem to have one anymore. As students of public administration, we have been motivated by John F. Kennedy's call to public service. Throughout our careers, we have chosen to "ask not what our country could do for us," asking instead "what we could do for our country." Steve Cohen joined the Environmental Protection Agency (EPA) in the late 1970s, but six months into Ronald Reagan's presidential term, after he defined government as a problem rather than a calling, Cohen left the EPA and did not seek another government position. He was not alone; many left and many who were needed never arrived. State and local governments continued to attract the best and brightest of our young people, but fewer and fewer seemed interested in working in our nation's capital. Most headed for private nonprofits and for-profits. In Washington, public service went out of fashion, and was replaced by the ambition-fueled revolving door.

Today, Washington seems a place of palace intrigue, arcane policy debates, campaign cash, and a political spin on everything and everyone. In some respects the final breaking point may well have been the Obama administration's failure to launch a functioning web-based sign-up system for national healthcare. Over a half-century of struggle to establish national healthcare culminated with a sign-up process that didn't work. We now have a federal government so incompetent that it can't manage the contractors it hires to set up a website. President Reagan set in motion a self-fulfilling prophecy; government, at least the federal kind, has become a problem.

With this as the backdrop, we have a planet that is trapped in an economic system based on the one-time use of fossil fuels and other material resources. The population of our planet has grown from three billion when JFK took office to over seven billion today. We need to develop and deploy the technology to create a renewable resource-based economy. We simply cannot continue using up materials and dumping the waste in a hole in the ground.

The private sector cannot make the transition from a waste-based economy to a renewable one by itself. This transition can only happen if we can create a public–private partnership. This is nothing new; we've been through this before. The transformation from an agrarian economy to an industrial economy could not have been done under the *laissez-faire* economic philosophy of the early industrial age. Teddy Roosevelt and his allies understood that and began to regulate the marketplace. Food, drugs, labor, and monopolies were regulated at the start of the 20th century. Franklin Delano Roosevelt continued the process of increasing the role of government in our mixed economy. Government was needed to establish the rules of the game, a social safety net, transportation, energy, and water infrastructure. Now, as we begin the transition from a fossil-fuel–based economy to one based on renewable energy and other reusable resources, government has a critical role to play again.

While we are focusing here on the role of government, it is important to understand that the private sector has a much larger and even more important role to play in the transition to a sustainable economy. It is the private sector that produces the goods and services that modern life relies on. We like and want these goods and services, and without capitalism's power to motivate people and reduce inefficiency, there would be far fewer of these goods and services to consume. This is not an argument that government knows best. It is the argument that effective competition requires rules, referees, and meaningful penalties for anti-social, criminal behavior. We are saying that in a complex economy on a crowded planet, we need a set of rules that respond to the international stress and complexity that our global economy has created. Just as the regulation of Wall Street builds confidence in the public marketplace for capital, we need rules to ensure that economic life does not destroy the planet that provides us with food, air, and water.

The role of government in building a sustainable economy includes:

- Funding basic science needed for renewable energy and renewable resource technology.
- Using the tax system, government purchasing power, and other financial tools to steer private capital toward investment in renewable energy and other sustainability technologies and businesses.
- Investment in sustainability infrastructure, such as smart grids, electric vehicle charging stations, mass transit, waste management facilities, water filtration systems, and sewage treatment systems.
- Regulating land use and other private behaviors to minimize destruction of ecosystems.
- Working with private organizations as well as state and local government to ensure that the transition is well managed in the real world.
- Measuring our society's progress toward sustainability by developing and maintaining a system of generally accepted sustainability metrics. This in turn should facilitate the integration of sustainability into our overall management of organizations as well as the national economy.
- Selling or transferring sustainability technologies to the developing world.

## Funding Science and Providing Incentives for Private Investment

One of the fundamental tasks that can be done only by government is to fund the science needed to build the technological base for a sustainable economy. America's research universities remain the best in the world. They are funded by peer-reviewed, competitive, government grant programs. When coupled with the creativity hard-wired into American culture, they create a unique asset that can be used to develop a leadership position in sustainability technologies. The work of our scientists and engineers could not be more important. We need to develop a way to get off of fossil fuels and more efficiently store and use energy. We also need more effective ways of managing and recycling our waste stream. Government must fund the basic research and enough of the applied research to demonstrate possible profitability. The tax code must then provide private firms with incentives to invest capital in these new and speculative technologies.

## Funding Infrastructure

Just as government built ports, canals, dams, and highways—the infrastructure of the 19th and 20th centuries—it must build the energy, communications, and waste- and water-management infrastructure needed for the 21st century. Constructing and operating these facilities will probably be the work of private firms, but the vision and financing will need to come from taxpayers and their government. Infrastructure requires an imaginative and aggressive government. It cannot be seen as a residual category. The neglect of investment in infrastructure is obvious to even the most casual observer of America's political economy. Our roads, railways, water systems, electric grid, broadband speed, bridges, airports, and schools show signs of disinvestment and neglect. Our anti-government and anti-tax ideology has made investment difficult and will make the transition to a sustainable economy even more difficult.

## Setting and Enforcing Rules to Protect the Environment and Maximize Resource Efficiency

Anti-tax and anti-government sentiment is also reflected in reflexive opposition to so-called *job-killing* environmental regulations. Even though the economic benefits of environmental rules are far higher than their economic costs, our delegitimized federal government has not enacted any new environmental laws in over two decades. Many sustainability-oriented local officials understand the clear connection between environmental quality and economic growth; however, there is also a prevalent idea that economic growth must come at the expense of environmental quality. True financial gain can be secured through sustainable practices, which are much less costly—from an economic and societal standpoint—than remediation costs to fix polluted air, water, and land.

Our economy is more complex than ever, and more toxics have made their way into production processes than in the past. These facts mean that our country and world require rules that can keep pace with economic, demographic, and technological change. The food, water, and air that sustain human life must be protected, and only government oversight can ensure that such critical resources are maintained. Rules must prevent damage to the environment, and also ensure that energy efficiency, recycling, and environmental stewardship are integrated into our structures, institutions, and daily routines.

## Working to Ensure the Transition is Well-Managed

Making policies and setting rules is only the start of the process; these rules must be flexible in order to be adapted to a changing world. Implementing these policies will require the development of new organizational capacities. Very few new activities match the plans they are based on. Edicts from faceless bureaucrats reinforced by arrogant, tough-enforcement attitudes almost always backfire and should be avoided. As Steve Cohen's friend and retired EPA manager Ron Brand used to say, "Focus on the real work. There are no cash registers in headquarters." Revenues and expenditures are driven by the people on the production line delivering services and manufacturing goods. Once policies and strategies are developed and the money to implement them is allocated, the action shifts to operational management, assessment, and learning. It is a mistake to ignore operations management.

## Sustainability Metrics and Management

As management guru Peter Drucker famously stated, "You can't manage something if you can't measure it." Without metrics, you can't tell if the actions taken by management are making things better or worse. In some respects, sustainability metrics are as primitive as accounting was before the Great Depression. While the imposition of income and corporate taxes at the start of the 20th century resulted in the growth of the accounting profession, early accounting principles were not consistently applied. According to financial writer Andrew Beattie:

> In 1917, the Federal Reserve published *Uniform Accounting*, a document that attempted to set industry standards for how financials should be organized both for reporting tax and for financial statements. There were no laws to back the standards so they had little effect. The stock market crash of 1929 that launched the Great Depression exposed massive accounting frauds by companies listed on the NYSE. This prompted stricter measures in 1933, including the independent audit of a company's financial statements by public accountants before being listed on the exchange (Beattie, 2009).

Sustainability metrics are still under development. Each corporation, locality, and think tank seems to have its own favorite measures and methods. Some focus on physical issues such as water, waste, and energy, while others include issues of equity, fairness, and environmental justice. In the end, government will need to set reporting standards. Perhaps they will be integrated into standard accounting definitions and practices as the U.S. tax code evolves to encourage sustainability, or maybe a separate set of measures will be developed. We have proposed that the U.S. government establish a National Commission on Sustainability Metrics to bring academics, government officials, industry, labor, and environmentalists together to develop a set of generally accepted sustainability metrics.

## Transferring Technology to the Developing World

As the developed world makes the transition to a more sustainable, renewable resource-based economy, it is important that newly developing nations are provided with incentives to use the new technologies instead of older ones that might get cheaper as they are discarded by the developed world. Coal and coal-fired power plants could get very inexpensive as they are replaced by cleaner sources of energy, and if the United States lowers its greenhouse gas emissions while developing nations increase theirs, the climate will continue to be degraded. We believe that the mitigation of climate change will require new energy technology, but without effective technology transfer, the problem will remain. Fortunately, a variety of financial tools could be used to lower the cost of new technology for export to the developing world.

## Government Needs a Sophisticated, Agile Sustainability Policy

The issues identified here cannot be addressed by the private sector and the free market alone; they require government action. Unfortunately, it requires a degree of management savvy we have not seen in the United States' federal government in decades. The people that rolled out Obamacare, bailed out the financial system at the expense of the middle class, and invaded Iraq to destroy non-existent weapons of mass destruction will not be able to handle the management challenges of this transition. Nevertheless, there is no choice. The U.S. government will need to assume global leadership of the transition to a sustainable economy. The probability of this happening today is low. We see far more evidence of this capacity in local government than we do at the federal level.

The future well-being of this country and of the planet as a whole depends on the U.S. government playing a more strategic and future-oriented role to bring about the transition to a renewable, resource-based economy. This country seems to do its best work when confronted with a crisis. While this crisis has arrived, many people do not believe it is here. We need a national leader willing to communicate the need for change and a strategy for getting from here to there. While no one immediately comes to mind, perhaps someone will emerge.

# Acknowledgments

This book represents the work of a number of people, and we would like to acknowledge them here. First, we would like to thank Columbia University, where we all work, and President Lee Bollinger and Provost John Coatsworth. In particular, we'd also like to thank the School of International and Public Affairs (SIPA), under the leadership of Dean Merit E. Janow, as well as the Earth Institute, under the direction of Jeffrey Sachs. We would like to thank the staff of the Research Program on Sustainability Policy and Management, including Satyajit Bose, Dong Guo, Kelsie DeFrancia, and faculty advisory council members Michael Gerrard and Tanya Heikkila. We would also like to thank the research and editing efforts of our team of student and staff assistants that helped tremendously in the making of this book, including Earth Institute staff Hayley Martinez and Yasmin Williams, and research assistants Jacob Kaden, Kyle Marsh, and Rachael Lubitz.

**Steve Cohen** would also like to acknowledge a number of people that have taught him about public and environmental policy, especially the late Lester Milbrath, and Sheldon Kamieniecki, Marc Tipermas, Tony Khater, Bob O'Connor, and Tom Ingersoll. Steve would like to thank his family; his wife, Donna Fishman; his children, Gabriella Rose and Ariel Mariah; his parents, Marvin and Shirley; his brother, Robby; and his sisters, Judith and Myra.

**Bill Eimicke** thanks former New York City Mayor Ed Koch and former New York Governor Mario Cuomo; New York Governor Andrew Cuomo; FDNY Commissioner Salvatore Cassano; and Columbia University Provost John Coatsworth. Bill is grateful for the support and advice of his wife, Karen Murphy; his daughter, Annemarie; his dog, Balsam; and his horses, Clef, Just Foxy, and Golden Hare; and donkey, Paco.

**Alison Miller** would like to thank her co-authors—Steve Cohen, professor, mentor, boss, and colleague, and William Eimicke, colleague and advisor. Alison also acknowledges the other teachers and mentors who have had outsized impacts on her academic and professional careers: Matthew Hoffmann, whose undergraduate course on global environmental governance first led her on the path of environmental policy; Andrea Bollyky, Michael Klein, and Louise Rosen. She thanks her colleagues, past and present: Allison Ladue, Sarah Tweedie, Natalie Unwin-Kuruneri, Alix Schroder, Annie Hunt, Courtney Small, Davida Heller, and all of her professors and classmates in the MPA ESP program, who helped shaped her understanding of the world. She is ever grateful for the constant love and support of her family: Carol, Gary, Richard, Jaclyn, and Jonathan.

# 1

# What is Sustainability Management?

## Introduction

After decades at the periphery of public and private agendas, sustainability and environmental protection have emerged at the center of our economic and political dialogue. As consumption and population rise, the planet's resources are showing signs of strain, and energy, water, and waste management have added significant costs to the budgets of government and private organizations. Whereas many environmentalists are motivated solely by their love of nature, sustainability managers (who very well might love nature) focus on environmental preservation because they understand the importance of functioning ecosystems to human well-being. Safe water, air, and food are necessities, not luxuries. The ability to achieve sustainability is increasingly seen as an indicator of a well-run organization. As the private sector shifts toward sustainable practices, it brings us close to achieving the type of critical mass that can have a major effect on the global economy. In this chapter, we define sustainability management in public and private enterprises, describe its evolution, and introduce the management case for sustainability.

We will also take a look at the challenges that sustainable practices can present. In this chapter, we will discuss the evolution of the environmental movement, starting with its initial focus on preserving nature, then moving on to its expanded concern for public health and eventual focus on the transition to a renewable economy. The chapter then places sustainability management in the broader context of the evolution of the field of organizational management. In our view, no organization, and therefore no manager, can ignore what we term the *physical dimensions of sustainability*. Next, we will discuss the increased use of sustainability principles in management and the growing momentum behind these practices, especially in well-managed corporations and sophisticated municipal governments. This is followed by an analysis of the importance of sustainability metrics. It is difficult to manage the transition to a sustainable, renewable economy without knowing precisely what one looks like. Metrics are the key to setting concrete sustainability goals and tracking an organization's progress. The chapter then concludes by identifying some of the specific needs that must be met if we are to develop a sustainable, renewable economy.

## The Challenges of Sustainability

In the past several decades, we have developed what we sometimes call a *brain-based economy*. The high-value–added elements of modern economic life involve analytic concepts, technological development, mathematical models, communications, and creativity. We have developed a highly mechanized, energy-intensive, high-throughput economy that is using up the planet's resources at a ferocious pace. This has resulted in rising prices of raw materials and massive destruction of environmental resources that we rely on for "ecological services" such as clean water and air, which is provided free of charge. Shutting down this economy to prevent further damage is not an option. Instead, given the needs of the developing world, international economic production and consumption will grow dramatically through the 21st century. The only way this growth can be both achieved and maintained is if we pay far more attention to the natural resources affected by our economies and the impact of economic development on self-renewing, interconnected ecological systems.

The cost of mistakes such as the BP oil spill, GE's dumping of PCBs in the Hudson River, or America's toxic-waste clean-up program will continue to grow if we do not learn how to manage our organizations and their production according to the principles of environmental sustainability. Our planet is more crowded and resource-stressed than ever, and our global economy is more interdependent. Combined, these factors place increased demands on organizational management and inter-organizational networks. Consider that in the 1940s waste products were freely released into the air and water in unpopulated areas where they, supposedly, would not pose a risk to humans. Steel mills emitted so much pollution that people in Pittsburgh would often need to dust off their vehicles in the morning to see through the windshield. A more populous planet means that there aren't many remote places to dispose of waste, and we also now understand that toxics can stay in the atmosphere or water supply for decades and have a long-term impact on people and the environment. Coordination among the decentralized networks that produce the goods and services we depend on requires well-functioning transportation, water, and energy infrastructure. Our use of energy and consumption of raw materials dwarfs the consumption rate of that from a century ago. The management of our complex and interconnected economy and the maintenance of the planet that it depends on requires sophisticated sustainability managers in the private and public sectors and a set of environmental rules that can't be bargained away for short-term material wealth.

## Sustainability Management

What is sustainability management? The term sustainability itself has numerous definitions and interpretations. Consensus on the interpretation of sustainability remains elusive, despite decades of scholarly work and practical applications. The most commonly used definition is from the 1987 Brundtland Report, *Our Common Future*, which defined sustainable development as "development that meets the needs of the present without compromising the ability of future generations to meet their own needs" (World Commission on Environment and Development, 1987). Since then, the concept of sustainability management has developed from a conceptual understanding of development to prescriptive strategies that minimize environmental impact and maximize resource conservation. In Steven Cohen's 2011 work, *Sustainability Management*, he observed that: "Sustainability management is simply the organizational practices that result in sustainable development" (1).

Sustainability management is economic production and consumption that minimizes environmental impact and maximizes resource conservation and reuse. The depletion and degradation of our natural resources has changed the cost structure of production in all organizations. Leaders and managers must now double down on efforts to make efficient use of energy, water, and other raw materials, and must pay attention to the content and full cost of the waste produced by their production processes. The issue of sustainability is no longer an add-on to other factors routinely addressed by management; it has moved to the core of management concerns (Unruh, 2014). Following the lead of both private sector corporations and public sector policymakers, the field of sustainability management is focused on strategic analysis and implementation of the most effective technologies and policies.

This new field of study combines organizational management with the field of environmental policy (Cohen, 2011). Sustainability management is both a practical and long-term approach to organizational management. In some respects, a focus on sustainability is an effort to correct modern management, moving it away from the abstract world of financial manipulation and back to the concrete world of physical resources and constraints, which had traditionally been at the forefront of management's concern. The principles of sustainability management are built on an understanding of human dependence on nature for our well-being. Nature is not protected for its own sake, but for ours; this is a key difference between environmentalists and sustainability managers. These physical dimensions of sustainability can no longer be ignored. The field of sustainability management can help us manage our global economy, ensure long-term growth, and secure a sustainable material future, but we need public policies that encourage private management innovation and accelerate the transition to such a sustainable economy.

## The Evolution of the Environmental Movement

Many pundits and politicos are stuck in a 20th century notion of environmental protection and seem to have missed the transition to sustainability.

When the environment emerged as a political issue in the early 20th century it was all about Teddy Roosevelt–style wilderness conservation. The environment was thought of as a beautiful and even mystical resource, and its protection was seen as an issue for the elite. This definition is out of date, but has persisted since that time. In the 1960s and 1970s we became aware of the interconnectedness of the environment due to the superb analytic and communication skills of environmentalists such as Rachel Carson and Barry Commoner. Their work led to a redefinition of the environment as an issue of public health. We began to worry about environmental quality not because we loved nature, but because a polluted environment could make you sick. Commoner and Carson focused on the transport of toxics through the delicate interconnected web we call ecosystems. The connection of toxics to cancer and other diseases coincided with greater focus on public health by both governments and citizens.

While the issues of conservation and environmental health remain with us in the 21st century, the transformation of the environmental argument to one of sustainability has changed the issue's definition and brought it from the fringe to the center of the political agenda. Environmental quality was initially defined as something that might be expensive, but, if pursued, would bring benefits such as higher quality of life and better health. Just a few decades ago, environmental protection was an afterthought and was often done after production was complete by treating waste, effluent, or emissions at the end of a pipe. Similarly, waste treatment and disposal and site remediation were undertaken after consumption had taken place, but production processes remained the same. The sustainability perspective turns this traditional definition upside down.

In contrast to the outdated political debate regarding environmental protection—which incorrectly claims there is a trade-off between environmental protection and economic production—the sustainability management framework demonstrates that continued economic prosperity is dependent on the health of the environment. As the population of the planet grows and the consumption of land, food, water, energy, and raw materials grows along with it, we are learning that we cannot simply use stuff up, destroy the landscape, and move on to the next mountain or valley. The current approach to economic life has created a lifestyle previous generations couldn't even dream of, but it cannot be sustained without a revolution in management, technology, and scientific understanding of our home planet.

## The Sustainability Perspective

Sustainability is an effort to sustain production today without impairing our ability to produce in the future. Our goal is not conservation of resources, but the continued productive use of them. We do not conserve resources for posterity, but we manage resources for their continued use. If a resource can be used only once, we try to learn how to reuse it for another purpose or try to avoid using it when possible. Burning fossil fuels for energy is an excellent example of a one-time use of a natural resource. Once it is burned, it is gone. A sustainability perspective might try to reserve the use of these resources for plastics and building materials. Our goal is to base our consumption on resources that can be grown or renewed. A sustainability perspective would lead a CEO to question an entire production process to see if there was some way to manufacture the same good or service without generating pollution and waste in the first place.

The sustainability perspective is an effort to use design, engineering, and public policy to make economic production and consumption efficient and effective. Pollution that poisons people or the planet may have some short-term benefits, but our experience with environmental remediation and restoration tells us that these short-term benefits expire quite rapidly, and are soon replaced by longer-term costs (Lubber, 2008). We might make $50 million selling the good that resulted in pollution, but the pollution might well cost $500 million to clean up. If you are in doubt, ask BP about the costs of restoring the Gulf of Mexico, or ask GE about the costs of dredging PCBs from the Hudson River. Organizations may benefit in the short run, but someone must eventually pay to clean up the mess. When looking at business practices from the sustainability perspective, we ask if there is a way to make the $50 million without paying the $500 million in clean-up costs. Clean-up costs may seem optional, but if the alternative is to allow a key resource to be destroyed, the cost must be paid. Since 1980 and for the foreseeable future, America's military, industries, and citizens will be paying hundreds of billions of dollars to clean up the toxic wastes dumped throughout the 20th century. China will soon be facing a similar clean-up bill (*The Economist*, 2013).

In sustainability management, environmental protection and efficient use of resources are central throughout the production process rather than a clean-up step tacked on at the end. The best run organizations try to minimize their use of non-renewable resources and reduce their environmental and carbon footprints. Companies like Walmart do this because they see it as a way to reduce costs and increase revenues. Sustainability becomes yet another cost advantage that helps a company beat the competition. The best, most effective managers will be sustainability managers, and the best-run organizations will adhere to sustainability principles because they lead to stable, long-term production and, in the private sector, profitability (Locke, 2009, 2).

Corporations traditionally focus on short-term gains over everything else, but sustainability management requires that organizations learn how to think about the long term instead of focusing exclusively on weekly, quarterly, or daily reports (Lubber, 2008). In a world of global, 24/7 electronic media; never-ending financial exchange; and low-cost information and communication, the pressure for immediate information, accomplishment, and gratification is overwhelming. Election cycles in politics have become endless, and corporations are no longer managed to the quarter or year, but to the minute. If we are to achieve a sustainable economy and learn how to consume without destroying this planet's productive capacity, we must figure out a way to slow down the management merry-go-round.

## Evolution of Organizational Management

Sustainability is simply the latest step in the past century's evolution of the field of organizational management. The development of the modern field of management began in the 19th and early 20th centuries with the development of mass-production techniques, like the assembly line, followed by the start of modern human resource management. Later, we saw the development of generally accepted accounting principles (GAAP) and the evolution of the chief financial officer (CFO). From the 1960s to the 1990s, advances in computing and communications technology resulted in the growth of non-financial performance indicators in nearly all organizations. Well-run organizations established chief information officers (CIOs) to manage the exponential increase in information pouring in and out of the organization. By the end of the 20th century, the growth of the global economy required that many organizations increase their capacity to operate internationally. The modern CEO must now understand all of it: production, finance and financial management, human resource management, information management, and international trade and commerce.

Now, more than a decade into the 21st century, organizational management needs another dimension: *a physical one.* In the mid-20th century, water, energy, and waste were minor factors in an organization's cost equation. Those days are gone. On an increasingly crowded planet, the scale of production of everything has grown and with it we see an increased draw on the earth's finite resources. The costs of water, raw materials, and energy are an increasingly important part of the cost calculus for the modern organization. Waste disposal is no longer cheap or free and the organization that figures out a way to reduce and reuse waste has a significant cost advantage over organizations that do not.

Organizations that seek to cut costs without sacrificing quality can simultaneously become more efficient while becoming sustainable. Making investments in sustainable projects are similar to other investments, for which you measure a return on investment. The return on investment is sometimes slower to develop and less certain than traditional technologies, presenting a challenge to early adopters. However, often these sustainability strategies lead to a more holistic shift in thinking, resulting in "reorganizing, redesigning processes, [and] investing in process improvement" (Sterman, 2009, 5). Moreover, corporations are learning that wasting energy and other resources costs money and can make them less competitive (Haanaes et al., 2012, 3). This paradigm shift is the move from pure environmentalism to sustainability management.

What are these physical dimensions? First there is resource use: water, air, energy, and other materials used in production. Are these resources used efficiently and returned to the ecosphere undamaged? Second are the processes used to produce goods and services. Do production processes pay attention to the use of resources and work to minimize their ecological and carbon footprint? Or does the organization's culture dismiss waste and pollution as necessary "breakage," arguing that you can't make an omelet without breaking some eggs? If you think this way of thinking is only limited to manufacturing, you have not considered the vast amount of energy used by data farms that host "cloud" computing; or that all organizations work in a built environment and some office buildings are green and others are not. Finally, there is the impact of the organization's product and waste on the environment. Does the organization pay attention to its environmental impact and seek to minimize it?

All of these physical issues are now central to routine management. They cannot be dismissed with the old economic cop-out of "assuming all things are held equal." Environmental and physical factors cannot be "assumed away." These factors can be as important to management's decision making as issues of finance, labor, and strategy. Managers can no longer focus all of their attention on finance, marketing, information, labor, and communication; they must also focus on the physical dimensions of organizational life. The paradox is that in the early and pre-industrial age, physical resources were of paramount importance. Wars were fought for raw materials and good farmland. In some respects, the sustainability perspective simply reasserts the centrality of physical or material factors of production.

The physical dimensions of sustainability require that modern managers learn some science. Management education must include some of the basics of ecology, environmental science, engineering, design, hydrology, and, possibly, toxicology, so that managers can better pay attention to the use and cost of natural resources, the costs of waste production and disposal, and the environmental impact of organizational outputs and waste. These physical dimensions of sustainability are an increasing percentage of an organization's cost structure. They can no longer be wished away; too many people are at risk of exposure to industrial poisons. Under the sustainability framework, organizations:

- Efficiently use raw materials to reduce the creation of waste;
- Shift to renewable or recycled materials;
- Look for innovative materials or processes that have a softer impact on the environment; and
- Seek to build structures that take advantage of their location and use design and engineering to minimize their environmental impact and use of natural resources such as water and energy.

The idea, based in part on an engineering field called industrial ecology, is to manufacture goods without emitting pollutants. This is accomplished through the use of closed systems that ensure that all resources end up in some form of production (Gallopoulos, 2006, 10). Sustainability does not trade off environment and wealth; it is built on the premise that the environment is a major source of our wealth. Careful use of natural resources makes a company, organization, or city more efficient and more profitable. Wasting energy and water does not add to a company's profits, market share, or return on equity. Examples abound. Walmart requires its vendors to demonstrate sustainability to keep costs down along with environmental impacts. Hewlett-Packard collects empty toner cartridges and re-manufactures them, making money on the exchange rather than losing it. New York City is in the process of planting one million trees, and by doing so, it not only reduces air pollution and global warming, but also makes the city a more attractive place to live, which lifts housing values and tax revenues. The city also saves money by relying on New York's natural upstate ecosystem for water filtration rather than building a multi-billion–dollar filtration plant.

We believe that within a decade the definition of effective management will include sustainability management. In the same way that financial reporting and information technology were once new and distinctive management functions, today they are fully integrated into management routines. Sustainability management will develop in the same way. Corporations are taking substantive action, leading to the gradual development of industry standards, reporting frameworks, and standardized accounting practices. The field has developed from a defensive strategy to a competitive one.

## The Growing Momentum behind Sustainability Management

As noted earlier, the sustainability ethos that has entered our culture should not be confused with environmentalism. There are several forces within our marketplace and culture that are driving the sustainability agenda. First, there is the public relations value of being seen as a green company. No one wants to be known as an indifferent destroyer of nature and human health. Second is the growing cost of energy, materials, and waste management and the fact that a more carefully designed product that requires less energy to manufacture reduces costs and can lead to a higher profit margin and market share. A third factor is the growing body of environmental liability law and the costs of the liability defense and court-imposed penalties borne by corporations (Locke, 2009, 2). However, while dollars and image are important drivers of sustainability, a deeper change is underway in our culture and dominant social paradigm, our shared view about how the world works. People are starting to pay more attention to their impact on the planet, and the planet's impact on people. We are paying more attention to nutrition, exercise, and to the environmental impact of our lifestyles. The importance of this cultural shift should not be underestimated, and managers should see this type of social intelligence as a business asset that guides day-to-day decision making (Unruh, 2014).

A growing number of people are concerned about our ability to maintain and improve our quality of life on an increasingly crowded and resource-stressed planet. Young people have heard their parents speak about these issues in their daily conversations. They have grown up hearing about the price and occasional scarcity of gasoline, higher energy and water bills, the increased level of auto traffic, and changed patterns of land use—places where their parents once hiked and camped now house strip malls and residential developments. The U.S. population is now 317 million (United States Census Bureau, 2014). In 1960 it was about 179 million. Over the same half century, the planet's population grew from about three to seven billion. People understand what population growth means, and the idea that we should consume lower levels of energy, water, and raw materials in our daily lives is increasingly conventional wisdom. This does not mean we don't want the latest iPad or smartphone, nor does it mean we are going to live off the grid, but it does mean that we like it when the companies making these products are working to reduce their environmental impacts. Moreover, we are more likely to buy products that reflect green principles and we are starting to consider green design to be an element of higher quality. A product designed to ignore sustainability factors is seen by some as shoddy and second rate.

Mass culture both drives and sets the boundary conditions for political agendas and political legitimacy. Consumer purchasing behavior drives top companies like Walmart, Cisco, and HSBC to take sustainability seriously. A 2009 study by the Aberdeen Group found that top performers in sustainability had a 16 percent increase in customer retention rates (Environmental Leader, 2009). Nike, for example, wouldn't be doing this without the support of the marketplace. A politician ignoring these trends is asking for trouble come Election Day. Gay rights, the changing role of women in the workplace and society in general, healthier diet and exercise regimens, and increased concern for sustainability are reflections of how we live today. Public concern for environmental sustainability is now hardwired into our culture. Companies and elected officials are beginning to understand this and many believe that their continued success is built on this understanding.

The desire for quick profits, rapid development, and massive fossil fuel use is a tidal wave that is built on a set of values and beliefs that will take generations to reverse. Still, the slow process of change is underway. Here in America and certainly in Europe, we have seen a limit to the public's tolerance of overt and obvious environmental destruction. China and India are beginning to learn those lessons too, although a commitment to sustainability has not yet taken hold.

## The Expansion of Corporate Sustainability

A common method of examining and understanding the growth of sustainability and the green economy is to look at the expansion of corporate sustainability at the executive level. Organizations that integrate a framework of sustainability into their operations emphasize long-term planning from the top levels of management. These organizations:

- Examine operations from a long-term perspective in addition to their concern for daily, weekly, monthly, quarterly, or even annual analyses;
- Integrate costs of environmental damages into their financial analysis; and
- Integrate this thinking within organizational routines and standard operating procedures.

The fundamentals of sustainability require large organizations to think through the long-term impacts of their strategies and actions. It may help the next quarterly financial report if an organization dumps waste into a river instead of learning how to reduce waste and even reuse it, but the organization could eventually be required to pay for the costs—financial and reputational—of this destruction.

The fact that companies are institutionalizing sustainability is supported by a variety of surveys and studies over the past few years, indicating a significant increase in only a decade. A 2011 study by MIT Sloan acknowledged that sustainability management was no longer on the fringe of a company's operations (Haanaes et al., 2012). Respondents to their annual survey of global executives reported that they would continue to adopt sustainable strategies and that they were profiting from these strategies. The study reported growing commitments from companies, with resource-intensive industries continuing to lead the way. It also reported a new group of sustainability actors, which they termed "harvesters," or companies that generate profit from their sustainability actions. They also found that those organizations that have strong executive commitment for sustainability projects reported greater profitability (Kiron et al., 2013). Their report stated: "68% of respondents say their organizations increased their commitment to sustainability in the past year. That's a dramatic increase from 2009, when only 25% of respondents said that . . . 67% say that sustainability strategies are necessary to be competitive. That's a 12 percentage point increase from last year" (Brokaw, 2011).

A similar 2012 study conducted by Siemens and McGraw-Hill Construction also reported a growth in the importance of sustainability. This study tracked progress in sustainability and reported that 42 percent of companies "say sustainability plays a key role in their business operations," which was up from 18 percent in 2006 (Environmental Leader, 2012). In addition, a growing number of analysts are beginning to equate a company's capacity to include environmental factors in decision making as an indicator of excellence in management.

Private corporations will typically seek higher profits, return on equity, and market share. That is a given and must be understood. Corporate sustainability officers describe how they work with their colleagues to demonstrate the financial benefits of resource efficiency, recycling, and effective waste management. Engineers are starting to understand and apply the principles of closed-system industrial ecology. The growing costs of energy and waste management have caused industry to not only reduce waste but to make capital investments needed to accomplish efficiency and other sustainability goals.

## Sustainable Cities

We have learned the importance of ecological resources the hard way, but the good news is that there is growing awareness of the importance of protecting the environment; the same cultural sentiments that have pushed corporations to become more sustainable have driven local governments to take action as well. This increased awareness does not see environmental protection as an end but as a means, particularly with the wide acceptance of the realities of climate change. Local level sustainability plans are being developed to address infrastructure issues; improve use of materials, water, and energy; and to enhance our systems of waste management and waste reduction. New York City and other places have made the clear connection between environmental sustainability and quality of life. They are looking to lower costs and improve services from interruptions due to climate and extreme weather impacts or congestion. Cities are pursuing energy efficiency, cleaner air, enhanced parks and mass transit, greater availability of local and organic food, and recycling as ways to make urban areas more attractive places to live. Local governments are doing this because they believe they are in a global competition with other cities for businesses, residents, and tourists.

Local municipal governments have emerged recently as both laboratories for sustainability policies and programs and as leaders in creating and implementing sustainability and climate change action plans. This trend is significant for a variety of reasons, most notably that the global population is increasingly urban and that cities uniquely control important policy levers that many national governments do not. In 2007, for the first time in history, a majority of the world's population lived in cities, and the United Nations has estimated that urban populations will almost double by 2050 (WHO, 2014). In addition, the world's cities consume between 60 and 80 percent of energy production worldwide and account for roughly two-thirds of global carbon dioxide emissions (Kamal-Chaoui and Robert, 2009). More efficient water and energy use, more cost-effective waste management, reduced traffic congestion, and cleaner air are all needed to make cities more sustainable in the long run. Cities provide many important local services and operate related facilities, giving them a unique ability to take specific measurable action to reduce the use of fossil fuels and to develop a more ecologically sound water supply and sewage and solid waste management system (Svara, 2011). They have direct control over critical systems like water, waste and recycling, and public transit, and they also determine building and zoning codes, local smoking regulations, and other rules that govern commerce and citizens' behavior.

Adopting sustainability practices is central to urban vitality and to making cities desirable places both for businesses and residents. Cities are turning to sustainable solutions that will attract residents, stimulate economic growth, and encourage healthier lifestyles based on renewable resources.

## Measuring Sustainability

It is clear that businesses and nonprofit organizations increasingly value sustainability and are acting on it more each year. But, how do they measure this growth and how do they define the success of sustainability efforts? Similar to measuring the size of the green economy and the number of green jobs, measuring sustainability is both complex and essential to the long-term transition to a renewable-resource–based economy. Sustainability efforts are measured in many ways and by many organizations, including companies themselves, external standards groups, non-governmental organizations, government agencies, consulting firms, and academics. The goal of these efforts is to provide clarity and reduce confusion among consumers, investors, and shareholders who are trying to distinguish real sustainability performance from greenwashing or mere symbolic acts. The measurement of organizational sustainability is critical for several reasons:

- By measuring which sustainable technologies are being adopted, corporations, investors, and the government can gear policies accordingly.
- By comparing efforts within specific types of organizations, standards can emerge, collaboration can occur through working groups for innovative solutions, and organizations can gauge their own progress by comparison to similar organizations.
- Individuals and organizations can make better, more informed purchasing decisions.
- Increased participation and promotion will incentivize organizations to continue to act in meaningful ways.

To overcome the perceived barriers to change, decision makers need clear metrics that demonstrate the benefits of sustainable practices to help guide their strategies. There are lots of case studies, consumer and corporate executive surveys, and anecdotal material on sustainability management. Fortunately, we are also finally starting to see some more quantitative performance analyses. Unfortunately, there is no common method to measure sustainability. A large array of sustainability reporting and measurement standards, scorecards, and platforms has emerged, and organizations must decide how to navigate the increasingly busy terrain.

The ability to accurately measure sustainability is crucial to achieving sustainable development goals at every level, and the need to quantify concepts of sustainability into metrics or indicators has been well documented in the academic literature over the last decade (Azapagic and Perdan, 2000; Székely and Knirsch, 2005; Tanzil and Beloff, 2006). On the applied side, a variety of organizations have developed their own scorecards, indices, ratings, tools, and programs to help organizations measure, track, and report sustainability. Building on frameworks and aggregation methodologies outlined in the academic literature, some sustainability practitioners have attempted to select relevant indicators and develop "global" indices or frameworks to measure sustainability.

For example, since 1999, the Global Reporting Initiative (GRI) has been working to establish a credible set of sustainability indicators using four key areas of performance and impact: economic, environmental, social, and governance. These guidelines are among the most commonly used for sustainability reporting, and GRI aims to become the leader in universal standards for organizations of every size, sector, or location. GRI provides general indicator guidelines as well as sector-specific guidance, both of which are refined and updated over time. The Sustainability Accounting Standards Board (SASB) is a nonprofit engaged in the creation and dissemination of sustainability accounting standards for use by publicly listed corporations to disclose sustainability indicators for the benefit of investors and the public. SASB is developing sector-specific standards that it hopes will allow all stakeholders to understand environmental, social and corporate governance (ESG) metrics and ensure reliable comparison. By focusing on industry-specific standards, they expect to be able to compare apples to apples.

Despite these notable efforts and many other organizations like them, sustainability metrics in general lack universal comparability, assurance of reliability and rigor, and materiality. Each organization interested in improving sustainability must still determine what to measure, how to assess and differentiate between important and irrelevant information, what organization(s) they should report to, and what reporting or benchmarking organizations they can depend on for reliable sustainability frameworks and analysis. We have a long way to go if we are to develop adequate sustainability metrics.

According to Arthur Lyon Dahl, President of the International Environment Forum, "These multiple initiatives have all helped to advance the science of sustainability measurement, but we are still far from what most would consider adequate indicators of sustainability" (Dahl, 2012, 15). No sustainability metric has emerged as a standard. The theoretic work by academics to understand sustainability measurement systems and sustainability indicators, and the practical tools built by companies and various other actors across sectors are all important steps towards advancing sustainability, but they are not enough. We need to do more. We need a generally accepted set of definitions and indicators for measuring sustainability.

The loose boundaries of the definition of sustainability leave decision makers at a disadvantage as they try to understand how and what to manage to improve their sustainability performance. To facilitate the shift toward a more sustainable economy, an improved system of measurement and management tools are needed. Ultimately, we need to develop, for the physical dimensions of environmental sustainability, a set of generally accepted metrics that replicates the applicability and universality of traditional financial indicators and generally accepted accounting principles (GAAP). Best practices in sustainability management need to be based on solid evaluation research and systematic benchmarking studies rather than mythology and anecdotes. Without measurement, you cannot tell if your management action is making the situation better or worse. Sustainability metrics must be further developed and must guide decision making in businesses and organizations, as well as chart local, state, and even national progress toward a sustainable economy. In our view, these measures will need to be developed and codified by governments, and their validity, reliability, and accuracy will require the same enforceable system of audit and control that the financial data of publicly traded corporations are subject to.

## Toward a Sustainable, Renewable Economy

In the past several decades, we have developed a highly mechanized, energy intensive, high-throughput economy that is rapidly chewing up the planet's resources. There is a fundamental need to understand basic environmental processes in order to effectively manage anything in an increasingly challenging world. If we do not develop an economic system less dependent on the one-time use of natural resources, then it is inevitable that energy, water, food, and all sorts of critical raw materials will become more and more expensive. The development of a sustainable, renewable resource-based economy has become a necessity. Endangered sea turtles and polar bears need healthy ecosystems, but so does the species we all belong to—the human species. Energy and climate are just some of the first places we see the strain on the global biosphere, but they won't be the last.

If the status quo continues, we will outpace our capability to extract enough natural resources to sustain our economy and our quality of life. Currently, we do not have the capacity to manage the planet. We do not yet know how to produce the food, energy, water, air, and other biological necessities required to sustain human life and maintain a healthy global ecosystem. In order to develop those capacities, we need to invest resources in:

- **Earth observation:** Earth, atmospheric, ocean, and ecosystem science. We need a better understanding of the impact of our productive technologies on the planet.
- **Technology:** We need to learn how to make and use renewable energy, food, air, and water.
- **Organizational capacity:** We need people with the skills to understand and overcome obstacles to sustainability. This will require enhanced scientific literacy and a new rulebook that rewards and does not punish long-term thinking.
- **Public policy:** Government must develop a regulatory structure and set of proactive programs that promote sustainability technology and rules of the game that punish organizations that plunder the planet.

We have begun the effort to develop the technological and organizational capacity needed for sustainability, but we have a long way to go before we have completed this work.

It is easy to dismiss sustainability as a fad; globalization, information technology, and the Internet were similarly described in their early years. On a planet with a population of seven billion people, it is a fact that we need to conserve and reuse resources and build a renewable global economy. The rapid growth of nations in Asia and Latin America and the continued consumption in the developed world makes sustainability a necessity. From a sustainability standpoint, the environment is not a luxury that we should preserve so we can enjoy its beauty; our very survival depends on it. The serious attention being paid to the emerging green economy by government and business is not a public relations exercise, but a paradigm shift. It is clear evidence that the transition to a sustainable economy has begun. What we need now is a policy framework that recognizes these new realities and moves beyond the environmental legal structure we created between 1970 and 1990. This new framework must promote innovative policies at all levels of government.

A major goal of this book is to provide an overview of the public policies that encourage the transition to sustainability management. In the subsequent chapters we analyze regulatory structures, tax policies, government programs, and public–private partnerships to demonstrate what works and what does not. We want to debunk the anti-government bias we see by identifying effective public policies along with less effective or ineffective ones. Sustainability also requires public–private partnerships and we are determined to focus attention on public actions, private actions, and the interactions between them. We also highlight the important work of private organizations in sustainability, and discuss the political factors that can facilitate or impede the transition to more sustainable organizational behaviors and, ultimately, to a more sustainable economy based on renewable resources.

We seek to present an overview of policies to encourage and support sustainability. We will use case studies and examples to introduce what is working, what is not working and what is possible. While our focus is on the United States, we examine policies, legislation, and programs from cities and nations across the globe. This is because we understand that we are all part of a global economy, and the economic, cultural, and political happenings in one place affect other places in ways like never before. We as a nation do not work in isolation, so we need to understand what is happening in other parts of the world, especially considering the rapid economic growth in countries like China and India that is leading to a greater use of energy and more harmful emissions released into the atmosphere. Our interconnectedness and interdependency will only continue to rise.

We also understand that innovation is happening all over the world, and that some governments outside the United States are doing a better job at transitioning the economy to one based on renewable energy. Our attention here is also on policy tools feasible in the United States, with examples to demonstrate their current and potential application and capacity for innovation. The United States can learn from the policy options and innovative initiatives that are happening in localities across the world, from the European Union Emissions Trading Scheme for carbon, the largest of its kind, to TransMilenio, an award-winning bus rapid transit system in Bogota, Colombia. Our goal, to paraphrase Rene Dubos, is to look globally in order to act locally.

In this chapter, we have defined sustainability management and discussed the business case for sustainability. In Chapter 2, we present the role of the public sector in sustainability management, and why government is so important to the transition to a sustainability economy. Chapter 3 will describe the portfolio of policy tools at the federal level, while Chapters 4 and 5 will do so for the state and local levels, respectively. Chapter 6 will describe the efforts at measuring and evaluating sustainability initiatives within both private corporations and public sector organizations. In Chapter 7, we provide an analysis of the politics of sustainability at the U.S. federal level and how public opinion factors into sustainability policy. Finally, Chapter 8 concludes the book with a discussion of expectations of future sustainability management and policy in the United States and what we hope and expect to see happen in the next decade.

# 2 | Why We Need Sustainability Public Policy

## Introduction

Environmental sustainability is an important and growing field in the United States and globally, as stakeholders across private industries embrace sustainability efforts. Production processes based on renewable resources and consumption practices that reclaim waste products are vital elements of a sustainable global economy. The global economy is on a positive trajectory; we are investing globally in clean energy, displacing fossil fuel energy sources from the marketplace, and expanding efficiency like never before. A growing number of organizations value sustainability for its impact on the cost of production and the public is increasingly adjusting its habits in effort to become more sustainable.

Much of the work to advance sustainability will occur in the private sector; however, governments at all levels have immense influence on promoting sustainability across the private and within the public sectors. Government can support sustainability efforts in the same way the public sector has helped build other sectors of the economy such as agriculture, energy and housing. Through a mix of policy tools including tax credits, taxes, grant funding, and expedited permitting, and regulations such as zoning laws, building codes, and renewable portfolio standards, all levels of government are influencing the growth of sustainability. This chapter presents a brief survey of policies that have the ability to augment positive trends in the sustainable economy. While many of these policies focus on energy—a critical component of a sustainable economy—we look at policies that touch on all aspects of sustainability including energy, water, waste, ecosystem services, air, and so on. In subsequent chapters, we will analyze these policies in greater detail, examining them and presenting examples that demonstrate their actual or potential impact.

We begin by discussing why renewable energy is the key to a sustainable economy, and the critical importance and role of the public sector in making the transition to sustainability; we also consider why the private sector cannot achieve this transition without government assistance. We then turn to a discussion of the specific role we believe that government should play in the transition to a sustainable economy.

There are five government functions that are necessary to support the development of sustainable management practices in both the public and private sectors.

1. *Funding of basic scientific research:* The development of new technology is essential to this transition and most corporations cannot afford to engage in the level of research required to advance sustainability initiatives. Even in applied work, unless the payoff is rapid, private companies cannot justify the use of resources for this work.

2. *Funding of sustainable infrastructure:* Mass transit, water treatment, waste management, smart grids, and even research facilities are key here. These community resources have long been a responsibility of government and even in this era of U.S. anti-government sentiment, it is a critical role that only government can play.

3. *Use of the tax structure to provide incentives to direct private capital toward sustainability investments:* The goal here is to provide a positive environment to reinforce corporate sustainability.

4. *Use of regulatory rules and enforcement to prevent unsustainable economic activities:* Companies cannot be permitted to obtain short-term private profit at the expense of long-term public clean-up costs.

5. *Development and maintenance of a system of generally accepted sustainability measures:* We cannot manage what we cannot measure.

Sustainability is measured in many different ways. Government must work with private parties to develop acceptable common metrics.

## The Need for a Renewable Energy Economy

Energy is at the core of the sustainability challenge. Most of the production, transportation, and everyday processes that we depend on daily are energy intensive. We not only need to make these processes more energy efficient, but also need to power them with renewable sources if we are to develop a long-term sustainable economy. Enhanced energy efficiency can help us reduce demand as we reach peak production capacity. Energy efficiency saves money for consumers and lessens the pressure on utilities to increase their energy-production capacities. However, economic and population growth increase energy demand and, therefore, increasing energy efficiency will not be enough. We also need to develop renewable energy technologies to meet the growing global demand for energy.

With government investment in research and development, renewable energy technology can advance enough to become a low-cost alternative to fossil fuel use. This transition to lower-cost renewable energy is in progress, but we still have a long way to go. In the meantime, efforts to extract more fossil fuels using methods such as hydraulic fracturing (also called *fracking* or *hydrofracking*) and mountaintop removal for coal risk long-term damage to the environment. We need more government regulation of these practices in order to ensure the safety and health of our environment. The goal of government policy is not to raise the price of fossil fuels through regulation, but to lower the cost of renewable energy through research and development.

For decades we have been releasing greenhouse gases into our atmosphere (see Figure 2.1), and the result of our actions is becoming obvious. Human-induced climate change is a scientific fact. We must consider carefully how we deal with the impact of climate change. To prevent further global warming, we are going to have to develop the technological, institutional, and financial capacity to put the carbon genie back in the bottle.

Simply addressing the output of our energy processes is, of course, not enough. We also need to develop a form of energy that is cheaper, more reliable, and less dangerous than fossil fuels in order to drive those problematic resources out of the marketplace. The only solution to the climate

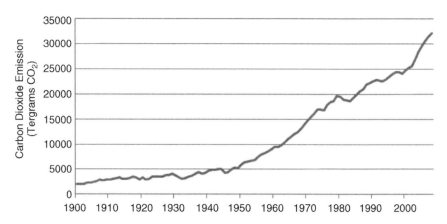

**Figure 2.1    Global Carbon Dioxide (CO$_2$) Emissions from Fossil Fuels 1900–2008**

*Source:* Boden, T.A., G. Marland, and R.J. Andres (2010). Global, Regional, and National Fossil-Fuel CO$_2$ Emissions. Carbon Dioxide Information Analysis Center, Oak Ridge National Laboratory, U.S. Department of Energy, Oak Ridge, Tennessee, U.S.A. doi 10.3334/CDIAC/00001_V2010.

problem that has any potential to work is the development of a renewable energy source that outperforms and underprices fossil fuels. No single technological challenge is more important for the future of our civilization.

Our political stability depends on economic development. Our economic development depends on low-cost, plentiful, and reliable energy. Our planet's ecological health and sustainability require renewable energy. Human well-being requires food, water, and air that have not been poisoned by industrial pollution.

The demand for energy is global and growing rapidly. China and India are moving aggressively to catch up with the economies of more developed countries and, in order to do that, they need to bring massive amounts of energy facilities online. They are grabbing for whatever energy source they can find, and for the most part they are relying on fossil fuel technologies. There is some nuclear power in the mix, but coal is cheaper to run and less expensive to build. In our view, no international treaty will stop increased use of fossil fuels, and only new technology will prevent it from damaging the planet.

In the 21st century version of the energy crisis, we face problems with both power generation and distribution. In some places, during certain times of the year, energy use puts a strain on generation facilities. In addition, energy generation poses risks to human health and ecological systems, first when we extract fossil fuels from the earth, and again when we burn the fuel.

Seeing this danger, some environmentalists have taken another look at nuclear power, but the Fukushima nuclear disaster in Japan reminded the world of its risks. There is a low probability that a disaster related to nuclear energy production will occur, but when one does—such as at Fukushima or Chernobyl—the damage can be catastrophic. If nuclear power is adopted as part of a sustainable energy strategy, it must be strictly regulated and monitored.

In our view, new technologies are essential to solving the sustainability challenge. Without continued breakthroughs in science and engineering, we cannot solve the problems we are facing. There is hope for the 21st century, especially when you consider that human civilization, and the United States in particular, spent most of the 19th and 20th centuries achieving scientific and engineering marvels. The economic opportunities and threats of the past two centuries were nearly all the results of technological advances; however, when new technology solves problems, it creates them as well. Here are two examples of this push and pull:

1. **Automobiles:** We invented cars, which meant that people died in car accidents. Thanks to safety research, we learned how to develop seat belts, air bags, and safer cars and roads.
2. **Indoor plumbing:** We invented modern toilets and sewage systems to carry waste from our homes, but sewage polluted our water. We then learned how to treat sewage and reduce pollution in our rivers and lakes.

There are many other examples, but the key point is that we often fix the problems caused by technology by applying new technology. We know how to apply technological fixes and we remain capable of developing solutions to the problems brought about by our economic and technological successes. In cases where development brings about massive changes and advances in society, we often find that problems are created along with progress. In response, government policies should be devised to enforce new rules designed to address problems, thereby ensuring the safety and health of our citizens.

## The Different Functions of the Public, Private, and Nonprofit Sectors

Before we introduce the role of government in sustainability, it is important to consider the role of government in society in general. What can and should the government do and not do? What activities and actions should it take on and what should be left to the private sector? Whom does the government serve? What role do nonprofits play in all of this? The distinctions between the sectors and their respective roles are not always easy to determine. The public and private sectors often have similar or even overlapping functions; for example, both provide services in health care and education, but there are discernible differences between them.

One way to understand these differences is what author Steven Cohen has termed "functional matching," meaning that the private, nonprofit, and public sectors are each in a position to serve the general population in different ways (Cohen, 2001). Differences in the nature of their missions, incentive systems, organizational cultures, and the kinds of talent that they attract mean that each sector has different strengths.

The private sector is motivated by profit, and may have to answer to shareholders as well as employees and clients. Unlike in the public sector, existence in the private sector is not guaranteed. Competition is steep and organizations that do not adapt to changing times and tastes can go out of business. To compete, organizations in the private sector have great incentive to reduce costs, and therefore may have greater levels of efficiency. This focus on cost-reduction might also encourage some organizations to engage in research and development that supports more efficient—and sustainable—processes. Manufacturing and certain service-support functions are probably best performed by the private sector.

Organizations in the nonprofit sector typically get their motivation from a mission, and they excel at infusing their employees and volunteers with dedication to this cause. Unlike organizations in the private sector, some nonprofits do not have paying customers; for example, Homes for the Homeless in New York City serves the homeless by providing them with free housing. For funding, nonprofits rely on a combination of contracts from government, grants, and gifts from donors, which can be individuals or other organizations. The nonprofit sector may be most effective in industries that require a great level of compassion, such as nursing, education, and social services. Governments often rely on private and nonprofit organizations to assist in analyzing policies, delivering services, solving public problems, and filling gaps in certain capacities; in turn, governments can lend these organizations a sense of legitimacy (Schuman et al., 2002).

The public sector in the United States is led by officials who are democratically elected, or appointed by elected officials. This means the government is more sensitive to political pressure, but they are able to do things that private organizations cannot, such as incarcerate people. Government performs best in circumstances where public accountability is crucial, such as in policing and establishing and enforcing the law. Government is necessary any time rules are developed to regulate or restrict the freedoms of individuals or organizations. The government, however, is hindered by fiscal restraints, as well as rules designed to prevent fraud and may draw on a nonprofit organization's network of volunteers as well as their greater flexibility of action (Feiock and Andrew, 2006). Both nonprofits and private companies assist the public sector with delivery of services, or planning and program development. But there are some essential functions that no one but government can fulfill, and we will see that this is especially true for sustainability.

## Limitations of the Private Sector in Addressing Long-Term Sustainability

Both the private and public sectors play important, often complementary roles in the transition toward a sustainable economy. Government regulation led the private sector to develop technologies to purify polluted water and produce cleaner air. Governments have an opportunity to ensure that whenever fossil fuels are extracted from the ground, the process results in minimal environmental damage.

Unlike in the public sector, global competition makes it difficult for private firms to finance basic research in sustainable energy technology. Therefore, government needs to allocate funding for research and development (R&D). The private sector may see no immediate benefit in investing in energy efficiency measures and infrastructure, so government must build this infrastructure and creatively balance carrots and sticks to encourage private firms to use resources efficiently and minimize negative externalities.

Each sector does certain types of things the best, and some goals are so massive, important, and difficult that they require government leadership, resources, and authority. Building a sustainable economy requires that government take the lead, fund the required basic research, regulate private firms, build infrastructure, and reward sustainable practices. The move to a sustainable economy requires that we generate far more energy tomorrow than we generate today. We do not yet know how to do that safely, but we need to learn.

If we leave issues of sustainability to the private sector alone, it will eventually come, but it will probably come too late to preserve our ecosystems. It will follow the typical boom and bust cycle we all experience at the gas pump. Only government has the capacity to take the lead. It will need to work with all of us to develop a vision of a sustainable economy and then invest and elicit the resources needed to achieve that vision.

## Role of the Government in Building a Sustainable Economy

### Funding Basic Science

One of the public sector's most important influences on the future of sustainability comes in the form of support for basic science. Why? Because in an increasingly challenging world there is a fundamental need to understand basic environmental processes in order to effectively manage anything, be it a household, a nonprofit organization, a multinational corporation, or a government agency. Decision makers must have insight into the resources and inputs that sustain their organizations or businesses. The resources we currently rely on most heavily are fixed and finite. Environmental and earth system processes are complex and not yet completely understood. Scientific research is required to continue to advance our knowledge of these systems so that we can ensure our ability to sustainably utilize them in the long run.

We are significantly more advanced in understanding the functioning of our economy than we are about how our environment is working. The gross domestic product (GDP) indicator has been around since the 1930s but there is still no such all-encompassing measure for environmental quality and planetary health. Basic environmental science and earth observation are the prerequisites to developing such an overall sustainability measure. Therefore, we must expand the collective understanding of natural resources, earth and environmental processes, and biological systems through additional public funding of basic research (U.S. Congress Joint Economic Committee, 2010, 4).

Many innovative cost-saving public programs would not be possible without a solid understanding of science. If we do not make the investment in the basic scientific research needed to make complex decisions regarding the planet's finite resources and sensitive services, a reduction in the planet's ability to produce goods and services is only a matter of time. We need to dramatically increase funding for basic and applied science, and focus attention on research and development in earth observation, energy, food, water, and other areas that can have an impact on sustainability.

One of the great strengths of the United States is our large number of research universities. In the post–World War II era, our country established an effective partnership between government-funded basic research and it's application by the private sector in a range of technologies, including computers, cell phones, the Internet, and, of course, a host of breakthroughs in medicine and medical technology (Bernanke, 2011). Much of the economic growth of the past hundred years directly results from this type of technological development. Government is especially crucial in funding basic science that is too far upstream from products and profits to generate significant private R&D investment (U.S. Congress Joint Economic Committee, 2010, 2). Government is also needed to help bridge the often wide gap between basic and applied research.

Government-sponsored research can make a tremendous difference to qualified scientists. Let's look at an example from the field of earth systems science. The scientists at the Earth Institute's Lamont-Doherty Earth Observatory are among the world's top environmental scientists, but they are spending an increasing amount of time away from their laboratory and field-based research projects to draft the numerous research proposals required to keep their teams funded. The competition for limited science research funding is getting more intense all the time. While resource scarcity can stimulate important discipline and can help ensure efficiency, too much funding scarcity can endanger the quality and creativity of science.

We also need to develop the organizational and institutional capacity to both understand the planet's conditions and to develop the technology needed to mitigate the damage we do to it. These measurement and research tasks are basic governmental functions that must be funded and directed by public policy. The private sector and universities will do much of this work as contractors and grantees, but the long-term perspective requires government funding, and the connection to our long-term security and safety makes planetary science and basic research a government concern.

The private sector is clearly best at making and marketing renewable energy resources, and it will play an important role in commercializing government-funded research; however, it will not fund the necessary R&D on its own. Government must fund the basic science, research, and development of new renewable energy and energy efficiency technologies. A number of analysts and elected leaders have called for a "moon-shot" project to develop renewable energy technology. This is a focused effort, funded by government to develop a few specific technologies. Laptop computers, jet engines, cell phones, satellites, and the Internet are all examples of government-funded technologies that have grown into massive private businesses. We need the same resources once spent on shrinking computers for missiles and spacecraft to be devoted to developing low-cost, non-fossil fuel–based energy.

Support for basic environmental science research should not be seen as a conservative or liberal issue. Supporting scientific research is a fundamental role of government similar to national security, emergency response, infrastructure, and criminal justice. The quest for fundamental knowledge has allowed us to improve our standard of living and holds the promise of a sustainable planet, free from extreme poverty. Reducing the funding base of this research is a threat to our long-term economic growth. As former Federal Reserve Chairman Ben Bernanke stated in a speech on promoting research and development, "innovation and technological change are undoubtedly central to the growth process" (2011).

Basic and applied scientific research can uncover new policy options, lead to cost savings in unexpected ways, and can help make sense of sometimes conflicting data or information. Keeping the public safe and secure is the quintessential governmental function. Damage to the environment needs to be seen as a life-threatening risk to the security of our families and communities.

### Funding Infrastructure

Just as government built ports, canals, dams, railroads, and highways—the infrastructure of the 19th and 20th centuries—it must build the energy, communications, research, waste, and water management infrastructure needed for the 21st century. The issue of funding infrastructure becomes even more important as we consider the impacts of extreme weather events due to climate change. As we work to transition to a sustainable economy and begin the long process of reversing the causes of climate change, we will also need to adapt to the impact of the climate changes already under way—changes such as powerful hurricanes that can bring down power lines, intense rain storms that can inundate soil and cause rivers to overflow their banks, blizzards that can damage our roads and buildings, and droughts that can cause fires and famines—threatening our lives and livelihoods. As these events are predicted to happen with greater frequency and intensity, government will be expected to meet those challenges with smart and timely action.

Think about the public sector's leadership in building the U.S. transportation infrastructure, from the Erie Canal to the interstate highway system. In our home city of New York, government worked with the private sector to build the mass transit, water, and sewage systems. During the Great Depression, President Franklin Delano Roosevelt created an expansive public works program to put men back to work. The Public Works Administration (PWA) electrified rural America; it built airports, roads, bridges, tunnels, sewage systems, hospitals, and schools, many of which continue to serve local communities. After World War II, President Eisenhower asserted that "a modern, efficient highway system is essential to meet the needs of our growing population, our expanding economy, and our national security" (White, 2012).

Today, not only do we need to repair and rebuild existing infrastructure like dams and bridges, we need to invest in the infrastructure of the future such as:

- Smart grids
- Public charging stations and related infrastructure to support electric vehicles
- High-speed railroads and other advanced public transportation systems
- High-speed internet access
- New, more efficient waste and water systems
- Green infrastructure systems that utilize natural ecosystem services to support traditional infrastructure systems

Much of the need for government investment in infrastructure is centered on renewable, smart, distributed energy systems. We know that renewable energy has the potential to radically change the energy business. While some large-scale organizations will always be part of the energy industry, we are seeing the start of decentralized, distributed generation of energy. Although the conventional wisdom tells us that solar power, battery technology, and smart grids are far in the future, we are only a breakthrough or two away from a new age of decentralized energy technology. Large-scale implementation of smart grid technology would make it possible to accelerate this trend. This indicates a latent market that could expand rapidly following a major technological advance in solar generation or energy storage technology. The proper infrastructure to take advantage of these breakthroughs must be in place, and we need government to assume its historical role to help make this happen.

An important advantage of decentralized, distributed generation of energy is that it is less vulnerable to catastrophic, large-scale disruption (Umberger, 2012, 191). As our lifestyles require more and more energy, even a few days of disrupted supply can have a significant negative effect on quality of life. After Hurricane Sandy, many suburbanites in the Northeast went out and bought electric generators and gasoline tanks to keep their homes powered during and after storms. A solar generating system in the home, with an advanced storage battery, would be a cleaner, more convenient way to do the same job.

Climate resiliency or adaptation is one area of focus that lately puts the spotlight on the need to improve our national, state, and local infrastructure, and also consider the role that government plays. The risk of disaster does not mean we should abandon our coastal communities and head for higher ground. It's not clear that any area is truly out of danger, but recent events make clear that we must develop more resilient homes and infrastructure along with a more robust national program of emergency response and insurance.

Our buildings and infrastructure must be made more storm resistant. Over the past decade, most of our shore communities on the East Coast have been changing building requirements. For example, since the devastation of Hurricane Sandy in October 2012, new homes in Long Beach, New York, are required to have their living quarters raised off the ground (City of New York, 2013). Similarly, many people plan to create utility rooms to keep hot water heaters and boilers above the basement to protect them from flooding. Building new infrastructure (and enhancing our current systems) is one of the key building blocks toward a sustainable economy, and the public sector must embrace its critical role in developing these systems.

### Providing Incentives for Private Investment

Government ought to employ a variety of market-based tools to support renewable energy and a more sustainable economy (Caperton, 2012, 2). Some of this comes in the form of direct taxes, while in some cases, government uses other incentives, like tax credits to promote or discourage certain behaviors. One way to address the energy issue might be to have energy prices reflect their true cost, so consumers and businesses directly absorb the costs associated with fossil fuel extraction and burning, including climate change, poor air quality, and serious health conditions. This would adjust the cost calculation for both renewables and fossil fuels. Examples of indirect taxes on fossil fuels include efforts to limit car emissions (e.g., fuel taxes, purchase or registration taxes, and congestion charges). Similarly, taxes on electricity or water consumption (e.g., electricity taxes and water fees) can be used to charge for externalities associated with wasteful or excessive usage. Taxes are almost universally recommended by economists as the most efficient mechanism to induce change in the market, and taxes are among the most transparent policy mechanisms available to governments; however, they are often politically infeasible (like a federal carbon tax in the United States) and resisted by elected officials.

The federal government has the extremely powerful tool of the tax code to adjust the cost-benefit calculus of organizations seeking to implement more sustainable practices. The goal should be to provide incentives that encourage the more rapid development of sustainability practices. This is not a new idea. Our very complex tax code is used to motivate a wide variety of economic behaviors. In the case of sustainability, communities, households, and businesses must be encouraged to become renewable energy generators and, when used properly, tax incentives can be extremely effective in changing behavior. One visible example is that of home ownership. In 1940, 43.6 percent of all American households owned their own homes. By 1960 that had reached 61.9 percent (U.S. Census Bureau, 2011). This was made possible by making mortgage interest and local property taxes deductible from income tax, and by the development of government-backed mortgage insurance.

During the past two decades, lax government regulation of the financial services industry led to high-risk behavior and, in some cases, outright abuse of the financial systems, which caused massive foreclosures over the past several years. The program had worked exceptionally well for more than 60 years, but when government abandoned its critical oversight, the private sector indulged in excesses that prioritized short-term gains with little regard for negative long-term impact. To advance sustainability, we need ongoing oversight as well as the creative policy to increase the percentage of people generating energy from renewable sources.

The transition to lower cost and plentiful renewable energy will happen and the private sector will deliver the necessary new technology. But the pace of change can be accelerated with carefully designed and targeted government policies. Subsidies, which are already characteristic of energy exploration and production policy, can be revisited to encourage the adoption of clean and smart technologies (UNEP, 2008, 2). For example, the current oil depletion allowance enables oil companies for tax purposes to treat reserves in the ground as assets that will eventually be exhausted (Leber, 2013). A percentage of the value of the asset is subtracted from a company's taxable income. The rationale for this subsidy is that once the oil in a well is pumped out, we want to encourage industry to dig another well. This made good sense when fossil fuels were our best option for generating a resource as critical to the economy as oil. It may even make sense as we begin the transition away from fossil fuels, but we must rethink this overall strategy and look to similar long-term methods to support renewable energy and the technologies that support it.

In the case of energy the important issue is: What types of subsidies are needed? The issue of the oil depletion allowance revolves around the need to attract capital to oil drilling and the degree to which our energy mix continues to require petroleum. Since capital flows toward the highest or safest rates of return and need not be invested in America, public policy must sometimes be used to encourage private sector investment in areas of national interest. We believe renewable energy and the supporting technologies of sustainability are worthy of such national investment.

Public policy can also be used to address challenges with financing energy efficiency and renewable energy. Financing remains a significant hurdle for widespread adoption of low-carbon energy technologies despite availability of capital for other purposes. Tax credits and mechanisms like guaranteed loan programs can help overcome this by lowering financial risks associated with clean technology development. These types of programs leverage public dollars into larger investments in the private sector. Feed-in tariffs, which provide long-term contracts to producers of renewable energy and offer price certainty needed to finance projects, are one of the most common policies to encourage renewable energy generation. At least 90 countries, both developed and developing, have some system of feed-in tariffs (REN21, 2012, 118). The U.S. does not have a national feed-in tariff, though many states are adopting feed-in tariffs or similar programs.

It is time for fact-based public debate on the type of policies that are needed to speed the transition to a fossil fuel–free economy. We need policies that encourage companies, localities, and even families to adopt new technologies as they are brought to market. Market-based tools can help move the United States toward energy sustainability.

## Setting and Enforcing Rules to Protect the Environment

In the United States, we've learned that there is no such thing as complete freedom to do whatever we want to do. In order for democratic values to persist successfully, we also need laws, rules, and regulations to provide structure and safety. In a democracy, citizens are free to voice their opinions and contribute to the development and enforcement of those laws and regulations. Those who enforce laws are also subject to and held accountable for those rules (Stroker, 2012). In a democracy, citizens are involved in the process to adopt new legislation, which aims to confirm that people are willing to accept society's rules and ensure that people are well served by laws that benefit the general public (Bakken, 2014). The government provides societal structure in a way that is meant to serve citizens' values and interests, and contribute to the public good (Tomain and Shapiro, 2014). We may want to drive fast, but we follow the rules of the road because these rules benefit everyone—ourselves included.

These same concepts apply to protecting the environment. In the United States we've learned that protecting the environment requires laws, rules, and regulations. Why should a company be able to pollute the air that we breathe or the water we drink? Valuable and vulnerable natural resources and public health must be protected from those that ignore or neglect the negative environmental externalities associated with their actions. Incentives to stimulate behavior are not always sufficient. Sometimes we need the rule of law to draw a line in the sand distinguishing right from wrong. In addition to making our environment less toxic, environmental regulations reduce the cost of health care attributed to environmentally induced illness and stimulate technological innovation.

Environmental regulations follow the same logic as traditional limits on the free market. Economic regulation and rules on fraud and protection of private property limit free enterprise. Businesses know they must operate within a system of law; that system both constrains and protects them. The regulatory process is a bargaining process where rules are proposed and adjusted to minimize costs while maximizing benefits. All environmental rules go through a process of give and take. Some disputes are settled by changes in rules as political leaders respond to industry demands. Some are settled in the courts when the Environmental Protection Agency (EPA) cannot find a way to get environmental groups and industry to compromise.

During nearly half a century of back and forth, we have developed an imperfect but effective process of environmental regulation that has resulted in cleaner air, safer water, and a nation that knows how to reduce pollution while growing its economy. While economists and policy analysts will advocate more creative and economically efficient climate policies such as carbon taxes and cap and trade programs, there is something to be said for a policy approach with a proven record of success. The landmark environmental policies formed in the 1970s—the Clean Air Act, the Clean Water Act, the Resource Conservation and Recovery Act, and Superfund, among others—continue to serve us well, enabling us to grow our economy while ensuring environmental quality.

Overall, the U.S. EPA has done a reasonably good job of developing, enacting, and enforcing environmental regulations. Policies made in Washington are coordinated by the agency's 10 regional offices and then implemented by state governments under delegated authorities. Local businesses and environmental groups weigh in and sometimes sue during the implementation process. No one would ever call this process rapid and efficient; but it does work. The effectiveness of U.S. environmental rules are dramatically demonstrated by pictures of Pittsburgh, Pennsylvania, in the 1970s (dark at noon on a Sunday) or modern-day Beijing, particularly in the winter.

While corporations and communities do incur costs for protecting the environment, resulting in some short-term pain, this is typically followed by long-term gains. American governments at all levels are very careful and quite flexible when imposing new rules on private parties. When the EPA designs environmental programs, they generally provide long adjustment periods that allow regulated parties time to gradually modify their practices. Auto fleets are given many years to meet fuel economy standards. Local governments are given long compliance schedules to meet water quality standards.

Regulations applied with firmness and care provide incentives for organizations to innovate and develop new ways of operating. Energy efficiency standards have created incentives for innovative engineers to build appliances that deliver higher levels of performance while using less energy. Start-up companies are launched to meet these new requirements, and established corporate giants such as General Electric reinvent themselves to compete under new rules. Industry opposition to technology-forcing environmental rules is nothing new. In the early days of air pollution control in the 1970s, American automakers argued that the catalytic converter could not be mandated because it was not ready for use. They maintained this argument until Congress began discussing banning the internal combustion engine. Suddenly prototypes of the catalytic converter began to appear everywhere, including in congressional hearing rooms.

On the one hand, it is true that regulation costs money, and some ideologues seem to have a reflex that causes them to oppose regulation whenever it is proposed. On the other hand, it's also true that lawlessness and an absence of rules can be quite expensive. Although many of the costs of regulation are borne by individual businesses and their customers, everyone pays the costs of the damage caused by a system operating without the rule of law.

Many of the complaints against regulation are that they are job-killing, anti-business policies. Rules of the game can create a level playing field that permits fair competition. The certainty and security of a fair business environment can actually attract competitors and creativity. Think of how badly traffic backs up when stoplights lose power and don't work. A world without rules and regulations is one of anarchy and chaos.

In fact, consistently over time, the total benefits of federal regulations far outweigh the total costs. The U.S. Office of Management and Budget (OMB) produces an annual report that monetizes the costs and benefits of major federal regulations. In 2013, their report concluded that the estimated annual benefits of major federal regulations over the ten-year period ending September 2012 were between $193 and $800 billion, while estimated annual costs were between $57 and $84 billion (OMB, 2013a, 3). For the EPA specifically, OMB estimated that the total annual benefits from its major federal rules over the same 10-year period were $112 to $637.6 billion and the costs were $30.4 to $36.5 billion (OMB, 2013a, 11).

Unfortunately, the old mindset persists: We must sacrifice environmental quality to achieve economic growth. While short-term benefits can be obtained by ignoring environmental conditions, polluted land, air, and water must eventually be cleaned if we are to remain healthy. The long-term costs of cleanup are far greater than the long-term costs of pollution prevention.

The result of our sophisticated and flexible system of environmental regulation is that we have learned how to grow the economy while protecting the environment. While some say this progress was due to the export of highly polluting industrial plants and jobs, the global economy, with its advanced communications and transport technology, were the real motors behind the export of manufacturing. Eventually, the standards we've applied here will come to be applied in the developing world as well. People will learn that no matter how rich you are, you can't build a walled community around environmental toxicity.

Our more complex economy and the increased use of toxics in production require rules that keep pace with economic, demographic, and technological change. The food, water, and air that sustain human life must be protected; only government rules and enforcement can ensure that those critical resources are maintained. Rules must prevent damage to the environment, but also must ensure that energy efficiency, recycling, and water efficiency are integrated into our structures, institutions, and daily routines.

## Sustainability Metrics and Management

One sign of the growing importance of sustainability management is the impressive number of efforts at the company level to develop and utilize sustainability metrics. This is also leading to the incorporation of standard operating procedures for sustainability into routine organizational management. A wide variety of organizations have developed and implemented an even wider variety of sustainability measures. Many companies are measuring and reporting their sustainability performance to their shareholders and the general public in annual reports; however it is not clear that the measures under development are appropriate, reliable, or valid. Moreover, the collection and reporting of these metrics is voluntary, self-completed, inadequately audited, and without penalty for deceptive, incomplete, or incompetent reporting.

Measurement may sound like an arcane, technical subject, but it is actually critical to action. Its importance to management decisions in a data-driven environment cannot be understated. Anything pursued in a serious way in a modern organization is measured. The most talented people in any organization tend to gravitate away from activities that lack metrics guidelines or measurability because it is difficult to review progress and justify decisions. Without measurement, you can't tell if your management actions are making the situation better or worse. As a result, such activities can fall from focus and be considered unimportant. More companies are beginning to measure sustainability, which is a sign of significant progress. We need these actions to continue and expand, but we need clearer rules on how to do it.

Just as we have generally accepted accounting principles (GAAP) and clear definitions of financial indicators, we need agreed-upon organizational sustainability indicators that everyone can use. These universal indicators would be incorporated into a manager's traditional set of organizational performance measures like market share, return on equity, and profit and loss. In the public and nonprofit sectors, those performance measures would be different than private sector measures, but they are similarly important to overall management and effectiveness. In this case, sustainability metrics would be measured alongside organizational process and output measures such as labor productivity and efficiency, value of goods and services delivered, employment, and labor turnover. The indicators to measure are not settled, but the need is clear.

In addition to organizational level indicators, we need to do some hard thinking about developing some multiple indicator scales that might chart local, state, and national progress toward a sustainable economy. An easy-to-understand measure like the gross domestic product (GDP) or the unemployment rate would help guide public policies encouraging sustainability management. One possible approach could include environmental benefits and costs in the GDP measure itself.

Some academics have attempted to calculate a *green GDP* by subtracting ecological costs from traditional GDP; however, this fails to capture the true economic value of ecosystem services and the benefits provided by environmental protection and sustainability efforts. While efforts to refine the notion of green GDP are sure to continue, its actual use and application today is extremely limited, remaining almost entirely within academia.

One example of a national sustainability metric is the Labor Department's effort to measure and report on green jobs beginning in fiscal year 2010. That year, 3.1 million U.S. jobs were associated with the production of green goods and services, accounting for 2.4 percent of total U.S. employment that year (BLS, 2012a). In March of 2013, this very important project was suspended in a shortsighted decision by the Department of Labor to respond to budget cuts imposed by Congress. We hope that this measurement effort will be restored, and that other aggregate measures of sustainability at the macro level will be developed and implemented.

One of the problems with the current drive to develop sustainability metrics is the absence of an authoritative and potentially objective moderator of the discussion. Corporations and environmental interest groups are key stakeholders in any metrics discussion, but they each have their own axe to grind and cannot be allowed to have the final word. Academics, business leaders, and government officials must work together to develop and refine acceptable indicators. A standardized system of data collection, verification, and audit needs to be put into place. Government again has a key role to play.

### Transferring Technology to the Developing World

As the developed world makes the transition to a more sustainable, renewable resource–based economy, it is important that newly developing nations are provided with incentives to use new technologies instead of older ones that might get cheaper as they are discarded by the developed world. Coal and coal-fired power plants could get very inexpensive as they are replaced by cleaner sources of energy. A variety of financial tools could be used to lower the cost of new technology for export to the developing world (World Future Council, 2009, 2). Technology transfer can include resources, but also expertise, knowledge, and training. If the United States and other developed countries lower their greenhouse gas emissions while developing nations increase emissions, the climate will continue to be degraded. The mitigation of climate change will require new energy technology, but without effective technology transfer, the climate problem will remain.

### Public–Private Partnerships

Rules, regulations, governance, and investment are necessary conditions for prosperity in the modern global economy, but they are not sufficient for generating the necessary level of progress. We also need a creative and competitive private sector, cutting edge research and educational institutions, and a sense of shared purpose and vision. The goal should be to create a sophisticated partnership between government, industry, and nonprofits. The technology breakthroughs required to transition from fossil fuels to renewable energy will likely be developed by university-based researchers, collaboratively funded and operated by government, nonprofit, and private organizations.

Public-private partnerships have been around since the start of the United States. That partnership built the transcontinental railroad, the interstate highway system, the air traffic control system and the nation's many ports and shipping terminals. Public–private partnerships exist at all levels of government, "and enhanced public–private collaboration and understanding are required more than ever" (WEF, 2014, 1).

In 1817, New York State Governor DeWitt Clinton invented a new kind of public–private partnership to build the Erie Canal. When the federal government refused to invest, New York State built the canal without federal funding. The canal was finished ahead of schedule and under budget—and it had a transformative effect on New York's economy. New York City became a commercial powerhouse when it was able to cheaply ship agricultural goods and natural resources from the Midwest using the canal and the port of New York. In modern times, since Ed Koch's mayoral administration and continuing to today, New York's city government has maintained a sophisticated relationship with local nonprofits who now implement most of the city's social welfare programs.

To be a community, America requires public institutions. To build and maintain public institutions, we must have a vibrant public sector. Government is not a beast to be starved, but an institution that requires nurturing. An active partnership between the public and private sectors will be needed to transition from a resource-consumptive economy to one that manages, reformulates, and reuses resources. This transition will depend on an active government, a vibrant research establishment, and a fully engaged private sector.

## Working to Ensure the Transition is Well Managed

It is difficult to improve government management when political forces attack the legitimacy of government. Government may not be perfect, but it is capable of doing some pretty wonderful things. Government is necessary. It performs key functions in our society and economy that cannot be performed by any other institution. It could, should, and must do a better job of delivering services and enforcing rules. Fiscal cliffs, budget sequestration, government shutdowns, and the other ideological games underway in Washington have the effect of chasing away talented government managers.

We need an effective government because we have some needs as individuals, communities, and a nation that cannot be provided by the market alone. While private companies are deeply involved in government's work, modern government requires a partnership between public and private organizations. Defense, police, fire, sanitation, water, pollution control, transportation infrastructure, education, and many health and welfare functions require substantial government participation and policy leadership.

At the present time we do not know precisely how to develop a sustainable economy, but we are on the road to figuring it out. In order to transition to a cleaner and therefore more sustainable economy, governments need to act aggressively through all the tools at their disposal. Local, regional, and national governments have control over aspects of the public and private sectors; they can help drive the shift to a more sustainable future. Without their leadership, the private sector cannot effectively deal with these issues. Cities are leading the efforts in sustainability and serving as pioneers in both climate mitigation and adaptation. State policies can serve as forums for innovative local programs. National policies can set broad standards for markets of scale to develop. No single policy can achieve sustainability. A tailored, multidimensional approach can make substantial progress toward a sustainable economy.

# 3

# Policy Levers for Sustainability

## *The Federal Level*

## Introduction

The transition to a sustainable economy will take activity and leadership from all sectors—public, private, and nonprofit. The United States federal government has many instruments to put in place to encourage sustainability and make sustainable options more viable in the marketplace by reducing risk and increasing competiveness. National sustainability policies aim to encourage sustainable energy use and other sustainable practices while discouraging dirtier, environmentally destructive, or unsustainable practices. None of these policies is a silver bullet; the environmental challenges that we face are too complex and too extensive for simple solutions. However, multiple policies enacted together can facilitate substantial progress. In fact, it is precisely that complexity that requires the federal government to play a leadership role. While today the U.S. national government is often ridiculed as inept, historically it has been capable of tremendous feats such as the transcontinental railroad, the mobilization of industry and society in World War II, and sending astronauts to the moon.

In a similar fashion, we need the federal government, through multiple coordinated efforts, to speed our transition to sustainability. Many of these policies focus on energy, a critical component of the sustainable economy. As discussed in Chapter 2, addressing the energy issue centers around reducing the price of renewable energy or, alternatively, making all energy prices reflect their true costs so consumers (both individual and organizational) must internalize the externalities associated with fossil fuel extraction and burning, which include climate change, poor air quality, and negative health impacts. Appropriate policies can also be developed to address other issues of sustainability such as environmental protection, water use, waste disposal, and recycling.

In Chapters 1 and 2, we made the case for sustainability and presented arguments in support of necessary public–private partnerships to bring about the transition to a sustainable economy. In this chapter, we will present an overview of the range of federal level policies that could be developed to encourage sustainability. First, we will present the type of policy tools that currently influence America's environmental approach, including the effective and innovative mechanisms that the U.S. has employed historically and continues to utilize today. This overview will examine a variety of approaches including public spending, market-based tools, and regulations. Then, we'll outline the policies that are not working, those that serve to discourage or undermine sustainability management, and discuss alternatives. Finally, we will turn to what is possible and introduce policy options that could be adopted at the national level in the near term, and use global examples to demonstrate the viability and effectiveness of these programs.

## What Is Working?

The United States has a long history in environmental sustainability. In the 20th century it established one of the greatest national park systems in the world. It developed some of the first environmental laws to protect our land, water, air, and health. It demonstrated that economic development does not need to be accompanied by declining environmental quality. The United States has achieved these notable successes via a series of policy instruments. We'll discuss a number of these initiatives here, though it is by no means an exhaustive list or history of environmental policy in the United States.

## Public Investment and Spending

The federal government has the capacity to directly fund key elements of the transition to a sustainable economy through a variety of programs and tools, specifically investment in scientific research and development (R&D) and direct spending through sustainable public procurement policies and programs. As we noted in Chapter 2, one of the most important roles of government is mobilizing resources into scientific research and discovery. We believe that advanced technologies (such as nanoscale solar and next-generation batteries) are the key to a sustainable future. However, substantial gaps exist between actual investments in these technologies and what is needed in order to achieve the transition to a sustainable economy. The U.S. federal government has traditionally filled this gap and must continue to do so. In fact, the U.S. government is one of the very few funders of basic science in this country, although we have seen an increase in private philanthropy in this area. For example private funding for science has grown dramatically over the past twenty years. At our own university, Mortimer Zuckerman donated $200 million for a new institute focused on mind, brain, and behavior that Columbia named in his honor. In Washington DC, where budget cuts have closed laboratories and forced the layoff of scientists, wealthy philanthropists have been able to rekindle and revitalize scientific exploration. According to Steven A. Edwards of the American Association for the Advancement of Science, science in the 21st century has been shaped more by the particular preferences of wealthy individuals rather than national priorities (Broad, 2014).

### Investment in Scientific Research and Development

Support for basic science and engineering is a fundamental role of government, similar to national security, emergency response, infrastructure, and criminal justice. Investment in basic research and development has historically been a high priority for federal governments. Government-funded research, coupled with private-sector application to commercial products and processes, has led to some of the most significant technological breakthroughs in the last century: computers, cell phones, the Internet, global-positioning systems (GPS)—all breakthroughs that have created enormous economic growth in the United States and globally. Public investment has been there, behind the scenes, for these important innovations, generating the basic scientific research and helping to bridge the gap between those scientific discoveries and applied research and development. This role is perhaps paramount in the sustainability transition. We know the outcomes of the investments made in science during the post–World War II era; we don't know what the innovations of the 21st century will be, but we are continuing to invest to ensure that those discoveries occur. We believe that they will change the way we think about the future of sustainability.

Over the last three decades, until recently, science funding has increased fairly steadily. The American Association for the Advancement of Science (AAAS) has tracked federal funding for R&D and found an increase from roughly $80 billion in 1978 to a peak of nearly $180 billion in 2009 before declining to roughly $130 billion in 2013 (AAAS, 2013). Over the last few years, funding for the government agencies that fund science has been roughly flat, with slight increases or decreases year to year, depending on the agency. For example, the president's proposed Department of Energy fiscal year 2015 budget represents a 2.6 percent increase above the fiscal year 2014 enacted level (U.S. DOE, 2014). Although funding for the Environmental Protection Agency (EPA) is declining—a trend that is expected to continue in the near future—other agencies responsible for investment in environmental science, such as the National Science Foundation (NSF), the U.S. Geological Survey, the National Oceanic and Atmospheric Administration, and the Forest Service, are expected to see slight increases in funding in the short term. Despite these small gains, funding for these agencies is far below other agencies, like the National Institutes of Health (NIH), which supports medical research, or the Defense Department; for example, the proposed budget for the NIH in the president's fiscal 2015 budget request was nearly $30.4 billion, compared to the $7.3 billion for NSF and $7.9 billion for the EPA, respectively (OMB, 2014).

In 2009, in efforts to bolster the global economy, countries across the globe increased federal spending through stimulus programs, which provided a quick boon to the sustainability field. In the U.S., the American Recovery and Reinvestment Act (ARRA or *the stimulus plan*) resulted in an increase in research funding across most federal agencies. That same year, President Obama announced a long-term goal for the United States to invest 3 percent of its GDP in research and development as part of "A Strategy for American

Innovation" (OSTP, 2010, 1–2). The proposed Plan for Science and Innovation, which was never approved by Congress, focused on three main federal agencies: the National Science Foundation (NSF), the Department of Energy (DOE), and the National Institute of Standards and Technology (NIST). President Obama aimed to put these agencies on a doubling trajectory by 2017. The 2011 budget sustained the administration's commitment with increased funding for these key science agencies, keeping the doubling path on track (OSTP, 2011, 1–2). However, in a 2013 report, the American Association for the Advancement of Science found that the agencies fell short of the doubling pace, despite receiving increases (AAAS, 2013, 4).

The impact of ARRA was particularly notable for clean technology. From the period 2002–2008, federal support for clean technology (across agencies) totaled an estimated $44 billion and grew to $150 billion from the period 2009–2014 (Banks, 2011, 40). Despite these gains from ARRA, funding has decreased since the peak in 2009. In 2009, the budgets for clean tech totaled $44.3 billion and then dropped to roughly $11 billion in 2014—a 75 percent decrease in funding for solar, wind, and other clean technologies (Jenkins, 2012, 6). This continued to decline as subsidies expired. By the end of 2014, 70 percent of 2009 programs had expired and non-ARRA funding declined by 50 percent (Jenkins, 2012, 4, 6).

So, what does this all mean? What did the Obama stimulus funding actually do? To understand the impact, it's important to understand what federal funding is allocated toward. The National Science Foundation supports the physical sciences, environmental sciences, engineering, mathematics and computer sciences, and life sciences. In fiscal year 2012, approximately 88 percent of its budget went to universities and colleges, the highest proportion of any federal agency (NSF, 2013, 9). The National Aeronautics and Space Administration (NASA) focuses one-third of its research on engineering, about a quarter on environmental sciences, and the remaining on physical sciences. Of the environmental science that NASA funds, a significant percentage flows to oceanography and atmospheric and geological sciences. For example, $1.8 billion of NASA funding in 2013 supported research for a fleet of Earth observation spacecrafts to better understand climate change, improve future disaster predictions, and provide vital environmental data to federal, state, and local policymakers (OMB, 2013, 183).

The National Oceanic and Atmospheric Administration's (NOAA) core responsibility is environmental science and stewardship and it supports critical weather and climate satellite programs. This includes better forecasting of ocean conditions and events; more and better data about severe storms and sea-level rise, which helps coastal communities prepare for threats; and restoration and protection of important habitats that protect communities and support healthy ocean ecosystems (National Ocean Council, 2013).

The Department of Energy (DOE), which proposed a budget of $27.9 billion in 2015, supports priority areas such as clean energy, advanced transportation, and grid modernization and resiliency (OMB, 2014). Most of the DOE's budget is devoted to nuclear weapons and nuclear waste and the part allocated to energy resources is less than 10 percent of the total. The fiscal year 2015 budget included increased funding for applied research, development, and demonstration in the office of Energy Efficiency and Renewable Energy (EERE), and expanded funding for the Advanced Research and Projects Agency-Energy (ARPA-E), with the hope of positioning the United States as a world leader in the clean energy economy, creating new industries and domestic jobs. "Within EERE, the Budget increases funding by 15 percent above 2014 enacted levels for sustainable vehicle and fuel technologies, by 39 percent for energy efficiency and advanced manufacturing activities, and by 16 percent for innovative renewable power projects such as those in the SunShot Initiative to make solar power directly price-competitive with other forms of electricity by 2020. The Budget provides funding within EERE to help state and local decision-makers develop policies and regulations that encourage greater deployment of renewable energy, energy efficiency technologies, and alternative fuel vehicles" (OMB, 2014, 74).

These investments symbolized the federal government's growing but, in our view, still small-scale effort to improve our understanding of earth, environmental, and climate science. Even so, the stimulus funding continued the U.S. commitment to international science experiments and support of the frontiers of energy research (OSTP, 2009, 2).

One program of specific note is the Advanced Research and Projects Agency-Energy (ARPA-E), which has funded a number of cutting-edge innovations in clean technologies. Created within the DOE and modeled after the Defense Advanced Research Projects Agency (DARPA), the military's primary division for new technology innovation, ARPA-E works toward developing new technologies to reduce dependence on imported energy, reduce emissions, and increase energy efficiency (Greenstone, 2011, 6). In 2009, Congress and President Obama allocated $400 million to the ARPA-E program as part of the stimulus, providing funding for their first initiatives (ARPA-E, 2014a). Over the next five years it funded 362 projects. Initiatives include projects in biofuels, thermal storage, grid controls, and solar power. "To date, 22 ARPA-E projects have attracted more than $625 million in private-sector follow-on funding after ARPA-E's investment of approximately $95 million. In addition, at least 24 ARPA-E project teams have formed new companies to advance their technologies, and more than 16 ARPA-E projects have partnered with other government agencies for further development" (ARPA-E, 2014b). It is not hard to see how investments in early stage research and basic science can lead to private sector investment during the commercialization and deployment stage. Still, considering the size of federal funding levels, allocations below $1 billion are so insignificant they are not typically mentioned.

While funding levels for basic science are not quite at post-2009 levels, they continue to be supported. Unfortunately, dysfunction in Washington, like the government shutdown in the fall of 2013, seriously impairs government's ability to do this important work. Scientists that depend on federal funding for their research cannot count on a government that could shut down at any moment over partisan squabbles. Federal funding cuts remain a significant challenge to research universities (like Columbia University, where we work), and can discourage scientists from pursuing key opportunities.

How does the United States compare to its international counterparts in federal investment in research? When examining the United States' public and private investment in R&D in terms of GDP, it represented 2.9 percent in 2009, placing it below several other developed countries including Japan (3.3 percent), South Korea (3.4 percent in 2008), and Sweden (3.6 percent) (AAAS, 2013, 21). China's continued increase in R&D investment is now on par with the European Union at 1.98 percent of their total GDP (OECD, 2014, 2). If the United States aims to be a global leader in the green economy, we must ensure that funding for science does not become politicized, and that it remains a top priority for the federal government, demonstrated through continued and increasing support.

*Public Procurement*

While investment in R&D will be the engine to invent the technologies of the future that will lead us towards a green economy, we must also focus on widespread adoption and implementation of both new and existing technologies and practices. Here too, the federal government has a substantial role. Fossil fuels can only be replaced by renewables when clean technologies become cheaper than dirty ones. To drive clean technology prices down, we need demand on a grand scale. Economies of scale for sustainable products and processes push those prices down, closing the gap between these new technologies and older traditional ones. The U.S. federal government is one of the few single purchasers that can use its immense spending power to be a market mover. Governments can use sustainable procurement practices to "create high-volume and long-term demand for green goods and services. This sends signals that allow firms to make longer-term investments in innovation and producers to realize economies of scale, leading in turn to the wider commercialization of green goods and services, as well as more sustainable consumption" (UNEP, 2011, 546). As is the case in many countries around the world, the U.S. government is the largest consumer of goods and services nationwide, and therefore has significant influence over the market. Christian Parenti, Professor in Sustainable Development at The School for International Training Graduate Institute, puts it clearly:

> The fastest, simplest way to do it is to reorient government procurement away from fossil fuel energy, toward clean energy and technology—to use the government's vast spending power to create a market for green energy. After all, the government didn't just fund the invention of the microprocessor; it was also the first major consumer of the device . . . A redirection of government purchasing would create massive markets for clean power, electric vehicles and efficient buildings, as well as for more sustainably produced furniture, paper, cleaning supplies, uniforms, food and services. If government bought green, it would drive down marketplace prices sufficiently that the momentum toward green tech would become self-reinforcing and spread to the private sector (2010).

Why is government procurement so important? First, they spend a lot. The average share of public procurement in GDP in OECD countries is about 11 percent, reaching 16 percent in the countries of the European Union (OECD, 2008, 41). According to the Council on Environmental Quality in the United States, "the federal government occupies nearly 500,000 buildings, operates more than 600,000 vehicles, employs more than 1.8 million civilians, and purchases more than $500 billion per year in goods and services" (The White House Council on Environmental Quality, 2009). Second, it can be directed and executed by the president and the executive branch. The ability to act without Congress is unfortunately the key to making serious shifts toward a green economy. We will probably never see a carbon tax, but we can use the federal government to purchase clean energy now. The United States has begun to make changes in this area, announcing a sustainable procurement strategy in 2009 through Executive Order 13514. It set sustainability goals for federal agencies, focusing on increasing energy efficiency, reducing fleet oil consumption, water conservation, waste reduction, and using their purchasing power to promote environmentally responsible products and technologies (The White House Council on Environmental Quality, 2009). The executive order also called for measuring, reporting, and reducing federal greenhouse gas emissions, and in 2010 President Obama announced goals for 2020: a 28 percent reduction of 2008's direct emissions (e.g., fuels and building energy use), and a 13 percent reduction of indirect emissions (e.g., employee commuting and business travel) (The White House Council on Environmental Quality, 2009). These efforts can have a significant impact. It's estimated that the federal government can save an estimated $1 billion a year through energy efficiency measures in federal buildings (Walsh and Gordon, 2012, 35).

Governments across the globe are using procurement to advance their environmental sustainability and climate change goals. In 2012, over 30 governments and institutions supported an initiative to harness sustainable procurement processes. The initiative promotes the benefits and impacts of sustainable procurement and encourages greater collaboration between key stakeholders (UNEP, 2012, 1–2). The United Nations Environment Programme has found that "sustainable public procurement has the potential to transform markets, boost the competitiveness of eco industries, save money, conserve natural resources and foster job creation" (UNEP, 2012, 1).

*Case Study: Defense Investments in Clean-Energy Technology*

In the United States, the military is one of the biggest clean technology proponents. Recognizing the security implications of our fossil fuel dependence and the energy savings potential of renewables and energy efficiency, the military has consistently served as a test bed for innovation in energy. In the Department of Defense's 2014 Quadrennial Defense Review, the military outlined its vision for environmental sustainability and the critical importance that it places on these issues, as well as their increasing relevance to our national security. "The impacts of climate change may increase the frequency, scale, and complexity of future missions, including defense support to civil authorities, while at the same time undermining the capacity of our domestic installations to support training activities. Our actions to increase energy and water security, including investments in energy efficiency, new technologies, and renewable energy sources, will increase the resiliency of our installations and help mitigate these effects" (DOD, 2014, vi).

These efforts have a global impact. The U.S. Department of Defense is the single, largest energy consumer in the world, passing the consumption total of more than one hundred nations (Adamson, 2012, 1). As part of President Obama's strategy to develop the United States' domestic energy resources, the Department of the Interior (DOI) and the Department of Defense (DOD) teamed up to strengthen the nation's energy security and reduce military utility costs. The two agencies formed a Renewable Energy Partnership Plan, agreeing to work together to facilitate renewable energy development on public lands, and other onshore and offshore areas near or adjacent to military installations (DOD and DOI, 2, 2012).

The U.S. government is also able to use military installations as test beds for new technologies, with the DOD serving as a sophisticated first-user evaluating the technical validity, cost, and environmental impact of advanced technologies before they enter the commercial market (DOD, 2012, 3). The DOD is working to improve energy efficiency of buildings, improve renewable energy technologies, and develop smart microgrids. The DOD is helping create a market for emerging technologies that prove effective and reliable, accelerating the availability of next-generation energy technologies for other federal agencies and the private sector (DOD, 2012, 3–4).

According to a 2014 study by the Pew Charitable Trusts, the deployment of clean energy technology continues to expand throughout the military. They found that the number of energy efficiency projects at military installations "more than doubled from 2010 to 2012, from 630 to 1,339 . . . the number of renewable energy projects increased from 454 to 700 during the same period" (Pew, 2014). These projects are reducing energy demand, increasing on-site energy production, and enhancing energy management (through smart grids), all of which save taxpayer dollars and advance the clean tech market. Pew, and its research partner, Navigant Research, predict that by the end of 2018, renewable energy capacity on military bases could increase by more than fivefold, putting it in position to meet its goal of 3 gigawatts of renewable energy by 2025 (Pew, 2014).

### *Market-Based Tools*

Direct public spending and investment is one set of tools that federal governments have at their disposal. Another option is to use market-based instruments, which employ markets, pricing, and other economic incentives or disincentives to induce change. These include taxes, subsidies, and cap and trade or tradable pollution permit systems. Robert Stavins and Bradley Whitehead describe how market tools are used to meet sustainability goals:

> Properly designed and implemented, market-based instruments—regulations that encourage appropriate environmental behavior through price signals rather than through explicit instructions—provide incentives for businesses and individuals to act in ways that further not only their own financial goals but also environmental aims such as reduce waste, cleaning up the air, or reducing water pollution. In most cases, market mechanisms take overall goals of some sort—say, the total reduction of emissions of a specific pollutant—and leave the choice of how to accomplish this up to the individuals or companies concerned (105–106).

Taxes are nearly universally seen as government's primary policy tool. They are also among the most transparent and effective policy mechanisms available. Taxes, designed to correct negative externalities, such as pollution, enable the government to incorporate some of those external social costs into the price of activities and products, allowing the market to play a critical role in changing purchasing patterns (OECD, 2008, 13). Compared to regulations, which require monitoring and enforcement, taxes, in theory, can work more efficiently because they allow for more flexibility from a household or firm. Carbon taxes are most frequently cited as a possible mechanism to achieve sustainability goals like reduced greenhouse gas emissions. However, unlike many other countries, notably in Europe, the United States imposes practically no green taxes. Some of the few U.S. green taxes imposed at the federal level include the "gas guzzler" tax on new automobiles that exceed fuel efficiency standards, a tax on ozone-depleting substances, and various minor taxes on fertilizers and pesticides used in agriculture. In a global economy, companies can avoid some forms of taxation by locating their firms abroad. Moreover, today, new taxes are political non-starters in the United States, so while they may be recommended by economists, students of public policy look to other mechanisms to achieve desired goals.

Instead, the United States uses other market tools, including subsidies like rebates, tax credits, and loan guarantees, to incentivize investment in the industries it wants to promote. To meet the scale needed to build a sustainable economy, governments must develop policy frameworks that encourage substantial private sector investment in lower-carbon energy options. According to the International Energy Agency (IEA), "financing remains a challenge for low-carbon energy technologies despite availability of capital" (IEA, 2012, 8). Government can facilitate this financing challenge using mechanisms like guaranteed loan programs, which helps lower financial risks associated with clean technology development. These types of programs leverage public dollars into larger investments in the private sector. However, they can face significant criticism when an investment publicly fails, as in the case of the Solyndra bankruptcy, which failed after receiving loan guarantees from the Department of Energy.

Tax credits can provide stable, multi-year incentives to encourage the private sector to invest in certain technologies. They lower the cost difference between renewables and fossil fuels. Providing medium- to long-term price certainty encourages investment in renewable energy and related technologies (like energy storage and smart grids), which in turn drives innovation, wider adoption, and further reduction in prices. These types of policies are critical to lowering costs for consumers, making it easier for individuals to choose renewables over fossil fuels. The investment tax credit (ITC), for example, is a key driver for solar energy. It provides a 30 percent tax credit for solar energy systems for residential and commercial buildings. Since the investment tax credit was implemented in 2006, annual solar installation grew by over 1,600 percent—a compound annual growth rate of 76 percent (SEIA, 2014b). As of 2014, the tax credit has been extended through 2016, providing a short- to medium-term time horizon for investors.

*Case Study: The Production Tax Credit*

Similarly, the Production Tax Credit (PTC) supports the development of renewable energy, most commonly wind, though also geothermal and some bioenergy. The PTC provides an incentive of 2.3 cents per kilowatt-hour (kWh) for the first 10 years of a renewable energy facility's operation (Union of Concerned Scientists, 2014). The tax credit has been a major driver for wind power. It facilitated the tripling of U.S. wind capacity between 2007 and 2012, with an annual average investment of $18 billion. It has also resulted in 550 manufacturing facilities across 44 states producing 72 percent of the wind turbines and components installed in the country (Union of Concerned Scientists, 2014). In 2012, wind power provided 42 percent of all new U.S. power capacity—more than any other single energy source (Steve, Severn, and Raum, 2013).

However, the tax credit for wind power, first enacted in 1992, has since expired three times, and has been temporarily renewed a total of seven times (Jenkins, 2012, 37). This on-again/off-again status has resulted in what has been described as a *boom–bust cycle* of development. In each of the years following expiration, installations dropped significantly—between 76 and 93 percent (Union of Concerned Scientists, 2014). The credit was scheduled to expire again in 2012, but Congress extended it at the very last minute, and it ran through the end of the 2013. However, the deal came so late in the year, that the market was unable to avoid a pull back from investors. As a result, 2013 saw a 93 percent reduction in wind installations in the United States, and the nation's lagging wind market led to a 20 percent drop in global wind development—the first decline in eight years (Eaton, 2014). By the time the extension deal arrived, it was too late to stop planned layoffs and project cancellations (IER, 2013). For example, the Danish-based wind turbine manufacturer Vestas laid off employees at their U.S. factories as a result of the tax credit expiration. In Colorado, Vestas cut its workforce by 40 percent in 2012 (Jaffe, 2013). The last minute deal to extend the credit was unable to revive the momentum that had built up over the previous years, and once again, the tax credit was not extended after it expired at the end of 2013.

This on-again/off-again extension cycle has tremendous impact on investors, price, and availability of renewable energy. Investors look for market certainty, and do not want to rely on the whims of Congress in any given year. While the industry benefited from the short-term tax extensions, they also created uncertainty, job layoffs, and higher-cost projects because organizations were unable to engage in long-range business planning. The absence of a long-term policy discourages manufacturers from investing in and expanding U.S. manufacturing facilities (Steve, Severn, and Raum, 2013), and also causes developers to rush to complete projects as they near the date of the tax credit expiration, leading to smaller projects, higher costs, and increased electricity prices. The planning and permitting process generally takes up to two years to complete, and with expirations looming, developers that depend on the credit to improve a facility's cost-effectiveness will be less likely to begin new projects. This uncertainty and last minute option for extension result in market instability and thwart efforts in wind development. Ultimately, this haphazard policy compromises long-term business investment. Solar power, biofuels, energy-efficient products, and other market segments have experienced similarly erratic expirations (Jenkins, 2012, 37). A study by Navigant Consulting in 2012 found that "a four-year PTC extension would create and save 54,000 American jobs, including growing the wind manufacturing sector by one-third." Unfortunately, congressional politics makes effective investment decisions difficult if not impossible.

## Cap and Trade or Tradable Pollution Permit Systems

Another successful market-based tool employed in the United States is cap and trade, also called tradable pollution permit systems. While often associated with greenhouse gases, pollution trading systems were originally conceived for more traditional air pollution challenges, and have been very successful to date. Cap and trade systems are designed to limit the total amount of pollutants emitted in a defined region by specified parties. Within the cap, parties either receive, or bid on at auction, emission allowances that they may use or sell for a profit. The *cap* sets the limit on emissions and is gradually reduced over time, while the *trade* creates a market for allowances, helping companies innovate in order to meet, or come in below, their allocated limits. Companies are penalized if they exceed their emission allowance. The specific reduction at each plant is not rigidly set by government regulation. The total amount of allowances each facility "owns" equals their cap, thus, a regulated entity may only emit as much of a pollutant as it has allowances for. Some initial emission allowance is given (or sold) to each facility by the government. If the facility is clean and doesn't need to use all of its allowances it can sell them; if it is dirty it can either buy allowances or clean up its facility. Since the cap is lowered on a gradual and predictable schedule, industries can plan ahead for reductions, using engineering and process innovations to meet the reduction. This option gives companies more flexibility by allowing them to make long-term investments instead of forcing a rapid change.

The cap and trade system allows companies to buy and sell allowances to match their individual needs, leading to more cost-effective pollution control and an incentive to invest in cleaner production. Each company decides the best method for its own emission reductions. If a company ends up with extra allowances, it can sell them to other companies, creating a powerful incentive to be a market leader and develop processes to reduce pollution generated by their practices. These types of market mechanisms spur innovation as companies engineer new methods to enhance efficiency and reduce pollution.

Cap and trade has been successfully implemented in the case of sulfur dioxide ($SO_2$) emissions. A series of studies in the 1980s found that $SO_2$ emissions, mostly from coal-fired power plants, were causing acid rain, which was responsible for damaging forests, lakes, and buildings in the northeastern United States and Canada. This discovery led to heated debates over how to reduce this harmful pollutant. Ultimately, policymakers concluded that directing every plant owner to cut their emissions in a traditional, top-down government approach would cost too much, impede innovation, and ignore the valuable insight and initiative of local plant owners (EDF, 2014a).

Instead, policymakers designed a unique approach—emissions trading, which is the result of collaborative efforts, led by the Environmental Defense

Fund (EDF), between environmentalists and government conservatives. The cap and trade system was implemented through the 1990 Amendments to the Clean Air Act as a way to harness the power of the market by allowing each plant to decide how to cut their $SO_2$ emissions. This has resulted in a significant reduction at a quarter of the cost initially projected (EDF, 2014a). By 2009, the Acid Rain Program, run by the EPA, reduced $SO_2$ emissions by 67 percent compared with 1980 levels and 64 percent compared with 1990 levels (EPA, 2010a). A similar program was later developed for nitrogen oxides, a primary contributor to ground-level ozone (i.e., smog). The acid rain emissions trading program has been very successful, exceeding its initial objectives and demonstrating the potential of this type of policy tool. According to EPA, "A 2003 Office of Management and Budget (OMB) study found that the Acid Rain Program accounted for the largest quantified human health benefits—over $70 billion annually—of any major federal regulatory program implemented in the last 10 years, with benefits exceeding costs by more than 40:1" (EPA, 2014b, 1). In 2002, *The Economist* termed it "the greatest green success story of the past decade" (2002).

### Regulations and Standards

Of course, while the success of the acid rain program provided proof of concept for emissions trading, many of the environmental successes of the last 50 years can be attributed to more traditional command-and-control regulatory policies. In the United States and other developed countries, federal environmental laws are typically advanced and cover a wide array of abuses and issues. U.S. examples include: the Clean Air Act, the Clean Water Act, the Resource Conservation and Recovery Act, the Toxic Substances Control Act, and the Comprehensive Environmental Response, Compensation, and Liability Act (CERCLA or Superfund). Governments use regulatory approaches, guided by science, to ensure current and emerging technologies limit pollution and its impacts.

The Clean Air Act (CAA), considered one of the most effective environmental laws ever enacted, was originally established in 1963 to fund the study and cleanup of air pollution. In 1970, a stronger version of the Clean Air Act passed in conjunction with the creation of the Environmental Protection Agency to carry out programs to reduce air pollution nationwide. The Act sets national standards for clean air. Despite clear gains—our air has never been cleaner—in 2011, conservative politicians attempted to prevent the EPA from enforcing the Clean Air Act by attempting to cut $3 billion from the agency's budget (EPA, 2011b, 14). In recent years the EPA has needed to defend itself against repeated attacks by Congress.

While directly regulating industry is often politically unpopular particularly with the businesses that are regulated, these types of laws benefit the broad public by ensuring their water is safe to drink and their air safe to breathe. In certain instances, existing laws may be expanded to compensate for the lack of new law. For example, while the EPA was created in 1970, the Clean Water Act was not enacted until 1972. In the early years, the agency used a 19th century statute designed to keep rivers and harbors free from debris to force cities to clean up their rivers. In a similar vein, the EPA is now regulating greenhouse gas emissions under the Clean Air Act. In comparison to newer proposed legislative solutions to climate change, like the failed Waxman-Markey bill that sought to establish a cap and trade system for greenhouse gas emissions, the Clean Air Act is a non-comprehensive approach to climate policy. It wasn't designed to deal with a problem like climate change, though it is being retrofitted for that purpose. Developing and implementing new rules for greenhouse gases will be a slow and arduous process under the Clean Air Act, with fights from opponents at every step. Nevertheless, with Congress unable to provide a modern tool to begin the process of reducing greenhouse gases, the EPA will simply have to use what is available. Though less than ideal to face the complex challenges of climate change, the Clean Air Act is far better than nothing. The fact that it was designed to adapt to take on new environmental issues as they emerge (many decades later) is a testament to the design of the law.

Another landmark environmental regulation was the first major U.S. law to address water pollution, the Federal Water Pollution Control Act of 1948, which underwent major amendments in 1972 and later became formally known as the Clean Water Act. The act established the basic structure for regulating pollutants and discharge into U.S. waters, and gave the EPA the authority to implement pollution-control programs, including setting wastewater standards and making it illegal to discharge any pollutant from a point source into navigable waters without a permit. It also funded construction of sewage treatment plants and recognized the need for planning to address critical issues as a result of pollution.

The federal government also commonly uses regulatory standards to enforce policy goals. For example, the corporate average fuel economy (CAFE) standards are designed to improve vehicle fuel economy. It was introduced in 1975 with the goal of reducing the U.S. dependence on foreign oil in the wake of the Organization of Petroleum Exporting Countries (OPEC) oil embargo (Anderson et al., 2010, 2). Upon inception, the fuel economy standards helped to nearly double miles per gallon (MPG) for double passenger vehicles by 1985 (Union of Concerned Scientists, 2012). They have dramatically altered vehicle attributes by increasing fuel economy and significantly decreasing the size and weight of passenger cars. After the adoption of fuel economy standards, fuel use by passenger cars had decreased by nearly one-third since 1975. Without these standards, motor-vehicle fuel consumption would have been approximately 14 percent higher that it was in 2002 (NRC, 2002, 13).

Fuel standards did not improve between 1990 and 2011, but in 2009 the Obama administration introduced the National Fuel Efficiency Policy, setting forth new standards requiring an average fuel economy of 35.5 MPG for model years 2012–2016 (Office of the Press Secretary, 2009). This achievement involved an unprecedented collaboration between the Department of Transportation, the EPA, the world's largest auto manufacturers, the United Auto Workers labor union, and leaders in the environmental community and state governments.

While this was a great success, the United States lags behind many industrialized countries in fuel economy standards. Europe remains the global leader in vehicle efficiency with 50 percent higher fuel economy than the United States. In 2020, the European Union has set forth a goal of 60.6 MPG; Japan hopes to meet 55.1 MPG, and China 50.1 MPG. The United States trails with a goal of 49.1 MPG in 2025, indicating the country still has some progress to make to meet the targets of its international counterparts (The International Council on Clean Transportation, 2, 2012).

## What Is Not Working?

We have outlined a number of policies that the U.S. federal government has deployed that serve to move toward a green economy. None are perfect, and most need more political support and resources than they currently have, but in general, they are effective and need to be continued, expanded, and championed. However, next we'll turn to the federal policies that hinder our progress on the path to sustainability. We'll look at the policies that financially support the fossil fuel industry, regulatory failure, and what President Obama calls his "all of the above" approach to energy strategy.

## Fossil Fuel Industry Support

We have already discussed the importance of subsidies for clean technologies—the energy generation, storage, and distribution systems of the future—but federal policy continues to subsidize the current fossil fuel–based energy system. According to the International Energy Agency (IEA), in 2011, global fossil fuel subsidies were estimated at $409 billion (up almost 30 percent from 2010), six times the amount allotted for renewable energy support (2012). The phasing-out of inefficient fossil fuel subsidies is estimated to cut growth in energy demand by 4.1 percent by 2020 (IEA, 2011a). Eliminating these subsidies globally would also cut energy-related carbon dioxide emissions by 13 percent, according to the International Monetary Fund (Ball, 2013). In the United States, subsidies for fossil fuels over the period 2002 through 2008 totaled $72 billion, while subsidies for renewable fuels totaled $29 billion during the same period (Environmental Law Institute, 2009, 3).

In the United States, the oil depletion allowance enables oil companies to treat reserves in the ground as assets that will eventually be exhausted for tax purposes. A percentage of the value of the asset is subtracted from a company's taxable income. This allowance can be traced back to the Revenue Act of 1913, in which the oil subsidy was written into the tax code. This allowed oil companies to write off 5 percent of the costs from oil and gas wells. Today, one hundred years after this policy was enacted, oil companies can deduct 15 percent. The rationale for this subsidy is that once the oil in a well is pumped out, we want to encourage the industry to dig another. While fossil fuels are our best option for generating a resource as critical to the economy as oil, it is not clear whether the depletion allowance is necessary to incentivize investment in exploring new energy resources. It may well be that the profits of the oil industry are incentive enough: "Exxon Mobil just missed setting a company—and world—record for annual profit in 2012. The No. 1 U.S. oil company posted full-year earnings of $44.9 billion" (Isidore, 2013).

The fossil fuel industry and many supporters in Congress argue that these tax breaks encourage domestic oil production and provide jobs for millions of Americans. Supporters see the tax provisions as comparable to those affecting other industries and supporting the production of domestic oil and natural gas resources. Opponents see these tax expenditures as subsidies to a profitable industry and impediments to the development of clean energy alternatives (Pirog, 2, 2012). In 2011, President Obama called on Congress to eliminate the oil depletion allowance along with a series of other tax breaks totaling $4 billion annually (Hargreaves, 2011). In a letter to congressional leaders, Obama wrote, "CEOs of the major oil companies have made it clear that high oil prices provide more than enough profit motive to invest in domestic production without special tax breaks. As we work together to reduce our deficits, we simply can't afford these wasteful subsidies" (Hargreaves, 2011). President Obama continued advocating the repeal of the $4 billion in fossil fuel subsidies in his proposed budget for FY 2015 (OMB, 2014).

Are these subsidies actually serving to keep costs down and serve the American public? Oil is a global commodity and prices are driven not by subsidies to U.S. companies, but by the global market. World energy consumption has nearly doubled in the last two decades. The simple laws of supply and demand will continue to drive the price of energy up as long as we continue to depend on fossil fuels that are expensive to mine and expensive to transport. Energy prices are increasing due to the control of energy resources by a few large companies along with massive increases in demand. Our addiction to energy throughout the economy contributes to the price growth and volatility experienced by the average American energy consumer.

In order to lower energy costs we will need to look to new technologies for energy generation and distribution. Not only does fossil fuel mining and burning damage the environment and cause global warming, but it also will be difficult for increased supply to keep up with increased demand. This is not to say that we will run out of fossil fuels in the near future, but even with new sources like shale gas and hydraulic fracturing, these fuels are not getting easier or cheaper to extract and transport. In our view, our goal should not be energy independence, but rather a reduction in the proportion of our GDP spent on energy. Lower-cost renewable energy, smart grid technology, distributed energy generation, and increased energy efficiency will enable us to reduce the cost of energy. If the goal is a sustainable economy we will need to readjust our subsidies from fossil fuels to renewable energy.

## All of the Above Energy Policy

Under the Obama administration, the United States lacked a coherent, clear national energy policy. President Obama's proposed *all of the above* energy policy, includes expanding domestic natural gas and oil production, promoting biofuels, supporting renewables, and investing in carbon capture and storage for clean coal (which these authors believe is an oxymoron). This approach was a way to avoid making clear policy decisions and developing a strategic direction. It was a political strategy designed to avoid choices that could alienate stakeholders—and in energy policy, anyone can be considered a stakeholder. Such a broad policy lacks focus, which makes it nearly impossible to put into action. As Jeffrey Ball, former environment editor at *The Wall Street Journal* and scholar-in-residence at Stanford University observed: "As a statement of fact, 'all of the above' neatly describes the nation's energy shift. But as a summation of strategy, it's so general as to be meaningless. It's so opaque that it's succeeding mostly in angering all the special interests involved" (Ball, 2014).

The question for governments is: What can be done to stimulate the rapid development and diffusion of advanced clean energy technology? The transformative potential of such technology is obvious. The political necessity for this technology should be equally obvious, but is not. It's really quite simple. Without an energy transformation, our way of life is in danger and the probability that the aspiring billions in the developing world will achieve what we have here disappears. In its place, we can expect a declining standard of living and political instability.

"All of the above" is more of a public relations phrase than a policy because it refuses to acknowledge the need to make choices. President Obama seemed to understand the energy issue, and understood the relationship of renewable energy to America's economic revival, but he was unwilling to pay the political price needed to make renewable energy a real priority.

There is no question that demand for energy will continue to increase, and that inadequate energy supplies could be economically devastating and politically destabilizing. It is easy to see why national leaders gravitate to the all of the above energy strategy, but we do not need governments to advocate or pursue all of the above. Without government leadership and direction, the market itself will deliver an "all of the above" approach to energy.

The political power of energy companies is an intense and central part of the environment of policy decision making in Washington. It would take unusual courage and skill to pursue government energy policy that resists this economic and political force. It may be too much to expect a U.S. president to push back against this force, but without strong and constant leadership in the Oval Office, rapid change is unlikely.

### Regulatory Capture and Regulatory Failure

In April 2010, the BP Deepwater Horizon drilling rig exploded, killing 11 people and releasing oil into the Gulf of Mexico for 87 days. It was the worst environmental disaster the United States has seen since the dustbowl of the 1930s, with 200 million gallons of oil entering the Gulf before the leak was contained. Along with our colleagues, we watched with horror as the live feed showed the oil spilling into the ocean day after day, despite the efforts of top industry and government engineers. No one knew how to stop the flow. Ultimately, it was closed, and we refocused our attention on the reasons this was allowed to happen. What we found was one of the most blatant examples of regulatory capture—and failure—in recent memory. *Regulatory capture* refers to the phenomenon when a public agency created to oversee an industry instead serves to advance the special interests of companies they are supposed to regulate. Regulatory capture is often paired with a revolving-door policy, wherein regulators leave their positions in government and assume executive positions in the regulated industry. The BP oil spill represents one example of this problem that occurs in many industries in the United States and around the world.

### Case Study: Regulatory Capture in the Minerals Management Service

The now-restructured Minerals Management Service (MMS) was an agency housed within the Department of the Interior that managed the nation's natural gas, oil, and other mineral resources on the outer continental shelf. Until its restructuring in 2010, the MMS was responsible for generating revenue by leasing land to extractive companies, overseeing the process, and protecting the environment. Created in 1982, the Minerals Management Service was given two goals: (1) to collect royalties from oil companies operating on U.S. soil, and (2) to protect U.S. soil and water from the companies operating on them. Its dual purpose put the agency in a difficult position and its two goals sometimes came into conflict, especially as its revenues soared.

In the 1990s, the Minerals Management Service was instructed to accelerate royalty collection, and at the same time, 10 percent of its staff was laid off in five years. In 1995, with royalty revenues at the center of its focus, the MMS adopted a regulatory style that used *performance goals* instead of *prescriptive rules* to protect the natural environment. "Performance goals leave it to the offshore drilling industry to prevent blowouts . . . Prescriptive rules detail how it's supposed to do so—and hold the industry accountable if it doesn't" (Blumenthal and Bolstad, 2010). In the Minerals Management Service's case, rewards were the royalties flowing from oil and gas companies to the federal government. The desired performance was twofold: (1) good oil-drilling practice, and (2) the maximization of revenue. Unfortunately, good drilling practice was sometimes sacrificed in favor of revenue maximization. Studies funded by the MMS that called for more regulation were often ignored or rewritten. This regulatory style explains why it did not regulate the number of blind shear rams on every oil rig or insist that oil companies perform regular upkeep tests on their safety equipment. By relying on a regulatory style directed by performance goals, the Department of the Interior essentially handed regulatory power over to the industry that it was supposed to be regulating.

In the case of the BP Deepwater Horizon disaster, the Minerals Management Service consistently allowed the industry to self-regulate and make its own choices when it came to safety. It failed to enforce measures that would have prevented oil companies and their contractors from choosing cost reduction over safety. The primary cause of the Deepwater Horizon oil spill was that resource-extraction technology outpaced effective government regulation of the industry. The Department of the Interior has an inherent conflict of interest because it generates revenue by leasing government land and water for mining and drilling, and regulates those activities that take place there. Under this arrangement, the mining and drilling companies are clients of the Department of the Interior, which must also act as an unbiased regulator. A similar conflict of interest would arise if a chief food inspector were also a partner in the same city's biggest restaurant.

In response to the Deepwater Horizon catastrophe in the Gulf of Mexico, the Obama administration decided to break up the Minerals Management Service to separate its regulatory and revenue collection functions in an effort to reform the government's regulation of offshore energy development. However, this may serve to simply move the conflict up the organizational food chain, as both entities are all still housed within the Department of Interior.

The BP spill is certainly not the only case of regulatory capture, but it is one of the most visible. The Fukushima Daiichi nuclear accident in Japan, which followed a 2011 earthquake and tsunami, was also due in part to regulatory capture and oversight failure. Some defenders of the close relationships between regulators and industry claim that only those with the deep knowledge and expertise that comes from working within the industry itself can enable a regulator to truly understand the technical challenges in the field. We argue that is not the only way to gain this expertise; for example, we could instead invest in our regulatory agencies and attract top experts in these fields.

*Federal Regulatory Failure*

When the technology to extract resources so significantly outpaces our ability to clean up or fix failures in that system, or even to understand the environmental and health implications of those activities, we are in trouble. We are beginning to see this with hydraulic fracturing (commonly called *fracking*) across the United States. Fracking is a process in which water, sand, and chemicals are injected under high pressure into deep earth wells to fracture shale rock formations, which release natural gas that can be extracted. Industry has devised an innovative new method to profitably extract oil and gas that were previously unreachable, but we are proceeding before we have had a chance to truly understand fracking's impact on the geology of the land, the toxicity of the chemicals used in the process, and the resultant impact on the local communities.

In the long run, we need to develop a fossil fuel–free economy, but in the short run, we are forced to choose between the energy sources now available. Natural gas pollutes the air and emits greenhouse gases, but it is not as dirty a fuel as either coal or oil. Every energy source has costs and benefits that need to be carefully weighed before it is dismissed or adopted. Hydraulic fracturing, deep-sea oil drilling, and mountaintop removal are risky and environmentally destructive, but it is infeasible to ban them until we develop a renewable energy source that is readily accessible and affordable. Our economic well-being and political stability depend on energy. The forces pushing to extract these fuels are far more powerful than the political and economic power of those in favor of leaving the fuels in the ground. If hydraulic fracturing is to take place, then it should be carefully regulated to reduce its impact on ecosystems and public health. We should carefully study the technology of hydraulic fracturing in order to develop a set of best practices designed to reduce fracking's impact on ecosystems and human health.

The federal government's abdication of its regulatory responsibilities in this area is a legacy of the Bush-Cheney years. Through loopholes and political maneuvering, hydraulic fracturing was exempt from EPA regulations in energy legislation enacted in 2005. Hydraulic fracturing cannot be successfully regulated without national rules, and in the long run that is what we will need to do. Fracking is allowed in 30 states, yet it is not regulated at the federal level. States with no rules and little accountability, like Pennsylvania, Ohio, and West Virginia, are said to be like the Wild West when it comes to gas drilling practices. Processes in these areas can be sloppy and poorly managed, and invite environmental catastrophe. Other states have seen a backlash against fracking. In 2008, New York State issued a moratorium on fracking until more studies could be completed. New York's Governor Cuomo has worked to avoid making a decision on ending the moratorium (Klopott, 2014).

If scientific study indicates that there is no safe way to extract shale gas from the ground, the practice should be banned. A more likely outcome is that a carefully managed fracking process can be designed, but it will cost more than the current version. Given the need for energy and the cost of other energy sources, fracking can probably be profitable, even if it is rigorously regulated at the federal level.

Fracking demonstrates the lack of ability at the federal level to take on new environmental challenges. We certainly see this in other areas. We have no federal policy on climate change. We have no federal policy on electronic waste recycling and that is a growing problem due to the rapid replacement and disposal of smartphones, laptops, and tablet devices. We have not had any major piece of federal environmental legislation since the early 1990s. We are relying on existing laws, agencies, and other mechanisms to deal with new problems not envisioned when those laws were designed. We need legislators who are willing to take on the complexities of global, regional, and local sustainability issues. We also need to enhance the ability of our regulatory structure to keep pace with the industries it is meant to be regulating.

## What Is Possible?

In this chapter, we've discussed the policies and programs we think the U.S. federal government is effectively implementing to address challenges of sustainability, and introduced some of the challenges that remain. While progress at the national level is stalled in the United States, other nations are moving forward. While many of the policies pursued outside the United States might be politically infeasible in this nation today, we still believe it is useful to analyze and learn from the rest of the world.

### Taxes

We have discussed the use of the tax code to help move the cost–benefit calculus toward sustainability. The federal government could expand its use of taxes and tax incentives to encourage more rapid development of sustainability practices; examples include tax credits, subsidies, local fees and charges for specific activities.

It is typically argued by economists that a carbon tax is a simple way to discourage fossil fuels, but despite being easy to implement, such a regressive tax would affect people, rich and poor, across the economic spectrum. Designing a rebate or dividend system to return collected revenues to poor people would not be simple. A second problem with a carbon tax is determining the rate. It is crucial to get it right at the outset because, as seen with the current tax on gasoline, it will be very hard to raise at a later date. The federal tax on gasoline was supposed to fund the entire interstate highway system and its operation and maintenance. Unfortunately, this tax has not kept pace with inflation and our roads have fallen into disrepair. A carbon tax would be equally difficult to change once it is established. The trend in environmental and safety regulation is that as we learn more over time, we make the rules more stringent. The political reality is that we often do not know what a safe level of a hazardous substance is, so it is probably best to set a standard that can be changed over time.

The probability of an American carbon tax is quite low. Nevertheless, other countries have successfully implemented carbon taxes and other green taxes. For example, the Nordic countries (Denmark, Finland, Norway, and Sweden) introduced carbon taxes in the 1990s. Other countries with taxes or surcharges on household electricity include Austria, Germany, and the Netherlands (OECD, 2008, 14). In many of these cases, taxes on electricity provide public funding for renewable incentives or are devoted to improving efficiency in the existing infrastructure.

Finland's carbon tax applies to gasoline, diesel, light fuel oil, heavy fuel oil, jet fuel, aviation gasoline, coal, and natural gas. In 2008, the Ministry of Environment in Finland estimated that the revenue from the carbon tax was approximately $750 million annually. All the revenue from the carbon tax goes directly into the government's general budget without any earmarking for climate issues (NREL, 2009, 9). In Norway, the tax rates vary greatly by sector, but are applied to the generation of approximately 68 percent of Norway's $CO_2$ emissions and 50 percent of total greenhouse gas emissions (NREL, 2009, 10). Norway directs the tax revenues to a general government account along with the revenue from offshore drilling licenses. In 2007, these revenues financed a special pension fund that contained $373 billion or $80,000 for every person in Norway. They've found that their carbon tax has led to industrial efficiency gains as well as technological innovation. From 1991 to 2003, emissions per unit of production have decreased by 22 percent (NREL, 2009, 11).

In 2010, Ireland began imposing taxes on most of the fossil fuels used by homes, offices, vehicles, and farms. Historically, Ireland had been among Europe's highest per-capita producers of greenhouse gases. However, since the implementation of the carbon tax, Ireland has seen its emissions levels drop by more than 15 percent since 2008 (Rosenthal, 2012). Of course, it is difficult to determine how much of that decrease was due to the global recession rather than the tax itself. The tax raised nearly €1 billion

($1.3 billion dollars) in taxes in the first three years of implementation (Rosenthal, 2012). When the tax was first introduced, the Minister provided funding for complementary measures to support retrofitting of homes to improve energy efficiency as well as a subsidy for the poor, though that subsidy declined over time (Convery, 2012). However, a large portion of the carbon tax revenue was used to reduce the Irish government's huge budget gap and deficit. The tax provided the government with 25 percent of the €1.6 billion in new taxes it needed, preventing an otherwise certain rise in income tax rates (Rosenthal, 2012).

National taxes may also be used to promote more efficient water, waste treatment, and recycling efforts. To discourage water waste and encourage water reuse, some governments tax water usage and wastewater. Australia, Canada, Mexico, and most European countries have implemented such charges and have seen success in reduction in water use and waste. The tax can be figured at the consumer level based on a number of factors, including the physical size of a home, the number of occupants in a household, or on a per-person basis (OECD, 2008, 14). In Denmark, "household water consumption was greatly reduced by a 150% increase in the price of water through a combination of taxes—water supply tax (41%), VAT (20%), variable water taxes (12%), green taxes (14%), variable taxes (9%), fixed wastewater charge (2%), and State wastewater tax (2%)" (OECD, 2008, 15). Again, while these efforts are being implemented successfully abroad, mostly in Europe, they remain extremely difficult to enact in the United States.

### Cap and Trade

The American Clean Energy and Security Act, also known as the Waxman-Markey bill for its authors, representatives Henry Waxman, of California, and Edward Markey, of Massachusetts, was an energy bill brought in front of Congress in 2009 that would have established a greenhouse gas emissions trading plan much like the European Union Emission Trading System. The bill was passed in the House of Representatives in June of 2009, but was defeated in the Senate, ending the only real congressional effort to address climate change in a comprehensive way. The hyper-partisan era that has overtaken Washington, DC, since that time means that a national cap and trade program is very unlikely. In Chapter 7, we'll discuss the politics of sustainability that make efforts like a carbon cap and trade program so difficult.

## *Case Study: the European Union Emissions Trading System*

Despite failing to pass federally in the United States, greenhouse gas cap and trade schemes exist elsewhere at the national and regional levels. One example is the European Union Emissions Trading System (EU ETS). Launched in 2005, the European system was the world's first and largest emissions trading scheme, operating in 30 countries, and covering emissions from power stations, plants, oil refineries, and cement, paper, and other factories. According to the Environmental Defense Fund, the cap and trade program has driven significant reduction in greenhouse gas emissions, led to the innovation of new low-carbon processes, and has done so at a fraction of the predicted costs—only 0.01 percent of GDP (Brown, Hanafi, and Petsonk, 2012, 5). In the program, the EU sets a legally binding cap on the amount of carbon dioxide emissions allowed by covered entities. The price of carbon allowances on the open market is determined by the price of the penalty and the need for extra allowances.

Since its inception, emissions in sectors affected by the trading system have decreased by approximately 13 percent between 2005 and 2010. By 2012, the EU trading system was responsible for the reduction of more than 480 million tons of $CO_2$, more than the entire 2009 $CO_2$ emissions of Mexico or Australia (Brown, Hanafi, and Petsonk, 2012, vi). However, some argue that the apparent results of the EU emissions trade may be inflated. The financial crisis of 2008 resulted in reduced energy use and industrial activity in Europe. The unexpected reduction in the energy usage due to the financial crisis created a surplus of emissions permits, which lowered the price of the allowances (Reed, 2014).

The EU trading system stipulates that the revenue received from the auction of allowances must be returned to the EU member states. Eighty-eight percent of the allowance revenues are distributed to the member states based on their relative share of emissions from regulated installations in 2005. Ten percent of the revenue is distributed to the least wealthy member states as an additional source of revenue for the purpose of solidarity and growth in the European Union. The remaining 2 percent is distributed to the members who had reduced greenhouse gas emissions by at least 20 percent from their respective Kyoto Protocol base year levels (European Commission, 2014). The use of the distributed auction revenues is mostly left to the discretion of the member states, although at least half of the revenues returned to each member state is meant to be dedicated to combat climate change. Although this provision is not legally binding, member states are obligated to inform the European Commission on how they use the additional revenues (European Commission, 2014).

While the EU system is the largest system of its kind, a handful of other countries are beginning to implement programs of their own. In 2008, New Zealand implemented the New Zealand Emissions Trading Scheme that covers emissions from forestry, stationary energy, industrial processes, and liquid fossil fuels (New Zealand Ministry for the Environment, 2012). Since 2005, Japan has been operating a voluntary emissions trading scheme that covers carbon dioxide emissions from fuel consumption, electricity and heat, waste management, and industrial processes. More than 300 companies take part in this voluntary program (New Zealand Ministry for the Environment, 2012). In 2012, South Korea enacted a trading scheme that requires about 500 of its largest emitters (covering approximately 60 percent of Korea's greenhouse gas emissions) to pay for their carbon dioxide emissions beginning in 2015.


## Infrastructure

The U.S. federal government built this country's ports, canals, dams, railroads and highways, and now must build the infrastructure of the 21st century. Travel through Europe or Asia and you see high-tech airports and state-of-the-art bullet trains; come to New York City and you see a run-down JFK Airport and the underground tunnel system we call Penn Station. Infrastructure spending is an essential function of government that has been financially starved since the start of the Reagan revolution in 1981. Many types of infrastructure are financed through public–private partnerships, and government planning, policy, and subsidies are typical. The long lead times of some infrastructure projects can make them relatively invisible, when compared to high-profile, hot-button issues that have an immediate effect. This makes infrastructure projects a low priority for elected leaders, although the failure to restore infrastructure can lead to inconveniences—such as potholes and flooded roads—and catastrophes—such as bridge collapses and gas-line explosions.

Anyone traveling via America's highways, deteriorating bridges, ramshackle airports, and underfunded mass transit facilities knows that we are not keeping up with infrastructure needs. There are, of course, some exceptions, such as New York City's addition of a new subway line on Second Avenue. However, there have also been less successful infrastructure projects, such as the Big Dig in Boston and the now-dead Trans-Hudson Passenger Rail Tunnel between New York and New Jersey. We seem to do better at public–private partnerships when we are building billion-dollar sports complexes than when we are improving our infrastructure. The problem with the sports facilities is that they do not have the same degree of positive economic impact that we get when we build a new bridge, train, or water treatment facility.

America's infrastructure gap is no closer to being addressed today than it was at the end of the 20th century. When we began the interstate highway system in the 1950s, we funded both capital and maintenance through a tax on gasoline. Unfortunately, that tax was set in absolute pennies per gallon rather than as a percentage of the price of gasoline. For the most part, that formula has remained, and the highway trust fund has not kept pace with the nation's highway capital or maintenance needs. Dedicated and adequate financing will be the key to sustaining our nation's infrastructure for the future.

Anti-tax sentiments and growing costs of the social safety net during the past three decades have made it impossible to develop long-term mechanisms to fund America's infrastructure. A system of user fees ought to be developed and must be made part of routine policy making. Cable TV and cell phone companies have managed to develop a new set of user fees that allow them to replace and upgrade communications infrastructure while generating substantial profits. Roads and other public goods cannot be privatized to that degree, but some type of routine methods must be developed to finance essential infrastructure. Water fees and, in some localities, waste management fees have been added to local property taxes and provide a regular revenue stream for those essential services. While no one wants to pay fees or taxes, no one wants to travel on dangerous bridges, or rely on an expensive, tenuous, and energy-inefficient system for transporting goods to market. Advanced infrastructure is needed if the United States is to meet its environmental challenges, ensure global competitiveness, and maintain long-term national security.

## High-Speed Rail

There is currently one high-speed rail line running in the United States—the Amtrak Acela Express, which travels along the Northeast Corridor between Boston, New York, Philadelphia, and Washington, DC. However, the U.S. definition of *high-speed rail* is generous. Even on the Acela train, it still takes approximately 3 hours to travel the 225 miles between Washington, DC, and New York City. The Acela is also expensive; the average price of a one-way ticket runs from $150 to $200. By comparison, in Europe, you can take the Eurostar from London to Paris (approximately 280 miles) in about 2 hours and 15 minutes for £77 ($126 USD), *round trip*.

For more examples of successful high-speed rail systems, we look to China, which is comparable in area to the United States. High-speed rail was introduced to China in April of 2007. In less than seven years, the high-speed rail system now carries twice as many passengers each month as the country's domestic airline industry (Bradsher, 2013). Over the first five years of operations, high-speed rail traffic has grown about 28 percent per year. In fact, airlines in China have more or less ended service on routes of less than 300 miles if high-speed rail is available between the cities. They have even reduced service on routes of 300 to 500 miles because so many people can travel by train. Projections from 2013 estimated that the number of passengers using China's high-speed rail line each month would soon exceed the number of people taking domestic U.S. flights each month (Bradsher, 2013). China's high-speed rail lines have had a significant impact on local economies: a World Bank study found that the Chinese cities connected to the high-speed rail network are more likely to experience broad growth in productivity because companies are a manageable ride from tens of millions of potential customers, employees, and corporate rivals (Bradsher, 2013). China's investment in high-speed rail has not come without expense. The government has accumulated approximately $500 billion in overall rail debt, and predicts they will continue to invest $100 billion a year in the system for many years to come

(Bradsher, 2013.) Despite the high price tag, China's rapid growth in high-speed rail is a tangible example of green growth that will serve the country for the next century.

High-speed rail is also a popular form of transportation in Europe. It has improved travel times on intranational corridors ever since it was first introduced in the late 1980s. In 2007, a consortium of European rail operators, known as the Railteam, formed to boost cross-border high-speed rail travel. Austria, Belgium, France, Germany, Italy, the Netherlands, Russia, Spain, Sweden, and the United Kingdom are just a handful of countries that are all connected via high-speed rail. These systems have a significant impact when it comes to reducing greenhouse gas emissions. An independent study commissioned by one of Europe's rail companies, Eurostar, found that a flight between London and Paris generated approximately 10 times more carbon dioxide emissions than the equivalent Eurostar journey (Eurostar, 2006). According to a study by the Center for Clean Air Policy and the Center for Neighborhood Technology, the United States could save around 6 billion pounds of carbon dioxide emissions per year by implementing high-speed rail between select major cities in the United States. If implemented, they project 112 million trips by 2025, resulting in 29 million fewer automobile trips and nearly 500,000 fewer flights (Center for Clean Air Policy, 2006, 1).

In 2013, President Obama requested $40 billion over five years for a new National High-Performance Rail System (Federal Railroad Administration, 2013, 6). However, almost all of the money in this program goes towards improving current rail service and infrastructure, leaving very little for research, development, and technology of new services, including implementation of new high-speed rail tracks.

*Electrification of Vehicle Transportation*

High-speed rail is one way to bring our transportation system into the 21st century while enhancing efficiency, advancing environmental sustainability, and improving the quality of life for riders. A second method is to transition from the internal combustion engine to electric vehicles (EVs). Electric vehicles release no emissions when operating, and are nearly zero-emission when they are fueled by electricity generated from renewable sources. Electric vehicles can also be used as batteries, storing electricity when they are not in use, and they can be charged when the grid has excess capacity late at night.

Up to this point, local and state governments have primarily led efforts to provide electric vehicle incentives and infrastructure (such as charging stations). The federal government made investments, but they have not been substantial. In his State of the Union Address in 2011, President Obama established a goal of 1 million electric vehicles on the road by 2015. The United States invested funds from the stimulus plan to help achieve this goal. However, in January 2013, the Department of Energy announced that they were easing off President Obama's goal and articulated a more modest goal of promoting advanced-drive vehicles over the next nine years and decreasing their cost as well as supporting research for new battery technologies and manufacturing methods (Rascoe and Seetharaman, 2013).

Despite this reduced goal, the federal government is building capacity for electric vehicle deployment with the EV Project. With funding from the Department of Energy, and partnerships with Nissan, General Motors, and over 10,000 city, regional and state governments, utilities and other organizations, the project deployed 12,000 electric vehicle chargers across the country. The project was tasked with installing chargers, collecting and analyzing data, conducting trials of revenue systems, and evaluating the effectiveness of charging infrastructure. It represents the largest deployment of electric vehicles and infrastructure in history (The EV Project, 2013; INL, 2014). "The data collection phase of The EV Project ran from January 1, 2011, through December 31, 2013 and captured almost 125 million miles of driving and 4 million charging events." The Department of Energy's Idaho National Laboratory is responsible for analyzing that data (INL, 2014).

While efforts have begun, what will it take to transition to a renewable energy transport system? Currently, insufficient infrastructure and uncertainty about the future of EVs have made consumers hesitant about making the switch. We need charging stations at workplaces and other public destinations so drivers know that they will not be stranded when their batteries run low. Public charging needs to be convenient and quick to compete with gasoline powered combustion engines; no one wants to wait six hours to recharge a car battery. The construction of a national electrified transportation system goes hand in hand with the country's effort to modernize the electricity grid. Investment in R&D to advance EV technology is also crucial to tip the scale in favor of widespread adoption.

## The Smart Grid

The United States needs to continue its progress toward enhancing our energy infrastructure and improving the production and distribution of electricity. By transforming the way we produce, distribute, and consume electricity, the smart grid offers the United States the opportunity to transition to a more sustainable energy future.

A smart grid leverages technology in order to produce and react to information in the electrical system. Smart grid technologies enable two-way communication between the consumer and supplier using switches, sensors, software, meters, and other devices that allow the electrical system to monitor and control in real time the available supply and demand of electricity. It will be able to conserve energy, facilitate integration of new decentralized energy resources, and make the grid more resilient, responsive, and reliable (Succar and Cavanagh, 2012, 3). For example, a smart grid enables grid operators to detect power outages in real-time, allowing them to redirect electricity, control the size of the outage, and decrease restoration times. In addition, smart grids enable consumers to understand how much electricity they are using and to choose to use the electricity at off-peak times when the prices are discounted instead of during periods of peak demand. Smart grids pair well with electric vehicles, which typically charge overnight when electricity demand and prices are low. Smart grid technologies will increase the flexibility of the grid, allowing smoother integration of renewable technologies such as wind and solar to replace current sources.

The federal government has made investments in the smart grid already, but it must decide how to proceed. The government could help develop a framework that establishes guidelines and protocols for smart grid development. There are concerns that, because the electrical grids differ by jurisdiction, nationwide regulation may be nearly impossible to implement and police. A successful undertaking with similar challenges can be found in the interstate highway system, which created a national system of transportation. To facilitate smart grid power, the federal government could modernize the transmission of electricity with a similar tax and grant structure.


## The Promise of Federally Led Sustainability

Our nation's history of environmental sustainability has always been gradual, and it has always required the accommodation of local economic and political interests. The Resource Conservation and Recovery Act is a case in point. Though the act was signed in 1976, some of the final rules for hazardous waste dumps did not go into effect until the 1990s. The increased quality of our air and water is the result of about four decades of incremental reform and progress. The organizational structure of the EPA itself is designed to ensure that state and local political and economic pressures are carefully accommodated. The EPA is a very decentralized agency. While national policy is made in its Washington, DC headquarters, much of the specifics of implementation are left to its 10 regional offices. The work of the EPA's regional offices is closely monitored by the congressional delegations representing the states within each region. These regional offices negotiate with local industries and governments on the details of environmental permits and must be responsive to local economic forces and the demands of local elected officials.

All of this serves to ensure that the implementation of environmental regulation proceeds at a deliberate pace. Progress has come step by painful step, and America's air, water, and land are all cleaner than they were when the EPA was created in 1970, but there is no doubt that this progress has been very gradual. The EPA is the regulatory tortoise—not the environmentalist hare—but just as in the children's fable, slow and steady wins the race. We continue to advance federal efforts to support sustainability at all levels and across all areas of society and the economy. There may never be a sweeping cap and trade bill, but there may be a partnership with private companies to build high-speed railways. There are funds for our top universities to develop the next generation of batteries. They might not be as exciting or catch as many headlines, but these are the efforts that will ensure progress toward sustainability.

In our view, the focus of climate and energy policy should be to lower the price of clean energy rather than to raise the price of dirty energy. Cap and trade, carbon taxes, and other forms of regulation could be supplanted by policies that directly promote renewable energy. As oil and coal become less plentiful and more difficult to extract and transport, their prices will rise. As renewable energy technology develops and is adopted, its price will fall. Eventually, renewables will be much cheaper than oil and coal, and fossil fuels will go the way of the cassette tape. This still requires government intervention, but it does not need new command-and-control government regulation or a carbon tax. While those policies remain sound ideas that would speed the transition, they are not an absolute necessity. There are two government interventions necessary for sustainability progress: (1) investments in the basic science and engineering of new renewable-energy technologies, and (2) tax incentives to encourage their adoption.

# 4

# Policy Levers for Sustainability

## *The State Level*

## Introduction

The U.S. national government plays a crucial role in sustainability management; however, in recent years Congress has gridlocked on these issues. As happened in the 1980s, state governments have stepped in and filled the gap. State governments have at their disposal many of the same tools and mechanisms that the federal government has but, given the dysfunction in Washington lately, they seem better able to use them.

For example, although Congress failed to adopt comprehensive climate change legislation, the U.S. is still on its way to achieving the target reduction of 17 percent from 2005 levels by 2020—the goal that President Obama announced at the 2009 U.N. climate talks in Copenhagen. Contributing factors include the economic slowdown, anticipated greenhouse gas (GHG) regulations under the Clean Air Act, and trends in relative fuel prices and energy efficiency. However, progress can also be attributed to a number of actions implemented at the state level over the past decade (Burtraw and Woerman, 2012, 1–2).

States have not waited for the federal government to take up sustainability agendas. They are designing programs that complement national programs and compensate for gaps in federal policy. They are going ahead with energy policies, climate plans, infrastructure upgrades, and transportation planning to enhance their sustainability and attract businesses and residents to their states. Many of these initiatives are undertaken within the context of broad state sustainability plans or state climate action plans, and some are taken up as independent policies.

This chapter summarizes some of the many innovative and exciting policy options, tools, and programs that states across the country are implementing, including regional and multistate initiatives. We've organized this chapter into three main sections: "Energy Policies," "Transportation Policies," and "Climate Adaptation and Infrastructure." Most of the chapter examines energy issues because they are central to the sustainability challenge; we look at what states are doing to reduce fossil fuel reliance, reduce carbon emissions, and encourage renewable energy and energy efficiency. We examine how states use regulations and standards, then move on to which innovative financial methods they have developed to facilitate these changes. Finally, we will look to transportation policies, including emission standards and fuel efficiency, and climate resiliency and infrastructure.

## Energy Policies

Climate change is often at the top of the sustainability agenda. Mitigating climate change is most often addressed in the form of energy policies aimed at encouraging use of renewable energy, reducing our greenhouse gas emissions. To achieve these goals, we assess two types of policy instruments: (1) regulatory tools and standards, and (2) financial tools and mechanisms. Both can serve to incentivize the behaviors and change needed to move toward more sustainable energy use.

### Regulatory Tools and Standards

Regulations and standard setting are key components of sustainability policy. Currently, there is no clear national energy policy, but states have developed a series of important energy regulations and standards to improve energy efficiency, encourage renewable energy, and improve system access and the grid. These efforts include cap and trade, renewable portfolio standards, energy efficiency standards, building codes, interconnection and grid standards, and feed-in tariffs. They are serving to advance the field of sustainability and clean energy, and to encourage investment, innovation, and the development of local clean technology industries in regional economies.

## Regional Cap and Trade Systems

Economists often point to carbon taxes as the most efficient and effective method for reducing greenhouse gas emissions, but new taxes are exceptionally difficult to enact. An alternative, achievable strategy is through cap and trade systems. Cap and trade programs have helped to reduce emissions, improve local and regional environments, and protect public health. A national cap and trade system for greenhouse gases is unlikely in the near term, but several multistate partnerships are having a positive impact. These programs can have a significant effect on pollution at the regional level that, when aggregated, can influence the performance of the country as a whole.

One of the most notable programs is the Regional Greenhouse Gas Initiative (RGGI, pronounced "Reggie"), which began as a collaboration between ten Northeastern states to cut their carbon dioxide ($CO_2$) emissions. The partnership initially included Connecticut, Delaware, Maine, Maryland, Massachusetts, New Hampshire, New Jersey, New York, Rhode Island, and Vermont, but New Jersey Governor Chris Christie removed his state from RGGI in November 2011. Starting in 2009, RGGI became the first market-based regulatory program in the United States to reduce carbon dioxide emissions from the power sector, focusing specifically on fossil fuel–based electric power generators with a capacity of 25 megawatts (MW) or greater. In the program, a cap is set representing the regional $CO_2$ limit. Participating states sell emission allowances through quarterly regional auctions, and the proceeds are directed towards energy efficiency, renewable energy, and other programs that benefit consumers. Each state has the flexibility to develop its own allowance proceeds plan. In the first two years of the program, the 10 states allocated 52 percent of proceeds to improve energy efficiency, 11 percent to accelerate the deployment of renewable energy technologies, 14 percent to provide bill payment assistance, and 1 percent for a variety of greenhouse gas reduction programs (RGGI, 2011, 4).

Under the RGGI program, states unanimously chose to distribute more than 90 percent of allowances through an auctioning process (Union of Concerned Scientists, 2007). Some policy analysts and industry experts advocate giving away some allowances for free (often as a method to get industry to support the program), but establishing and maintaining a market for the allowances is key to a program's long-term success. To ensure prices are in line with what buyers can pay, the RGGI program established a cost containment reserve, a fixed additional supply of allowances available only if prices exceed certain levels, which increase each year. To ensure program effectiveness, a tracking system is used to record data on both $CO_2$ emissions and allowance transactions. For transparency, reports and program data are available on the RGGI website.

Each RGGI state is allocated a percentage of the total allowances. In 2014, New York had the highest allocation (39 percent of allowances), and Vermont had the lowest (only 1 percent). The individual state budgets for allowances are based upon their own regulatory schemes. One of the benefits of a multistate partnership is that power plants can ensure compliance by meeting the $CO_2$ allowance established by any RGGI state. Another benefit is that several state programs comprise a single regional compliance market, which creates a greater level of efficiency in operations and flexibility for participants.

The program has been successful at both auctioning its allowances and meeting its cap. The cap is designed to decrease over time, lowering regional emissions. From 2009 through 2011, the cap was 188 million tons of $CO_2$ per year; this was lowered to 165 million tons per year for 2012 and 2013. In 2011, emissions were 44 million tons below the cap (Burtraw and Woerman, 2012, 9).

In 2012, the states conducted a review of the trading program, which resulted in a new 2014 RGGI cap of 91 million tons, a 45 percent reduction. The revised program is designed so that the $CO_2$ cap declines 2.5 percent each year from 2015 to 2020. In addition, states have agreed to work to address emissions from electricity imports, which is significant considering that imports make up between 10 and 52 percent of electricity consumption in these states (Welton, 2013).

An economic assessment by the Analysis Group concluded that this market-based carbon control mechanism has delivered positive economic benefits, helped states reach other environmental policy goals, and reduced payments for out-of-state fossil fuels (Hibbard et al., 2011, 6). Through June 2013, allowances generated $1.4 billion in revenue that, through reinvestment in energy efficiency programs, will generate $2.4 billion in the states' economies over the next decade, leading to an additional 23,000 job years of employment (ENE, 2013, 1). Over the next decade, RGGI's efficiency measures will save customers $1.3 billion in reduced energy costs.

There are economic and job losses in some industries, especially those most affected by the carbon reduction regulations in fossil fuel–related industries. For example, powerplant owners could experience a $1.6 billion reduction in net revenue over time because of reduced demand, but, overall, regulation can bring substantial benefits. One study showed that more than $765 million remained in the local economy defined by the RGGI states because of reduced fossil fuel consumption (Hibbard et al., 2011, 4, 6). By investing proceeds locally in efficient and renewable energy programs, states are generating jobs in these industries and encouraging innovations in technology and processes to reduce emissions. They are also saving people money on their energy bills, which can be spent elsewhere in the economy.

Establishing a regional system of cap and trade signals to small businesses and clean-tech entrepreneurs that the Northeast is serious about the green economy, and its member states represent good opportunities for growth. A regional partnership, like RGGI, and strong incentives within the participating states establish a positive investment landscape, encouraging businesses to establish operations in the region.

Not every regional effort has proven so successful. Another regional cap and trade–based initiative, the Midwest Greenhouse Gas Reduction Accord (MGGRA), was signed in November 2007 by the governors of six Midwestern states and one Canadian province, with the goal of reducing greenhouse gas emissions between 60 and 80 percent below 2007 levels through a multisector cap and trade program. However, after 2010, states were no longer collectively pursuing the goals under the accord (although some have their own plans for reducing GHG emissions).

Another regional effort, the Western Climate Initiative (WCI), began in February 2007 with a non-binding agreement between the governors of five western states: Arizona, California, New Mexico, Oregon, and Washington. These states developed a regional target for reducing greenhouse gas emissions based on existing efforts (specifically, the West Coast Global Warming Initiative and the Southwest Climate Change Initiative). The plan eventually expanded to include Utah, Montana, and four Canadian provinces, in addition to other state "observers" (WCI, 2014). First in 2008 and again in 2010, WCI released program designs that states could use to develop their own reduction strategies, and called for the program to be implemented by 2012 with a second compliance period to begin in 2015. However by 2011, only California and Quebec had adopted any regulations based on the recommendations.

Why was RGGI successful when the Western and Midwestern initiatives failed? In a survey of stakeholders involved in developing these three regional programs, interviewees said the main reason for starting a cap and trade program was political. States saw a need for response to climate change due to federal inaction. Katia Biendenkopf, an assistant professor at the University of Amsterdam, who studied the impact of the European Union's GHG emissions trading scheme on the development of the U.S. regional systems, found that "demonstrating that GHG emissions trading was feasible and successful as well as building pressure on the federal government to act were dominant drivers, both in RGGI and WCI" (Biedenkopf, 2012, 15).

The failed MGGRA agreement was slightly different because it was developed at a time when federal policy was seen as likely to happen, and the program was shaped to specifically reflect the concerns of the Midwestern states so they could stay ahead of the curve (Biedenkopf, 2012, 16). The Midwestern states eventually lost the political will for their own trading program. And even though the Western Climate Initiative failed, California continued its aggressive pursuit of climate mitigation through its own statewide system.

*Case Study: California's Cap and Trade*

In 2006, California passed the Global Warming Solutions Act, which required a 25 percent GHG reduction statewide by 2020, which is the equivalent of taking 3.5 million cars off the roads (EDF, 2014). The law spelled out a range of measures to expand energy efficiency programs, achieve a renewable energy mix, and develop a cap and trade program.

The California cap and trade program went into effect on January 1, 2013, with a cap on the largest polluters in the electricity and industrial sectors, applying to plants emitting 25,000 metric tons of $CO_2$ equivalent or more annually. At the program's start, this applied to approximately 300 plants throughout the state. The plan will gradually cover ground transportation and heating fuels, and come to include 85 percent of the state's GHG emissions (Burtraw and Woerman, 2012, 8). When fully implemented, California's program will be twice as large as the RGGI program, as measured by the size of the state's economy and the number of sectors covered (Bifera, 2013). The cap itself decreases by 2 percent annually before 2015, and will decrease 3 percent annually between 2015 and 2020. Based on the amount of emissions covered, the program is currently second in size only to the European Union Emissions Trading System (EU ETS) (C2ES, 2014a, 2).

All rules and market mechanisms are implemented and enforced by the California Air Resources Board (CARB). According to the cap and trade scheme, regulated companies must hold enough allowances to cover their total emissions, and can buy and sell allowances on the open market. Allowances are both given for free and sold at auctions. In contrast to RGGI, CARB gave a significant number of free allowances to electrical utilities in order to ensure that businesses remained competitive, facilitate a smooth transition, and prevent emissions leakage (Hsia-Kiung et al., 2014, 5). Leakages refer to increases in GHG emissions outside the state to compensate for reductions within the state.

The remaining allowances are auctioned off. Each auction has a floor price that increases every year; in 2012 it was set at $10 per metric ton. There are two types of allowances auctioned: (1) current-year vintage, which can be used in the year of their auction, and (2) future-year vintage, which can be banked by companies for later use. The first auction was held in November 2012 when close to 29 million allowances (including current and future vintages) were sold to more than 600 approved industrial facilities and electricity generators. The allowances were sold for $10.09, near the minimum price of $10, indicating initial demand was modest and that participants were confident they would meet the cap (EIA, 2012a).

The first year generated $525 million in auction revenues (C2ES, 2014a, 8). Similar to RGGI, investment of the auction proceeds is vital for the program to achieve its climate change mitigation goals. Two laws establish guidelines for the dispersal of this revenue; the first requires that it be spent for environmental purposes, particularly concerning air quality, and the second requires that at least 25 percent be spent on programs to help disadvantaged communities.

At the end of each compliance period, companies must return allowances to the California government to cover their compliance obligation. Those that do not meet the compliance requirement must pay a penalty through the purchase of four times the number of outstanding allowances (Bosworth, 2013). Regulated entities can also meet up to 8 percent of their obligations using offsets. Offsets are reductions of greenhouse gas emissions that compensate for an emission made elsewhere. This allows companies to reduce emissions by funding reduction activities that would otherwise not occur, such as improving forest management or capturing and destroying methane from livestock manure.

The standards used for the California offsets were carefully developed with input from a number of stakeholders and experts. For example, for forestry-based offsets, the standards require that carbon must stay out of the atmosphere for 100 years, ensuring long-term sustainable forest management.

The use of offsets is not without controversy. Two public interest groups—Citizens Climate Lobby and Our Children's Earth Foundation—filed a lawsuit against CARB, arguing that the offset program violated the requirements under the Global Warming Solutions Act. In their suit, they claim that the offsets do not represent any additional greenhouse gas reductions as required by law, but are preexisting activities. They fear that offsets provide a mechanism for oil refineries to buy their way out of cleaning up pollution without providing any actual environmental benefit.

In January 2013, a state trial ruled in favor of California's Air Resources Board. Our Children's Earth Foundation appealed the decision, but as of this writing a hearing date has yet to be scheduled (Hsia-Kiung et al., 2014, 18). It is important to remember that success with offsets (and many other features of environmental initiatives) depends on how a program is designed. In California's case, it includes some of the strictest rules in the world, giving most participants confidence that offsets represent activities that would not have happened without the program.

Beyond offsets, there are other criticisms of the California cap and trade program. The fossil fuel industry and its lobbyists criticize the complicated nature of the program and its vulnerability to fraud. However, according to an analysis by the University of California, Los Angeles, the program is unlikely to suffer from manipulation and fraud because California's government uses third-party verifiers to check reported emissions and tracks allowances to prove authenticity (Cutter et al., 2011, 8).

A number of environmental justice groups opposed the program early on, arguing that it focused on gases that are released high in the atmosphere, and overlooked the release of heavier pollutants, like fine particles from oil refineries, that are most likely to harm low-income communities (Barringer, 2011). While the groups were supportive of the Global Warming Solutions Act generally, they opposed the cap and trade program as the primary mechanism to achieve reductions. One critic stated "our communities are opposed to a trading scheme because of the inherent inequities for communities of color and low income communities, and the missed opportunities for real localized emission reduction" (Conant, 2012, 32).

Despite these criticisms, the program continues to progress and expand. In January 2014, the California program linked with Quebec, Canada's program so that allowances and offsets issued in one jurisdiction could be used for compliance purposes in the other—the first international carbon market in North America.

California's program also continues to evolve. In October 2013, CARB released a set of amendments to the program based on public meetings and comments, economic analysis, and administrative insight. According to Thomas Reuters' Point Carbon, policymakers still need to address the state's reliance on complementary measures, such as the Renewable Portfolio Standard and the Low Carbon Fuel Standard, so that the demand for allowances doesn't drop to the floor price and stay there (2013).

## Renewable Portfolio Standards

While cap and trade programs are growing, their application is still limited in the United States. Cap and trade programs work by directly limiting the amount of greenhouse gas emissions in a given region, but the remaining policies we discuss here limit emissions indirectly by encouraging the use of renewable energy, reducing reliance on fossil fuels, and enhancing efficient use of energy. Renewable portfolio standards (RPS) are one of the primary mechanisms to encourage the uptake of renewable energy in the United States. A renewable portfolio standard is a performance requirement for electric utilities that mandates a certain amount of electricity be generated from eligible renewable sources. As of 2013, 29 states plus Washington, DC, have some kind of enforceable renewable portfolio standard, and 8 other states have non-binding renewable portfolio goals (DSIRE, 2013c). Figure 4.1 provides a map of states that have RPS standards and goals as of 2012.

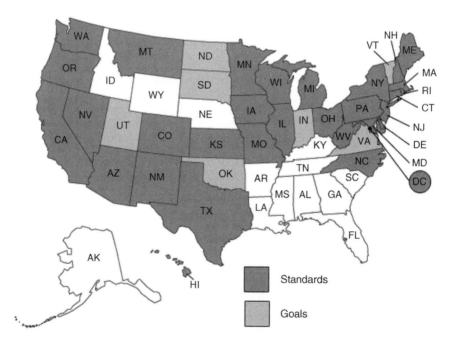

**Figure 4.1   States with Renewable Portfolio Standards or Goals, January 2012**

*Note:* West Virginia is noted as a Renewable Portfolio Standard State; however, the Interstate Renewable Energy Council categorizes it as a goal State.

*Source:* U.S. Energy Information Administration. "Most States Have Renewable Portfolio Standards." February 3, 2012. http://www.eia.gov/todayinenergy/detail.cfm?id=4850

Some states also include *carve outs*, requirements that a portion of their electricity portfolio comes from a specific source, such as solar. The first renewable portfolio standard was established in 1983 when Iowa passed the Alternative Energy Production Law (requiring that 2 percent of the state's energy be renewable), although most states passed their standards after 2000.

Massachusetts and Connecticut were among the first states to enact mandatory renewable portfolio standards. After it was clear that many states in the Northeast were considering these standards, the region decided to establish a coordinated system to track both renewable energy and emissions (Cory and Swezey, 2007, 10). Most renewable portfolio standard programs also allow renewable energy generation outside a state to qualify, so that non-renewable portfolio states can benefit from renewable energy policy in a nearby state. For example, Wyoming contains wind farms that participate in the Oregon RPS, even though Wyoming itself does not require renewable energy in its energy mix (Leon, 2013, 4–5). The Clean Energy States Alliance points out some of the key strengths and weaknesses of the renewable portfolio policy as compared to other types of clean energy policies. Some of the strengths of a renewable portfolio standard include:

- A straightforward and easy-to-understand concept;
- A market-based approach that leads to cost efficiency;
- A relatively long-term policy with clear future targets;
- Flexibility for each state;
- Compatibility with federal tax policies to support renewable energy; and,
- Modest costs (Leon, 2013, 8–11).

Weaknesses include:

- Volatility in the price of renewable energy certificates;
- Potential free riders who receive payments for projects that would be profitable without incentives; and,
- Need for modifications over time when revisions can be difficult (Leon, 2013, 13–15).

Each state sets its own standard, so policies can vary considerably. States differ on the level of the requirement, what they define as a renewable source, how it is measured, and how the requirement is enforced (Heeter and Bird, 2012). For example, California's renewable standard requires 33 percent from renewables by 2020, while Texas requires 5,880 MW of new renewable energy generation to be built by 2015 (Cory and Swezey, 2007, 1, 22). Minnesota requires 25 percent from renewable sources by 2025 plus 1.5 percent solar by 2020 (DSIRE, 2013a). Different states have different requirements depending on their capabilities and resources.

While political support for renewable portfolio standards is growing, there are also influential opponents. The American Legislative Exchange Council (ALEC) drafted model legislation in 2012 pushing for a complete repeal of renewable portfolio standards (Goldenberg and Pilkington, 2013). In this case, state legislators introduced versions of the model legislation in a number of states, though most didn't make it beyond an introductory stage. The Council's perspective is that a renewable portfolio standard is a tax on consumers and that it mandates utilities use sources that are expensive and unreliable, increasing the cost of doing business (ALEC, 2012).

In North Carolina, Ohio, and Kansas conservative groups sought unsuccessfully to reverse clean energy regulations. They argued that renewable portfolio policies have too great an impact on electricity rates, give an unfair advantage to certain energy technologies, and that a requirement for a type of energy source interferes with the free market (Leon, 2013, 20–21).

The effectiveness of state renewable portfolio programs can depend on federal policies, and the lack of a national framework makes it harder for businesses to develop separate models for each state. The state-by-state approach also increases regulatory uncertainty, and creates jurisdictional inconsistencies (Gallagher, 2013, 60). These standards permit states to determine what should be included, and these definitions vary widely and can cause confusion.

Increasingly, states are using alternative resources, such as energy efficiency, thermal, and even non-renewables, in their renewable portfolio policies (although non-renewables are typically capped). Michigan, Ohio, Pennsylvania, and West Virginia permit the use of non-renewable resources such as coal, natural gas, and nuclear. In fact, West Virginia's standard does not require a minimum contribution from renewable energy sources at all (DSIRE, 2012).

*Energy Efficiency Resource Standards*

An energy efficiency resource standard (EERS) or energy efficiency target is a policy tool developed to encourage more efficient generation, transmission, and use of electricity. These are long-term, binding energy savings target for utilities, expressed as a percentage of energy sales or specific energy units over a certain period of time (ACEEE, 2014c, 1). These are similar to renewable portfolio standards in that they require utility providers to reduce energy use by a specified amount that increases each year or so. An energy efficiency resource standard is like a renewable portfolio standard for energy efficiency.

In 1999, Texas was the first state to establish an energy efficiency resource standard, but the top five scoring states in energy efficiency are Massachusetts, California, New York, Oregon, and Vermont. A report by the American Council for an Energy Efficient Economy found that most states are on target to meet their goals (Sciortino et al., 2011). The policy advantages of this tool include simplicity, specificity, and economies of scale. States also often coordinate their renewable portfolio standards with energy efficiency standards to achieve higher energy savings. Eight states include energy efficiency as an eligible resource in their renewable portfolio policies. Authors of one publication found that states use the maximum amount of energy efficiency allowed when possible, making the specified level extremely important in policy design (Heeter and Bird, 2012, 10).

As of February 2014, 26 states have adopted an energy efficiency standard. These states represent 62 percent of electricity sales in the nation (ACEEE, 2014c, 1). The strongest energy efficiency standards are in Massachusetts, Rhode Island, and Vermont, which require nearly 2.5 percent annual savings (ACEEE, 2014b). Not surprisingly, the success of these types of programs depends on the clarity of the regulatory framework, the time frame allotted, and the commitment of resources of those involved (Sciortino et al., 2011).


*Building Codes*

States can help reduce energy consumption through requirements and incentives in their building codes. Buildings are a major source of greenhouse gas emissions (second only to the transportation sector). Nearly 5 million commercial buildings and 114 million residences in the United States account for approximately 40 percent of the nation's total energy use (US DOE, 2008, 4).

McKinsey & Company estimates that energy improvements in the building sector could reduce annual electricity consumption by 23 percent, thereby reducing consumer energy bills by $130 billion annually (Granade et al., 2009, 7–8). A major advantage of building codes is that they can be designed around local needs and climate—the most efficient and sustainable practices will vary from Wisconsin to Arizona. States can take full advantage of local distinctions that might be lost at the national level.

The first energy efficiency standards for U.S. buildings were adopted in 1978. After a relatively slow initial adoption phase, use of these tools expanded dramatically in the early 21st century. Building codes mandate materials, construction, engineering and related processes. New code provisions can enhance: sustainability and energy efficiency through minimum energy efficiency requirements; use of sustainable, energy efficient materials; and requirements for periodic reviews and updates. Future energy savings can also be locked in during times of new construction or renovation.

While there are federal requirements for building codes, many states have codes that are more stringent to yield greater benefits. Building efficiency codes can reduce peak energy demand, air pollution, and greenhouse gas emissions. Codes can also target building use—industrial, commercial, residential—size, and type of occupancy.

More than 275 American cities, counties, tribes, and states have created green building codes in order to conserve energy, water, and other resources, and to reduce power and water costs (EPA, 2014c). Building energy codes typically include insulation requirements, heating and cooling equipment standards, and lighting requirements. A cutting–edge code provision pertains to roofs, which can decrease power and cooling demand, and lower citywide air temperature in warm weather. Projections indicate that if all states adopted the most recent and stringent state codes and focused more on code enforcement, the United States could avoid construction of 32 new 400 MW power plants by 2020 (EPA, 2006, 4–37).

Massachusetts was named the most energy efficient state in 2013 by the American Council for an Energy-Efficient Economy. One reason is the 2008 Massachusetts Green Communities Act, which advises on best practices in sustainable building code design. The act requires that all commercial buildings in Massachusetts must be in full compliance with the national model building code within a year of any code update. Massachusetts also has an optional *stretch code*, which is up to 20 percent more stringent than the baseline state energy code. In Massachusetts, jurisdictions that adopted the stretch code as of 2013 house 50 percent of the state's population (Massachusetts' Businesses for Clean Energy, 2014). The state's lead-by-example program, which applies to all state agency new construction and major renovations over 20,000 square feet, has a LEED Plus green standard that is 20 percent more energy efficient than the state energy code.

Washington is another state that is using code compliance as an effective tool for sustainability. Its 2012 State Energy Code is one of the most stringent U.S. state codes, and elicits the highest compliance rate in the nation (ACEEE, 2014a). A residential cost compliance study by the Northwest Energy Efficiency Alliance from 2013 shows compliance rates of 96 percent (Cadmus Group and NEEA, 2013, 32).

California, another leader, has had energy standards for buildings since 1978. In response to a legislative mandate to reduce the state's energy consumption, the California Energy Commission approved new energy standards for both residential and commercial buildings more than 35 years ago. Currently, California's 2013 standards are the most stringent and among the best enforced in the nation (ACEEE, 2014a). California is moving toward zero-net-energy (ZNE) buildings, in which annual energy consumption will equal the production of renewable energy. All new residential buildings will reach ZNE by 2020, and all new commercial buildings by 2030. California is also committed to achieving ZNE for 50 percent of its existing state buildings by 2025 (Roth, 2013).

California's strict energy efficiency standards have helped keep the state's per capita electricity rate stay flat over the past 30 years, while rates in other states rose by 50 percent on average (Horowitz, 2012). Californians saved more than $65 billion on energy costs, and an additional 1.5 million jobs were created (Bacchus, 2012).

Despite these many efforts to improve U.S. building energy efficiency, a 2013 analysis by the Institute for Market Transformation found high rates of noncompliance in most states (Stellberg, 2013). Noncompliance can occur due to lack of resources, education, or political will. Improving enforcement of codes that are already developed could have a significant impact on energy efficiency. One analysis found that bringing just one year's worth of new construction up to full compliance with current energy building codes would save between $63 and $189 million in annual energy costs (Stellberg, 2013, 3).

Compliance can be supported by other state and federal programs, including tax credits and rebates, green banks, public benefit funds, and other financial mechanisms that enable individuals and business to finance energy upgrades. We see the importance of offering not only regulatory requirements but also other innovative programs using public policies to leverage and encourage individual initiatives. Combining code reform and financial incentives can multiply the overall impact on efficiency and sustainability.

## Grid Standards

Grid standards are requirements for connecting solar or other electrical generation systems to the electric grid, applicable to both utilities and customers (SEIA, 2014a). These standards encourage the connection of clean, distributed generation systems to the electric grid by establishing standard technical requirements and uniform procedures for utilities. This reduces the uncertainty and delays that these systems sometimes encounter.

For example, net metering enables residential and commercial customers who generate their own renewable energy to feed back into the grid the electricity that they don't use on-site (EPA, 2006, ES-17). It defines application processes and technical requirements for smaller projects and requires that electric utilities buy unused electricity back from customers at retail rates. With net metering, the meter runs backwards when a residential solar panel produces more electricity than is being used.

As of 2013, 44 states have some kind of net metering policy, whether through a law, regulation, or voluntary effort by utilities (Yim, 2013). While participation is increasing rapidly, the percentage of participating customers remains well below 1 percent (EIA, 2012b). Utility-industry trade associations and fossil fuel interests see net metering policies as lost revenue. They even argue that solar customers do not pay their share of electricity costs. The American Legislative Exchange Council (ALEC) recently proposed a resolution to weaken net metering policies. With the help of the Edison Electric Institute, they drafted model legislation outlining a fixed grid charge that would recover grid costs, and argued for the need to update net metering policies and restructure crediting mechanisms so that everyone who uses the grid pays to maintain it (ALEC, 2014). The Arizona Public Service Company took a similar position when it proposed that customers who install solar panels on their rooftops should pay an extra $50 to $100 on their monthly bill to cover the system's maintenance costs (Elsner, 2013). The final ruling was a lot lower than this—about $5 per month for customers; nevertheless, Arizona is the first state to charge customers for installing solar panels (Goldenberg and Pilkington, 2013).

*Feed-In Tariffs*

Feed-in tariffs (FITs) require electric utilities to pay pre-established, above-market rates to generators of renewable power that is fed onto the grid over a guaranteed period of time. The goal is to make renewable energy sources cost-competitive with fossil fuel–based technologies, by making the price of renewable energy known and reliable. Tariffs provide renewable generators with a set stream of income from their projects. They also reduce the *payback period*, that is, the time it takes to accumulate enough annual or monthly savings to recoup the original investment.

Feed-in tariff programs have been slow to emerge in North America, but they are widely used in Europe and other countries. California, Hawaii, Vermont, and Washington were the first states to establish systems of feed-in tariffs. Although only seven states have feed-in tariff programs as of 2013, a number of utility providers offer programs. For example, in 2013, a voluntary program started in Virginia, where residential and commercial owners of solar photovoltaic generators can receive 15 cents per kilowatt-hour (kWh) for five years (EIA, 2013).

Feed-in tariff programs were first introduced in Germany in 1991, followed by Denmark and Spain, and they are now the most widely popular policy to promote renewable energy worldwide (Zhang, 2013, 2). In the 1990s, project costs remained high due to fluctuating electricity costs, but in 2000, Germany and Denmark switched to a cost-base, fixed-rate model. This change was a "catalyst for the dramatic renewable energy growth witnessed by Europe, particularly Germany and Spain, over the past decade" (Institute for Building Efficiency, 2010).

In 2005, China introduced the first resource-based wind tariff outside of Europe. In 2012, Japan introduced a feed-in tariff for solar energy. The implementation of the Japanese program contributed to a 75 percent increase in clean energy investment; 97 percent of that was spent on solar (Pew Charitable Trusts, 2012, 21).

Feed-in tariff policies reduce the environmental impact of electricity generation, stabilize electricity rates, and facilitate economic development and job growth (NREL, 2013). The most effective of these programs set rates above the retail cost of electricity. In the United States, most feed-in tariff programs use a cost containment mechanism—they have a program and/or annual limit, to cap the dollar amount available (EIA, 2013).

Feed-in tariffs typically stimulate significant growth in the generation of renewable energy—some estimates credit them with stimulating approximately 75 percent of global solar photovoltaic and 45 percent of global wind capacity (Zhang, 2013, 2). Another study by the World Bank looked at wind feed-in tariff policies in 35 European countries to determine cost effectiveness. The researchers concluded that two main actions can increase wind investment: (1) extending the contract agreement and (2) providing guaranteed grid access (Zhang, 2013, 2).

Feed-in tariff policies work best in areas where the cost of retail electricity is low and cost of electricity from solar systems is high (The California Majority Report, 2013). In Germany, a country that led the way with these policies, there is now a contraction in the market, and other European countries have experienced FIT market turmoil (Trabish, 2014). With feed-in tariffs, solar customers sometimes build large systems to maximize their return, which can be unsustainable in markets where solar costs continue to drop. Net metering on the other hand, ensures that system size matches customers' electricity usage (Trabish, 2014). Some argue that feed-in tariffs remain beneficial to drive commercial and community-scale renewables, while net energy metering is more appropriate for residential scale projects.

## *Financial Tools and Mechanisms*

Financial tools and mechanisms provide incentives for the types of activities that support the government's policy goals. They can be used to meet many of the state requirements we've outlined so far. In the case of sustainability, Americans can take advantage of both federal and state tax incentives allowing them to leverage their own investment to an even greater extent. These types of funding programs and incentives are key activities that complement compliance programs like renewable portfolio standards or a state's cap under a program like RGGI.

Energy efficiency is commonly referred to as the low-hanging fruit of the sustainability challenge. No one wants to waste energy or money. Efficiency is nearly universally considered to be a positive thing, and energy efficiency programs have an important multiplier effect on local economies. In the Northeast region, one analysis found that every $1.00 spent on energy efficiency improvements creates $4.30 to $6.40 in economic activity (ENE, 2013, 2). Energy efficiency programs can reduce energy consumption, bring down electric bills and wholesale electricity prices, and decrease electricity demand from power plants. The challenge with energy efficiency comes from the initial high costs to retrofit existing systems and install efficiency upgrades.

## *Tax Credits, Rebates, and Subsidies*

Like the federal government, states can implement a range of tax credits, rebates, and subsidies to encourage businesses and consumers to take part in sustainability initiatives. According to the National Governors Association, every single U.S. state has created some kind of financial incentive to promote clean energy (2013, 2). These incentives range from deductions for renewable energy production and energy conservation, to deductions for wood-burning heating systems, biomass, geothermal, and bio heating oil use. Other incentives are offered for things like greater use of electric vehicles. These programs are important in making renewables as cost-effective as fossil fuels.

In 2013, California enacted the Green Tariff Shared Renewables Program, through which three major utilities will make renewable energy available to a whole new market of customers (e.g., renters, businesses that lease their spaces, low-income residents, and those with poor credit scores). Customers receive a credit on their utility bills for clean energy that they buy at off-site renewable energy facilities (without shifting costs to customers who do not participate). This program has the potential to create $2 billion in economic activity from the 500MW of solar facilities that will be constructed, generate $60 million in tax revenue, and create 7,000 jobs (Wolk, 2014).

Nebraska supports wind-farm development with tax incentives (C2ES, 2013b). A tax exemption for the purchase of wind-farm components like turbines and towers enables wind projects to stay competitive in the regional electricity industry.

Colorado provides tax incentives to support electric vehicle (EV) adoption. Their Innovative Motor Vehicle Income Tax Credit makes available up to $6,000 in tax credits for electric vehicle purchases/lessees until 2021. The Colorado Special Fuel Tax & Electric Vehicle Fee established an annual, flat fee for registration of plug-in vehicles, at a price lower than other states (C2ES, 2013a). New York State has also enacted three programs to expand financial incentives for solar energy projects, including tax credits to homeowners for the cost of solar installation equipment.

*Public Benefit Funds*

Public benefit funds (PBFs) are pools of public resources invested in clean energy supplies and programs. Public benefit funds are created by enacting a small fee, typically called a systems benefit charge (SBC), on customers' electricity bills.

Public benefit funds became popular in the late 1990s after the restructuring of the electrical industry. New York, California, and Massachusetts were among the first states to develop public benefit funds. California's was established in 1998 and generates more than $135 million per year for clean resources and consumer education (EPA, 2013a). In 1997, Massachusetts created a renewable energy and energy efficiency fund. The Massachusetts Renewable Energy Trust focuses first on identifying barriers to renewable energy growth and second on maximizing public benefit by creating high-tech jobs in clean energy.

Public benefit funds help states meet their long-term energy goals and may help them design a more cohesive energy strategy. They complement other clean energy policies at both the state and federal level and enable states to secure resources to meet their energy goals. The EPA has developed a number of best practices—ranging from establishing working groups and publicizing achievements, to designing complementary energy programs and drafting supporting legislation—from states that have such clean energy funds (EPA, 2009).

As of 2010, 30 states and the District of Columbia had public benefit funds (Glatt, 2010, 1). These programs are administered through state energy offices (California), through quasi-public agencies (Connecticut and Massachusetts), by public regulatory agencies (New Jersey), through nonprofit organizations (Pennsylvania), or through utility companies (Arizona). Public benefit funds have a number of advantages, they:

- Narrow gaps between market price of electricity and the costs of clean energy technologies;
- Lower regulatory and market barriers for emerging technologies;
- Help develop infrastructure needed for the success of clean energy; and,
- Promote awareness of clean energy to the public.

Utilities benefit from energy reductions, lowered customer electricity rates, and reductions in peak energy demands. Public benefit funds are often set up to provide assistance to low-income residents. For example, in 2007 in Illinois, $72 million of the state's $80 million public benefit fund went to low-income energy assistance (Glatt, 2010).

### Case Study: New York Systems Benefit Charge

New York is widely recognized as a leader in energy efficiency and renewable energy development (Morris and Stutt, 2012, 1). The New York Systems Benefit Charge (NYSBC) was one of the first of its kind established in 1996 by the New York State Public Service Commission. Originally funded from 1998 to 2001 at $78 million per year, NYSBC is administered by the New York State Energy Research Development Authority (NYSERDA), a public benefit corporation whose mission is to help New York meet its energy goals.

Two public power authorities not under the jurisdiction of the Public Service Commission—the New York Power Authority and Long Island Power Authority—offer their own programs funded by systems benefit charges. New York's Systems Benefit program, branded the New York Energy $mart program, was designed to generate funding for public policy initiatives not adequately addressed by New York's electricity markets. The program contains specific initiatives across four core areas: energy efficiency, research and development, programs for low-income customers, and environmental protection programs.

New York's Systems Benefit program was extended in 2001, with funding increased to $150 million annually, and an added goal of achieving peak load reductions to increase the stability of the electric supply. Extended again in 2006, funding was increased to $175 million annually. More specific goals and objectives were also set at that time: 54 percent of funding was specified for peak load, energy efficiency, and outreach and education programs; 23 percent to research and development; and 24 percent to low-income energy affordability programs (NYSERDA, 2010, 4).

The most recent extension of the program in 2011, through 2016, set total funding for the five-year period at $469 million (NYS PCS, 2014). In addition, some of the funding is provided to utilities that are also required to implement energy efficiency programs. This expansion also committed funds to power supply and delivery, building systems, and clean energy infrastructure. The portfolio of programs is designed to increase energy innovation through scientific research, market analysis, technology development, and clean energy technology adoption, more rigorous standards in codes, and promotion of a clean energy economy through business and market development. In 2012, programs in workforce development and combined heat and power were added (NYSERDA, 2013a, 2–1).

The fund's technology and market development investments serve to realize policy objectives in the energy efficiency portfolio standard (EEPS) and renewable portfolio standard (RPS) (NYSERDA, 2013a, ES-2). These initiatives help new or underused technology move into the marketplace and serve as feeders to help achieve energy efficiency and renewability goals (NYSERDA, 2010, 2). The fund is widely considered successful in moving New York to become a leader in the nation in this field (Morris and Stutt, 2012).

### Green Banks

State green banks are relatively new financial tools for sparking clean energy investment. Green banks use public debt to leverage private sector investment. Renewable energy technologies have great potential to meet the challenges of a low-carbon energy infrastructure, but require substantial amounts of capital and are often competing against government-subsidized conventional energy industries. Green banks bring elements of predictability and aggregation that reduce overall pricing, eliminating a significant market barrier that has long slowed the development of new clean technology (Hendricks and Bovarnick, 2014).

According to the Center for American Progress, national green banks have been successfully undertaken in Germany, the United Kingdom, and China. In the United States, New York, Connecticut, Hawaii, Massachusetts, and California all have or are in the process of establishing similar financial entities (although they are not all called banks). The Connecticut Clean Energy Finance and Investment Authority (CEFIA), established in 2011, was the first green bank in the United States. It provides a combination of loans, grants, and other credit in support of the state's clean energy industry. In 2013, Hawaii enacted a law to authorize the establishment of a renewable energy loan fund.

New York State Governor Andrew Cuomo called for the establishment of a $1 billion New York Green Bank, and in December 2013, the New York Public Service Commission approved funding for the bank from clean energy ratepayer funds, combined with funds from Regional Greenhouse Gas Initiative (RGGI) allowances for initial funding of $210 million. The green bank partners with financial institutions, energy service companies, project developers, and equipment manufacturers to support clean energy projects (NYSERDA, 2014).

Green banks can help overcome market barriers such as lack of capital markets and federal policy uncertainty. These institutions partner with private sector by providing credit enhancement, loan loss reserves, and loan bundling, in order to encourage private sector support of clean energy projects. Models show that these banks can double the amount of capital for clean energy markets within 5 years, and create ten times more capital within 20 years (New York State, 2013).

## On-Bill Financing

One of the barriers to introducing energy efficient retrofits is the high upfront costs these projects require. On-bill financing (OBF) can help overcome this barrier by leveraging the relationship between utilities and customers. Rather than directly paying the upfront cost to install an energy-saving project, on-bill financing enables customers to invest in energy efficiency improvements through a loan or tariff, and customers pay for upgrades over time as a charge on their utility bill. The utility or program administrator generally provides the loan funds, so they also hold the repayment risk. Many programs allow the utility to suspend service to those who do not make their loan payments. If the costs and benefits of energy efficiency measures are aligned properly, sometimes this can be *bill neutral* for customers, meaning the energy savings of the improvement make up for the charge; in fact, some programs require bill neutrality.

The earliest on-bill finance program was piloted in 1993 in Wisconsin. Today there are 23 states with on-bill financing programs, though not all have legislation to support it and many tend to have different provisions (ACEEE, 2012, 1–2). On-bill financing has a number of benefits including eliminating upfront costs for customers, generating positive cash flow for utilities, increasing the value of property, and creating new jobs. These types of programs are designed such that they can operate concurrently with other programs like rebate offers.

Importantly, on-bill financing can be tied to a property, often through a meter, so that debt can transfer between owners and tenants. This way if a customer paying the financing charge moves, the new occupant (not the building owner) must take on the payment obligation.

"In many buildings, without an OBF structure, the cost of utility services are borne by tenants, either directly with separately metered space, or indirectly with the owner passing charges on to tenants on the basis of square footage or some other formula. The owner typically bears the cost of improvements, such as a new boiler or better water pumps, but the tenants realize the benefits in the form of lower utility bills. This works to discourage the owner from making sensible investments in efficiency" (Henderson, 2013, 2).

On-bill financing can help encourage building owners to take part in energy efficiency projects, if both owner and tenants agree to improvements that reduce the total monthly bill (Henderson, 2013, 5). It also broadens the number of customers that can participate, having fewer eligibility restrictions than traditional loans; however, on-bill financing faces a number of barriers. Utility companies need the expertise and resources to act as lending institutions. Questions of equity may arise when programs are paid out of public benefit funds, which everyone pays into, while only some benefit from on-bill financing. There is also a risk that some borrowers will be unable to pay, especially because bill neutrality doesn't necessarily mean that individual customers will have lower payments (Henderson, 2013, 4).

*Property Assessed Clean Energy*

Property assessed clean energy (PACE) financing is a similar tool to overcome the barrier of high upfront costs and encourage renewable energy installations or energy efficiency retrofits in buildings. It also spreads the cost of the system over a longer time period than other types of energy financing (DSIRE, 2014). With property assessed clean energy, property owners borrow money from a local government to pay for energy improvements and repay the amount through a property tax assessment. What is unique about this type of financing option is that it attaches the loan obligation for these technologies to the property rather than the individual borrower, which encourages investment, even in projects with a long payback period (DSIRE, 2014). Homeowners who know that they may only be in their house for a few years may not want to invest in a solar photovoltaic system, for example, that has a payback period of 10 years. With the loan attached to the home, it transfers to the next homeowner, who receives the benefits of that energy upgrade, and continues making the payments.

As of March 2014, 31 states plus Washington, DC, had legislation that allowed for property assessed clean energy programs (Tweed, 2012). In 2012, California launched a program, allowing non-residential property owners in 14 counties and 126 cities to finance energy efficiency, renewable energy, and water efficiency projects. However, recent legal uncertainties have slowed down the growth of property assessed clean energy financing for residential programs.

The Federal Housing Finance Agency (FHFA) put residential property assessed clean energy programs on hold in 2010, claiming that the assessments violated securities agreements. They argued that since many of these programs are financed as the senior lien on a property, they create unacceptable risk of default on mortgages (FHFA, 2010). This means that property assessed clean energy loans rank higher than mortgages, giving them preferential right to foreclosure proceeds. In other words, the government that issued the PACE bond gets paid first. The FHFA advised Fannie Mae and Freddie Mac to avoid buying mortgages with property assessed clean energy loans. Lawsuits against FHFA came from Florida, New York, and California. A federal district court judge in the state of California ruled in favor of the state, saying that FHFA violated federal law by taking action without public notice or opportunity for stakeholder comment (US District Court, 2012). However, the Ninth Circuit Court of Appeals overturned this ruling, stating that FHFA could not be legally pressured into changing its opinion (Friedrich, 2013). Fannie Mae stood by its policy in a note to clients in November 2013.

The legal uncertainty may make some governments hesitant to start or restart property assessed clean energy programs, although some states and municipalities have found innovative ways to continue them. Vermont, Oklahoma, Maine, and Rhode Island chose to make property assessed clean energy loans a junior lien with lower priority than mortgage payments. A number of cities in California take part in the state's HERO Program, which provides disclaimers for homeowners enrolling in programs. According to PACENow, an advocacy organization, property assessed clean energy retrofits increase the value of homes, and evidence thus far shows that they may actually reduce the risk of default by making energy more affordable. In California, the default rate for mortgages of three of these programs has been less than 1 percent (Friedrich, 2013).

Despite the possibility that the bonds could suffer losses due to the risk that Fannie Mae and Freddie Mac might challenge the priority status of the liens, investors are moving forward in securitizing property assessed clean energy bonds. In March 2014, Deutsche Bank AG sold the first securities backed by these bonds. The Western Riverside Council of Governments in California issued the underlying bonds, which were given AA grade by Kroll Bond Rating Agency. The sale totaled $103.8 million and carried a 4.75 percent coupon (Shenn, 2014).

**Transportation Policies**

While the United States has gas mileage standards for motor vehicles, we do not have a national sustainable transportation policy. The nation's transportation system accounts for over two-thirds of oil consumption and,

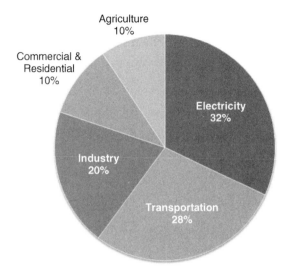

**Figure 4.2   Total U.S. Greenhouse Gas Emissions by Economic Sector in 2012**

*Source:* Environmental Protection Agency, "Sources of Greenhouse Gas Emissions." Last Updated July 22, 2014. http://www.epa.gov/climatechange/ghgemissions/sources/transportation.html

as Figure 4.2 illustrates, nearly one-third of U.S. greenhouse gas emissions (EPA, 2013b; Morrow et al., 2010). Increasing the efficiency of fuel used for transportation, reducing the amount of emissions released, and encouraging public and active transportation are all measures that states and municipalities can take to increase the sustainability of our nation's transportation systems. In this section, we'll look at some state efforts to reduce vehicle emissions, enhance fuel efficiency, and look at regional efforts to support transportation-related climate policies.

Several state transportation agencies are acting to reduce emissions by purchasing hybrids or electric vehicles for their own fleets. In 2010, Massachusetts launched GreenDOT to reduce greenhouse gas emissions, promote healthy transportation options, and support smart growth development (MassDOT, 2014). The program aims to reduce its transportation sector's greenhouse gas emissions by more than 2 million tons over the next decade, or 7.3 percent below 1990 levels. One aspect of this program is the Healthy Transportation Compact, which focuses on increasing bicycle and pedestrian travel. The program has procured hybrid-electric and natural gas fleet vehicles, retrofitted over 500 school buses, designed a project to reduce idling emissions from trucks, and required emission control devices on contractor vehicles (MassDOT, 2010). It is also pursuing renewable power projects, such as solar and wind, along state highways.

## Emission Standards

The U.S. Clean Air Act prevents states from adopting their own emission standards, but includes a unique provision that allows California to implement them for cars and light trucks (if those standards are at least as stringent as federal standards), and allows other states to adopt California's standards as well (Transport Policy, 2013).

The EPA has a history of granting the State of California these kinds of waivers; it has approved about 50 since 1968. According to Leslie Walker, an associate with Abbott & Kindermann, LLP, "California set emission standards prior to 1966 and therefore is allowed to adopt its own standards for new motor vehicles if the Administrator of the U.S. EPA, based on criteria set out in the statute, waives the general statutory prohibition on state adoption or enforcement of emission standards. The state waiver request must meet minimum criteria to be granted" (2009).

The states that are currently following California's emissions rules include Arizona, Connecticut, Florida, Maine, Maryland, Massachusetts, New Jersey, New Mexico, New York, Oregon, Pennsylvania, Rhode Island, Vermont, and Washington (Maryland DEP, 2014).

California also has a number of transportation policies that serve to reduce emissions and improve the state's sustainability profile (US DOE, 2013), including:

- **Low-Emission Vehicle (LEV) Standards:** These standards represent the maximum exhaust emissions that must be achieved by manufacturers for LEVS, ultra LEVS, and super ultra LEVs.
- **Zero-Emission Vehicle (ZEV) Promotion Plan:** Zero-Emission Vehicles are defined as vehicles that produce zero exhaust emissions of any criteria pollutant. This includes electric and hydrogen fuel-cell vehicles and plug-in hybrids. The California Air Resources Board

worked with state agencies to develop ways to support the rapid commercialization of Zero-Emission Vehicles in California, with benchmarks related to infrastructure, number of these vehicles on the road, and greenhouse gas emissions reductions.

- **Zero-Emission Vehicle Production Requirements:** Manufacturers of a certain size are required to produce a certain percentage of Zero-Emission Vehicles each year, increasing gradually until they reach 22 percent by 2025; there are a number of methods that can be used to reach compliance.
- **Heavy-Duty Vehicle Greenhouse Gas Emissions:** These regulations require that heavy-duty tractors/trailers be equipped with efficient tires and other devices to improve fuel economy whenever operating on California highways, regardless of where vehicles are registered.

The projected impact of these initiatives is that by 2025, new cars sold in California will emit 34 percent fewer greenhouse gases and 75 percent fewer smog emissions. Environmentally friendlier cars will be available for a wider range of vehicles styles and sizes and consumer savings on fuel will average $6,000 over the life of a car (CARB, 2012).

A number of other states are taking measures to reduce greenhouse gas and other emissions from cars. Oregon, for example, adopted California's emission standards, applying to vehicles newer than 2009, and requiring manufacturers to reduce overall fleet emissions. This will reduce greenhouse gas emissions from cars and trucks 30 percent by 2016 (State of Oregon, 2011). In October 2013, eight states in the Northeast signed an agreement to build a market for Zero-Emission Vehicles or electric vehicles, pledging to put 3.3 million Zero-Emission Vehicles on the road by 2025. These eight states represent 25 percent of the nation's automobile market.

The memorandum of understanding between these states outlines a number of actions they can take to reach their goal, including creating Zero-Emission Vehicles targets for government fleets, coordinating station equipment across states, providing financial incentives for these vehicles, and developing interstate standards (Georgetown Climate Center, 2013). This coordination is critical for the transportation sector. For significant numbers of electric vehicles to be purchased, car owners must be assured that they will be able to drive over long distances. This means they need to know where and how they can charge their car in different states.

## Fuel Efficiency

Increasing fuel efficiency in vehicles and other public transport systems can also have an impact on reducing greenhouse gas emissions. In California, a low-carbon fuel standard was enacted as part of the state's overall global warming bill. The oil industry must achieve a 10 percent reduction in the amount of carbon in fuels like diesel and gasoline by 2020 (CEC, 2014). The standard establishes a life-cycle–scale assessment of the carbon content used in fuel; the carbon intensity will be considered at stages of production, storage, transportation, and combustion.

Critics and major fuel producers like Chevron and the Western States Petroleum Association argue that this could result in a spike in gasoline prices. Nevertheless, the standard had support from environmentalists, clean air advocates, utility providers, and the auto industry (Hull, 2013). In 2011, a federal judge struck down the standard as unconstitutional, saying it violated the Commerce Clause and discriminated against out-of-state businesses, but it was later upheld in the Ninth Circuit Court of Appeals.

Oregon developed a similar program in 2009, the Clean Fuels Program, that requires the reduction of the carbon intensity of fuels by 10 percent over a 10-year period (OEC, 2014). Fuel providers can choose how to reach this requirement, whether through blending low-carbon biodiesel, switching to natural gas–powered engines, or purchasing credits from utilities. The Oregon Environmental Council estimates that this standard will create $43 million to $1.6 billion in fuel savings, and increase income in the state by $60 million to $2.6 billion over 10 years (OEC, 2014). The standard has not yet taken effect, as it was stalled by a requirement that the standards do not raise gas prices. In February 2014, Governor Kitzhaber directed the Department of Environmental Quality to move forward with implementation, and the state worked with stakeholders to draft rules for adoption.

New York State is also beginning to consider a clean fuel standard in coordination with other Regional Greenhouse Gas Initiative states and Pennsylvania. Opponents, including Americans for Prosperity, an oil industry funded group, and the Consumer Energy Alliance, representing oil and gas producers, worked to block this standard (Gallucci, 2012). They argued that gas prices would go up and cost the region hundreds of billions of dollars. There are also political hurdles, as more conservative legislatures don't consider clean fuel standards a priority. Hurdles like this and the politics of sustainability will be discussed in Chapter 7.

### Transportation & Climate Initiative

The Transportation & Climate Initiative (TCI) is a collaboration of 11 Northeast and Mid-Atlantic states and Washington, DC. The Georgetown Climate Center initiated this formal collaboration in 2010 to collectively commit the members to reducing greenhouse gas emissions in the transportation sector. Transportation accounts for 30 percent of the greenhouse gas emissions in this region (C2ES, 2010). The Transportation & Climate Initiative's goal is to facilitate collaboration in policy and program formation across participating states, within four main areas:

1. Clean vehicles and fuels,
2. Sustainable communities,
3. Freight efficiency, and
4. Information and communication technology.

The Initiative launched the Northeast Electric Vehicle Network in 2011 to encourage the use of electric vehicles throughout the region. They partnered with the Clean Cities Coalition, private sector companies, and utility providers to collectively remove barriers to electric vehicle expansion. They work to support efforts to deploy electric vehicle charging stations (TCI, 2014). These efforts include streamlining permits for installation, coordinating planning between different locations, and planning demonstration projects. Despite this initiative, a number of barriers to widespread electric vehicle deployment remain. Challenges include charging infrastructure difficulties and potential impacts on the electric grid (Zhu and Nigro, 2012, 27).

The Transportation & Climate Initiative also worked to develop policies that support sustainable communities and smart growth. Their actions include transportation investments to support alternative travel modes, land protection efforts, and infrastructure investments for sustainable transportation. They are also working to make freight movement more efficient. A study by the Rochester Institute of Technology showed that 80 percent of freight moved in the Northeast is transported by trucks, which release high levels of greenhouse gas emissions (Georgetown Climate Center, 2012). The Transportation & Climate Initiative is considering ways to reduce those vehicle miles traveled with technology, smart growth strategies, reindustrialization policies, and increased use of rail and water.

Transportation & Climate Initiative states are also committed to using information and communication technologies to improve the operational efficiency of transportation systems. They recognize that smartphones, GPS systems, and wireless sensors can promote public transit use and give information on traffic, which has the potential to reduce commuting times and traffic congestion.

## Climate Adaptation and Infrastructure Policies

The effects of climate change are tangible, as demonstrated through record droughts, precipitation changes, record global temperatures, and historic storms. In October 2012, Hurricane Sandy devastated parts of the Northeastern United States, exposing the vulnerability of our infrastructure to the effects of intense storms. Millions lost power for days and even weeks. Hospital staff carried patients down stairs when generators failed. People waited for hours to get gas in their cars. Fires destroyed homes because roads were flooded and fire fighters could not arrive in time.

### Climate Adaptation Planning

The concept of planning for climate change has grown over the past decade, and especially in the Northeast since Hurricane Sandy. According to the EPA, 32 states currently have a climate change action plan to reduce greenhouse gas emissions (2014). Each state has developed its own plan specific to its unique geographic and socioeconomic conditions.

The overall goal of these plans is to detail actions that can reduce greenhouse gas emissions and adapt to the impacts of climate change to become more resilient in the face of these changes. These plans outline goals and a variety of strategies, actions, and policy recommendations that span a broad range of categories such as air quality, energy efficiency, public health, land use, transportation, urban planning, and economic development.

The policy measures that we have discussed throughout this chapter represent many of the initiatives that are included in these plans. They focus primarily on climate mitigation—designing methods for reducing our carbon emissions, improving efficiency, and reducing reliance on fossil fuels. We'll now turn to the efforts in climate adaptation. This is a considerably newer focus as policymakers have begun to recognize the importance of increasing resiliency in the face of extreme weather events that are predicted to occur with greater frequency and intensity. State governments are looking to strengthen existing and new infrastructure including roads, power lines, energy supply, and buildings. We need to consider climate-related impacts that affect fragile infrastructure systems and public health.

Coastal states are particularly vulnerable to the impacts of climate change. These areas must consider sea-level rise and improve storm surge management, prepare for flooding impacts, and improve emergency evacuation plans for more intense hurricanes and other extreme weather. Energy, transportation, communication and other critical infrastructure must be reinforced to prepare for storms and other possible disruptions. In addition, certain areas of the country can expect more variable and intense periods of drought, like the drought California experienced in 2013 and 2014, which posed a significant stress to the water supply and regional agriculture.

After Hurricane Sandy, New Jersey's Disaster Recovery Bureau, in the Office of Emergency Management, began helping communities develop hazard mitigation plans, and looked at opportunities for climate resiliency. New Jersey devised flood mitigation strategies for high-risk communities, advanced beach and dune projects to protect the coast, and created housing programs to incorporate resilience in rebuilding efforts (State of New Jersey, 2014).

In the wake of Hurricane Sandy, the State of New York convened a commission to examine the vulnerability of critical infrastructure systems. The commission included representatives from academia, business, non-profits, engineering, finance, real estate, and government. The commission recommended strengthening transportation, energy, drinking water, and wastewater systems; rebuilding with better options and alternatives;

encouraging green infrastructure; creating reserves for critical infrastructure; improving information systems; and creating incentive programs
to encourage resilient behaviors (NYS 2100 Commission, 2014, 12–13).

Although climate action and resiliency plans are rising in popularity,
there are still barriers to developing these plans. Best practices have not yet
been established and the most effective plans and policies are not yet obvious.
The need for financial backing and multiple stakeholder cooperation, the
reality of intra-agency planning difficulties, and coordination across jurisdictions complicate these efforts.

Most states involve a wide range of stakeholders in their planning, and
work to share best practices with other state and city municipalities. Most
adaptation planning around the country is in the beginning stage, identifying
the local risks of climate change and conducting capacity and vulnerability
assessments. Because this field is so new, evaluation metrics don't yet exist.
Fortunately, a number of states have been able to implement what seem to be
effective plans that can serve as models for states that have yet to identify
resiliency as an issue worthy of attention. In the next sections, we'll examine
key infrastructure systems that are particularly susceptible to extreme weather
events and the impacts of climate change.

### Energy Infrastructure

The U.S. power grid is particularly vulnerable to climate impacts. Heat
waves can increase electricity use, overload the power grid, and lead to
outages. Hurricanes and other storms can down power lines, leaving residents without power. Major flooding can interrupt the supply of liquid fuels.
States are now working with utility companies to increase the resiliency of
our energy supply. Recently, the New York State Public Service Commission negotiated with Consolidated Edison (ConEd), a major utility company, to utilize a multiyear rate plan to protect the power system from the
effects of climate change. The state also advised ConEd how best to spend
a $1 billion storm-hardening fund (Funkhouser, 2014). This is the first
state utility commission that is requiring all the utilities it regulates to take
climate change impacts into account in operational and capital planning.

Options to make the electricity grid more resilient include implementing peak pricing, which makes it more expensive to use electricity when it is

most in demand. This pricing structure can also be used to reduce demand during heat waves and encourage people to be more mindful about their energy consumption in general. Utility providers can also create rate options to diversify their energy sources, identify areas where cogeneration systems or microgrids could reduce system load, and encourage smart charging of electric cars and trucks overnight when energy demand is low.

Cogeneration systems recover the waste heat that is thrown off when electricity is generated. That heat can replace traditional fuels used to provide heat and hot water in buildings served by the system.

A microgrid is a small-scale electricity generation and distribution system that can be connected to the main grid or act as a stand-alone source. Military bases as well as university and hospital campuses have typically been among the earliest sites for U.S. microgrids, which are often paired with cogeneration systems. Smart microgrids can be fueled by renewable energy and include smart grid technologies like net metering to enable campuses and buildings to operate off the grid when needed. They can include advanced battery storage and incorporate electric vehicles in their planning. These types of systems can avoid the need for on-site back-up generators, which are inefficient and polluting. During emergencies, microgrids are able to power themselves and provide islands of stable power for critical systems. The Department of Defense, which has long been a leader in implementing microgrids, and the Department of Energy are working with private companies such as Lockheed Martin and General Electric on standardizing technologies for microgrids.

The state of Connecticut is a leader in microgrids. After the blackouts that occurred following Hurricane Irene in 2011, the state created a statewide microgrid pilot program with $18 million dedicated to fund nine projects (Thompson, 2013). The program is managed by the state's Department of Energy and Environmental Protection, which selected facilities like police stations, hospitals, emergency shelters, and senior centers to be included on microgrids so they can keep operating during severe storms. Construction of these projects began in 2013 and includes cogeneration systems, natural gas, fuel cells, and solar panels. New Jersey and New York also plan to develop microgrid systems in their states.

Community-level microgrids can be difficult to implement because utilities have stringent rules and are closely regulated. New York State and its Public Service Commission are working with utility providers and other private developers to overcome this, and at the time of this writing are in the midst of a competition to award $40 million dollars to develop 10 community microgrids in areas with 40,000 residents (Energy Solutions Forum, 2014). Similar to the Connecticut program, these microgrids would disconnect from the grid during weather emergencies to ensure that critical operations (e.g., police, fire, etc.) continue.

Part of the New Jersey disaster recovery effort after Sandy included looking at technologies like cogeneration and solar power with storage to address the need for back-up power generation that combines energy efficiency with greater resiliency. New Jersey Transit has also designed the NJ TransitGrid, a transportation microgrids that can sustain operations in densely populated areas in the event of large grid failures.

As discussed in Chapter 2, public–private partnerships are key to the development of sustainability infrastructure. These types of partnerships increased significantly in recent years, particularly at the state level. For example, the New York State Energy Highway Blueprint outlined 13 recommendations to utilize public–private partnerships to bring the states' aging energy infrastructure into the future. The blueprint was developed by the Energy Highway Task Force, with input from utility providers, private developers, and investors, and outlined a $5.7 billion investment for a range of measures to provide up to 3,200 MW of electric generation (NYSERDA, 2013b).

The plan called for investment in new electric transmission capacity, new renewable energy projects, smart grid technologies, and studies of offshore wind development (NYPA, 2014). Importantly, it called for an expansion of transmission lines to carry excess power from upstate to downstate areas, and for incorporation of the latest engineering and technology to help transmission facilities operate during severe weather. When the task force was disbanded in 2013 with the release of the blueprint update, tasks were assigned to specific agencies and state authorities and all 13 recommendations were adopted (NYSERDA, 2013b).

### *Water and Wastewater Infrastructure*

Our water supply and wastewater systems are in danger from the impacts of climate change. Drinking water filtration plants and distribution systems, wastewater treatment plants, and sewer lines are at risk of being damaged or overwhelmed. Most of the water infrastructure in the United States was built more than 30 years ago, and most of the systems need to be rehabilitated or replaced. We need modern, reliable, and efficient wastewater treatment systems. The United States has one of the safest water supplies in the world, but water quality varies from state to state. States must continually consider the challenges of meeting the water needs of a growing population. Western states must also consider the threat of drought.

As with most infrastructure upgrades, the biggest issue is finding the money to invest in the repair and rehabilitation needed. Repairing one mile of water piping costs anywhere between $1 and $3 million, and some estimate that anywhere between 30 and 80 percent of the nation's pipes are due for replacement in the next 10 years (Columbia Water Center, 2014). New York State estimated that updating its municipal wastewater system would require $36.2 billion over the next 20 years (NYS DEC, 2008).

The American Water Works Association (AWWA) believes that rates and local charges are the best ways to sustain these water systems (AWWA, 2014). In some municipalities, up to one-third of energy costs are for water and wastewater purposes, reminding us of the centrality of energy. Therefore, improving and upgrading water, wastewater, and stormwater management systems can significantly affect energy efficiency and a region's greenhouse gas emissions. Energy, air quality, climate change, and water quality and quantity are highly interconnected systems.

In 2009, California passed the Water Conservation Act. The most notable requirement under this act is that all urban water suppliers increase their efficiency by 20 percent by 2020. In addition, it requires that all agricultural water supplies measure the quantity of water being delivered to the farm gate, and base the price of water on volume delivered. However, an NRDC analysis in 2012 found that water suppliers were not on track to meet their goals, and that many are taking advantage of loopholes in the law (Quinn, 2012).

In California, irrigated agriculture uses approximately 80 percent of the state's water supply. The 2009 law required that all large agricultural water suppliers develop a water management plan by 2012, submit a second plan by 2015, and update their plans every five years thereafter; however, as of 2013, only 30 percent of the water suppliers had submitted a plan (O'Connor and Christian-Smith, 2013, 3).

California is not the only state focused on water. In January 2014, the governor of Pennsylvania, Tom Corbett, announced a $60.1 million investment in water and wastewater projects throughout the state; $51.3 million will go towards low interest loans and $8.8 million will be offered as grants (Lundin, 2014). These projects include installing water distribution lines, making drinking water wells floodproof, improving water quality and pressure, and improving storage tanks to eliminate chemical contamination. While California and Pennsylvania's initiatives are only two examples of state efforts to improve water sustainability, they represent examples of what's possible and the types of activities occurring throughout the country.

## Facilitating Innovation

Effective policies, programs, and public managers are succeeding, quietly, at improving processes and procedures related to improving our sustainability. They are reducing costs, fast-tracking approvals, and coordinating and consolidating services. They are monitoring, evaluating, and improving policy design and program implementation—and, again, much of this is taking place at the state level.

Processes for approval and installation of renewable energy measures often involve overly complex permitting and regulatory requirements. Even as the equipment and technology costs fall, making renewable projects cheaper, the "soft costs" of bureaucratic processes significantly add to the overall cost of solar, wind, geothermal, and hydro projects. Many state energy offices are looking to reduce these soft costs, which can add weeks, months, or even years to project development. One report by SunRun estimates that permitting processes add an average of $2,500 to each installation, and that streamlining could save $1 billion over five years (Zeller, 2011).

These processes could be made more efficient with common permitting tools online, funds for efforts to streamline education, and standardized formulas for calculating permit fees. Germany and Japan are two countries that use streamlined permitting (Zeller, 2014). Sometimes reorganizing codes or simplifying code language can create a clearer path for proposals. Some jurisdictions offer a pre-application meeting to explain requirements and expedite the formal application process (Washington State Energy

Office, 2011, 6). Increased communication between departments and more formal memorandums of understanding (MoUs) can smooth permitting processes.

Minnesota's 2014 legislative agenda included cutting red tape to allow for more solar and wind energy use (Fresh Energy, 2014). In Colorado, a pilot program was designed to facilitate small hydropower projects through coordination among different stakeholders. The Federal Energy Regulatory Commission (FERC) is responsible for licensing all hydroelectric projects in the nation; low-impact hydropower projects go through an approval process that takes anywhere from six months to several years, reducing the likelihood that these projects survive (NASEO, 2014, 3). Colorado's pilot program enabled the Colorado Energy Process to oversee some of the stages in the prescreening process, which reduced delays. The pilot program issued five Federal Energy Regulatory Commission permits in the state, an improvement over the six permits issued nationwide over the prior two years.

Hawaii's Energy Office developed a set of online resource tools for developers and investors to expedite permitting processes for clean energy projects. Permitting processes are particularly slow in Hawaii, due to limited land area and competition for project siting (NASEO, 2014, 7). A unique program in Vermont includes a 10-day expedited permitting process for solar net metering systems. In 2011, the expedited process applied to systems of 5 kW or less, and expanded to 10 kW or less in 2012. Since this streamlining has gone into effect, the permitting time frame has gone from a minimum of 40 days to a minimum of 10 (NASEO, 2014, 10).

Sustainability is not easily defined, and it is not easily solved by any one state, sector, or organization. It requires portfolios of thousands of projects to move us towards a sustainable global economy. The state-led efforts discussed in this chapter complement those implemented by the federal government and the international community, and the many activities taking place at the municipal level. In Chapter 5 we will turn to these efforts, the city-led plans, which are rapidly advancing sustainability goals.

# 5

## Policy Levers for Sustainability

### The Local Level

## Introduction

For the purposes of this text, we define *local* as consisting of dense urban areas. These cities, both large and small, are capable of achieving substantial efficiencies and scale that can enhance the sustainability of built environments. City governments have emerged as laboratories for sustainability and as leaders in designing and implementing sustainability action plans. While environmental performance and sustainable development have been measured at the national level for decades, cities (and some U.S. states and other sub-national regions) are beginning to measure and manage their own impacts. Localities are aggregating sustainability actions at the micro level—in households, local businesses, and municipal operations—and incorporating those measures into strategic policymaking. Adopting sustainability has become central to urban vitality and to making cities desirable places both for businesses and residents. Cities were once considered to be environmentally unfriendly, but now they are turning to sustainable solutions that will attract new residents, stimulate economic growth, and encourage lifestyles based on renewable resources.

This chapter describes why innovative, local level policies are growing in the United States. Local initiatives are happening globally, but this chapter will generally (although not exclusively) focus on the United States. We discuss why localities are ideally suited for sustainability planning, including examples of successful city-led sustainability action. Many of these examples are from New York City, the authors' hometown, which is also one of the best examples of urban revitalization and resiliency when it comes to sustainability.

## Why Cities?

In the U.S. alone, over 83 percent of people live in cities and their surrounding metropolitan areas (NRDC, 2014). Cities are implementing a variety of sustainability plans, programs, and initiatives, from water policies to climate action to resiliency plans. They are increasingly important sustainability agents due to their considerable population size and environmental impact. According to Lamia Kamal-Chaoui and Alexis Robert, "Roughly half of the world's population lives in urban areas, and this share is increasing over time, projected to reach 60 percent by 2030. Cities consume a great majority—between 60 to 80 percent—of energy production worldwide and account for a roughly equal share of global $CO_2$ emissions" (2009, 9).

As we noted in Chapter 1, cities directly manage important public services that deal with water and wastewater, solid waste and recycling, public transit, and building and zoning codes. And because we live in an increasingly urban world, city level impacts, when aggregated, become major global impacts.

### *Why Are Cities Taking the Lead in Sustainability?*

One reason American cities lead on sustainability policy (particularly climate change policies) is that they fill a gap where the federal government has failed to act. More often, they exercise competencies relevant to sustainability strategies, particularly emissions reductions. Cities are especially vulnerable to the impacts of climate change and are reacting to these threats. Municipalities often serve as innovation centers and laboratories for policies. They have also been less ideological on these issues than political actors at the federal level.

U.S. local governments have emerged as sustainability leaders in part because national institutions have not. Despite recent energy and climate proposals from the Obama administration in the United States, most notably the greenhouse gas regulations proposed in June 2014, the most significant activity associated with climate change policy has occurred at sub-national levels (Dierwechter, 2010, 60). Local and regional actors in the United States have attempted to "fill the void left by the absence of leadership at the federal level" (Betsill and Bulkeley, 2007, 449). While acute in the United States, this policy void is not unique to this country, as many cities throughout the world have taken proactive sustainability action prior to federal mandates—or taken steps that go further than national requirements.

Local governments often have greater control over a wide variety of key actions that affect sustainability directly than do state and federal governments. According to James Svara: "City and county governments are uniquely positioned to make a significant contribution to the effort. They are directly involved in providing or regulating many of the human activities that affect resource use, promote economic development, and affect the protection and inclusion of persons from all economic levels and racial and ethnic groups" (Svara, 2011).

Cities can influence climate change mitigation and adaptation through their responsibilities over land use zoning, transportation, natural resources management, buildings, and waste and water services. Cities also have significant power over public transportation systems, the built environment, renewable energy and energy efficiency measures, and the sustainability of services delivery (Kamal-Chaoui and Robert, 2009, 11). Mayors and other local officials can set out a vision and then drive an overall policy agenda (Arup and C40 Cities, 2014, 18).

Local governments are often more willing to tackle issues like climate change because they deal directly with the consequences illustrated by disasters like 2010's flooding in Pakistan and heat wave in Moscow, and 2012's Hurricane Sandy on the U.S. East Coast. According to Jan Corfee-Morlot and her colleagues: "Metropolitan regions are particularly vulnerable to climate change, given their relatively large populations, exposed infrastructure, high degree of economic activity, and concentration of poor populations" (Corfee-Morlot et al., 2009, 7). Sea level rise, flooding, and increased storm surges can heavily damage local infrastructure. Most of the largest cities in Europe (70 percent) have neighborhoods that are less than 10 meters above sea level (Kamal-Chaoui and Roberts, 2009, 9). Precipitation changes can also have serious impacts on critical water supplies to urban areas. Further, as climate change begins to take its toll, climate refugees could flood into cities, increasing the strain on local infrastructure.

Ellen Bassett and Vivek Shandas have written that cities can create "robust place-based strategies that reflect local biophysical, political, and economic realities rather than needing to conform to federal standards that may not be applicable to each location" (Bassett and Shandas, 2010, 436). Individual municipalities can address challenges and identify opportunities using tools and programs matched to their local needs. Because their policies are implemented at the local scale, cities have more freedom to experiment with policy options and test out different strategies (Corfee-Morlot et al., 2009, 11).

Finally, political reasons often allow city governments to take greater risks in designing policies and strategies than the federal government. Cities tend to be free from the heightened political polarization seen at the federal level. Local policies typically do not draw the media frenzy that can contribute to the partisan bickering that stagnates progress at the federal level. To paraphrase former New York mayor Fiorello LaGuardia, there is no Republican or Democratic way to pick up the garbage.

## What Makes City Efforts So Successful?

There are a number of key features that are critical to successful urban sustainability policy: 1) networks for information sharing and partnerships; 2) political support from the top; and 3) holistic policymaking, linking sustainability and the high quality of life that comes with a clean, safe environment to local efforts at economic development.

### Networks for Sustainability

Getting technical knowledge right is a critical foundation for successful sustainability policies. Networks facilitate this type of information exchange.

For climate, transnational networks invest heavily in creating tools through which local authorities can create emissions inventories and forecasts, to determine where policy interventions are likely to have the most success (Betsill and Bulkeley, 2007, 450). Knowledge sharing provides baseline information and lays the groundwork for important working relationships and partnerships. This interaction allows the experts (scientists, legal and insurance professionals, and risk specialists) to engage with stakeholders and policymakers and benchmark the efforts of other cities (Bulkeley and Betsill, 2005, 47).

One indication of the growing importance of sustainability planning is the sheer number of coalitions that have formed to address sustainability and climate challenges, both domestically and internationally. Climate change provides an excellent example. In Copenhagen in December 2009, while United Nations (UN) talks to negotiate an international climate treaty were disintegrating, the Copenhagen Climate Summit for Mayors delivered calls to action, with cities pledging greenhouse gas reduction targets and offering climate action plans. Climate change is often considered a global issue to be solved by national obligations in international treaties, and yet, as international negotiations remain at a standstill, cities have taken many steps forward.

The C40 Cities Climate Leadership Group is a strong global coalition on climate change. It is a network of 63 of the world's megacities (11 in the U.S.) that are taking steps to reduce greenhouse gas emissions and increase urban resilience to address climate change both locally and globally. This network facilitates exchange of information and collaboration across major cities worldwide. The C40 provides technical, project, and purchasing assistance; financial advice; network access; and analytical and measurement tools for cities to lower their GHG emissions (C40 Cities, 2014). Former New York City mayor Michael Bloomberg has played a leadership role in the C40 group, and even after his term as mayor ended, he continued to devote time, energy, and resources to its work.

C40 Cities is one of the most wide-reaching networks, but it's not the only one. The Urban Sustainability Directors Network is a coalition of municipal members that share information, network, and build projects around sustainability. This network was started in 2008 by a small group of sustainability directors, and by 2013 it had 120 members. Members work together to do things like expand funding streams for bike sharing, better

integrate climate preparedness into city departments, improve communication about sustainability, and implement best practices for reporting
metrics and outcomes (USDN, 2014).

Another organization, the International Council for Local Environmental Initiatives (ICLEI), is a network of more than 1,000 cities and local
governments around the world. Officials of these cities have signed onto
initiatives such as the Resilient Communities for America Agreement and
the U.S. Mayors Climate Protection Agreement.

The National League of Cities, a membership of 2,000 municipalities
of various sizes, contains a Sustainable Cities Institute arm, to give guidance
and information to local governments on sustainability issues. These types of
coalitions are evidence of the increasing emphasis that cities of all sizes are
placing on sustainability planning.

## High-Level Political Support

Buy-in from prominent leaders at the local level can improve the chances
that sustainability plans and goals are implemented. Leadership is needed
to take action. The presence of local champions and the political will to
address emerging conflicts was a key factor affecting the extent to which
the rhetoric of climate policy was translated into local realities (Betsill and
Bulkeley, 2007, 452). Leadership from city mayors was important in
developing climate action plans in New York City, London, Mexico
City, Rotterdam, and a host of others. As Ellen Bassett and Vivek Shandas
observed: "A political champion appears critical to the decision to plan
and, among the climate action plans we reviewed, we found mayors'
names all over the plans, even in their titles, as in Denver or Chattanooga"
(Bassett and Shandas, 2010, 441).

In the spring of 2013, a group of graduate students in Columbia
University's master's program in environmental science and policy analyzed
sustainability efforts in 30 American cities and 6 cities outside the U.S.,
specifically examining the impact of political transitions on sustainability
initiatives. They found that while these programs might change shape or
direction under a new mayor, they nearly always continued and very often
advanced to a new stage of institutionalization. So, while a political leader
can be important in launching sustainability plans and programs, once

established, they often continue their paths, further advancing local initiatives (Earth Institute ESP Workshop Group, Spring 2013, 54).

## Sustainability as a Driver of Economic Growth

Sustainability programs must compete for local support against economic and social issues, like education and health policy. Cities that most successfully communicate sustainability emphasize the co-benefits that matter to different audiences (such as green job creation, utility-bill savings, green space, or transit availability). Effective programs focus on policy integration, incorporated holistically into broader goals involving other aspects of authority and planning. This means recognizing that the environmental sector alone will not be able to secure climate and other sustainability objectives (Lindseth, 2004, 333). Utilizing a holistic or systems-based approach incorporates the co-benefits that are important to local residents. Linking city transportation infrastructure decisions to public health objectives by creating walking and cycling lanes may create significant co-benefits to human health and traffic congestion. In addition to these local impacts, reductions in traffic and outlays for new roads reduce greenhouse gas emissions, a co-benefit related directly to global climate change (Bai et al., 2010, 130).

Cities are beginning to bring elements of sustainability into normal planning operations, and are building roadmaps to achieve sustainable operations and, ultimately, sustainable cities. While they vary by city, one survey identified 12 common sustainability activity areas across U.S. cities: recycling, water conservation, transportation improvements, energy use in transportation, social inclusion, reducing building energy use, local production and green purchasing, land conservation, greenhouse gas reduction, building and land use regulations, workplace alternatives to commuting, and alternative energy generation (Svara et al., 2013, 130).

What most of these long-term sustainability plans have in common is the emphasis on the close connection between environmental sustainability and economic development (Geary, 2011, 1). Local leaders see sustainability as critical to long-term growth. They are investing in their future by supporting these efforts. They have taken steps in sustainability as a strategy for financial savings and are explicitly tying sustainability measures into broader economic goals (AIA, 2009, 5; Zborel, 2011, 1).

According to the Natural Resources Defense Council, "creating a smart and sustainable city means ultimately attaining a high level of economic efficiency, a high quality of life, a highly desirable place in which to live and do business, and a meaningful commitment to environmental responsibility" (Epstein, 2013). Research has also found that a sustainability approach can be beneficial to every major urban area, rich or poor (Newman, 2006, 293).

## The Growth of Sustainability Plans in the United States

As of November 2009, 56 cities, towns, and counties in the United States had completed or were in the process of completing a sustainability plan, while 141 had completed or were in the process of completing a climate action plan (ICLEI, 2009). We expect that number has already grown and will continue to grow. According to a survey by Living Cities, a collaboration of 21 large foundations and financial institutions, four out of five cities are reporting that sustainability is among their top five priorities, with over half of the large cities surveyed in some stage of a sustainability planning process (Living Cities, 2009).

Portland and Seattle were among the first cities in the United States to tackle issues of climate change and sustainability. In the early 1990s Portland recognized the importance of slowing the buildup of greenhouse gases and participated with other local governments around the world in the Urban $CO_2$ Reduction Project, coordinated by ICLEI (City of Portland, 1993). In 1994, Seattle issued a comprehensive sustainability plan called Toward a Sustainable Seattle, to become a more healthy and vibrant city (City of Seattle, 2014).

San Francisco started a sustainability planning process in 1995. Sustainable San Francisco is a collaboration of city agencies, including the Planning Department, Recreation and Parks Department, Solid Waste Management Program, Energy Conservation, and businesses, environmental organizations, elected officials, and residents. This team developed goals, objectives, and actions modeled after the European Community's Agenda 21 Implementation Plan. The Sustainability Plan was finalized in 1997, and acted as a blueprint for actions the city could implement on a regulatory or legislative level; an environmental department was formed to oversee implementation of the plan (Sustainable City, 2014).

Denver was one of the first cities to link sustainable and economic development. Sustainability planning in Denver began in 2005 when the Mayor signed a nationwide pledge under the U.S. Mayors Climate Protection Agreement. When Denver hosted the 2008 Democratic National Convention (DNC), it announced that it would be the greenest DNC ever. These greening efforts were housed in the mayor's office within the Greenprint Denver Office, established by an executive order (Geary, 2011, 2). The city's experience with the DNC was able to demonstrate that sustainable practices were good for both the community and for businesses, which eased the transition into green economic development after the convention ended (Geary, 2011, 3).

New York City's PlaNYC 2030 is one of the most notable sustainability plans in the nation. It was developed in response to projections that the city would house another million residents by 2030. Michael Bloomberg, mayor at the time, understood that the city needed to act immediately to initiate plans to accommodate this growth while ensuring NYC remained an attractive place to live and do business.

Created in 2006, the NYC Mayor's Office of Long-Term Planning and Sustainability brought together more than 20 city agencies to develop PlaNYC 2030's 10 overarching goals and 127 initiatives to address issues of land use, parks and open space, affordable housing, transportation, air and water quality, energy supply and demand, and climate change mitigation and adaptation. Since its release in 2007, PlaNYC has been upheld as a global model for best practices. Some of the key factors in the success of the plan included:

- Strong buy-in from the mayor;
- Central management and coordination from the mayor's sustainability office;
- A fact-driven plan based on research and analysis (and specific milestones and metrics identified in the plan);
- Guidance from stakeholders across sectors;
- Aggressive but achievable initiatives;
- A transparent and inclusive planning process; and
- Institutionalization of the plan in city law (ICLEI, 2009, 7).

New York City's sustainability agency, the Office of Long-Term Planning and Sustainability, was institutionalized in the city charter through a new local law, which also requires that the office issue both an updated sustainability plan every four years and annual progress updates (City of New York, 2013, 410). PlaNYC has contributed to achieving New York City's cleanest air in 50 years, planting over 750,000 new trees, and passing the city's halfway mark of reducing GHG emissions 30 percent by 2030.

## Urban Energy Initiatives

Cities have focused their limited resources on energy efficiency infra-structure and practices and increased use of renewable energy. These urban energy initiatives tend to be practical and operational, with a focus on short-term results.

### *Energy Efficiency and Conservation*

Increasing energy efficiency reduces energy consumption and saves money. For example, cities can upgrade incandescent signal and traffic lights with light-emitting diodes (LEDs) and also develop plans to optimize the timing of traffic signals (C40 Cities, 2011b). LEDs are brighter and last longer than incandescent bulbs, so they require fewer replacements, and save money on both electricity and maintenance costs. Chicago initiated an LED traffic-light program, installing new lighting at 2,900 intersections. Chicago projected this program would generate $2.55 million annually in energy savings and reduce yearly carbon dioxide emissions by 23,000 metric tons (C40 Cities, 2011b).

Similarly, Los Angeles (LA) retrofitted over 140,000 streetlights with LED bulbs (City of Los Angeles, 2012). This project will save the city over $7 million annually. The project was made possible by collaboration bet-ween the LA mayor's office, the Bureau of Street Lighting, C40 Climate Group, and the Clinton Climate Initiative. This partnership proved to be particularly important in providing technological and financial advice and public-private implementation models (City of Los Angeles, 2012). The project cost was funded primarily through a loan from the LA Department of Water and Power, which will be paid back through cost savings from the project itself.

PlaNYC 2030, New York City's long-term sustainability plan, specifically targets energy efficiency in large existing buildings. In 2009, the city released the Greener, Greater Buildings Plan, an effort that covered 15,000 buildings in the city. These large buildings consumed 45 percent of all energy used by New York City buildings and accounted for 74 percent of the city's greenhouse gas emissions (City of New York, 2014). The plan projected greenhouse gas reductions of 5 percent, a savings of $7 billion, and the creation of more than 17,000 jobs over 10 years (City of New York, 2014). The plan was institutionalized through a series of four local laws, which require energy benchmarking, energy audits and retrocommissioning, and sub-metering.

These laws were only one part of New York City's broader efficiency strategy. In 2008, then-mayor Michael Bloomberg asked the Urban Green Council, the New York chapter of the U.S. Green Building Council, to make recommendations on how to make the city's codes and regulations more sustainable. The New York City Green Codes Task Force included architects, corporate tenants, public health experts, city agencies, and environmental organizations. Their 2010 report made 111 recommendations for changes in the city code; 48 were incorporated into local laws and practices (UGC, 2014).

Zone Green amendments were proposed in 2012 by the Department of City Planning based on recommendations from the Green Codes Task Force. Building owners who wanted to install solar panels had faced obstacles such as building height requirements and area-of-insulation requirements; Zone Green amendments removed many obstacles faced in the construction and retrofitting of green buildings (NYC Department of City Planning, 2014). Zone Green supports technologies such as energy efficient building walls, which can better insulate buildings and reduce heating and cooling demands; sun control devices and awnings to reduce cooling and lighting demand; solar energy installations in strategic areas; eased bulkhead rooftop provisions to allow for more equipment to be placed on roofs; and wind turbines that can exceed building height (Larsen, 2012).

In 2003, the mayor of Boston and the Boston Redevelopment Authority (BRA) formed a task force to study how to encourage green building practices; the group released a set of recommendations under Article 80 of the Boston Zoning Code (AIA, 2009, 36). These zoning code changes were an important policy change to encourage greener practices in both commercial and residential buildings. The Boston Redevelopment Authority is now required to review the design of real estate developments and their effects on the community and city. In 2006, Boston became the first major city to require new buildings larger than 50,000 square feet to earn a certain number of construction points from Leadership in Energy and Environmental Design (LEED) (BRA, 2014, 5). LEED is a nationally recognized green building certification program that assigns ratings to buildings based on certain criteria. The Boston building amendments also encouraged green building materials as part of an affordable housing program (AIA, 2009, 37). And, since 2013, all projects subject to Article 80 reviews are now required to complete a climate change preparedness and resiliency checklist (BRA, 2013).

Seattle is considered a leader in green building programs, particularly for residential buildings (AIA, 2009, 15). In 2000, its High Point neighborhood was one of the first communities in the nation to incorporate sustainable design techniques on a neighborhood-wide scale (AIA, 2009, 58). These standards were rare at the time, but the basic principles used in this pilot neighborhood—such as eliminating lead paint, asbestos, and other harmful materials—are now much more widely incorporated in urban sustainability planning. Seattle also had a green building team as early as 1999, which eventually joined with the Office of Sustainability and Environment in 2012 to combine urban sustainability policy development with the permit and code development functions (C40 Cities, 2011e).

Globally, we see similar trends. In 2003, the city of Melbourne, Australia, set an ambitious goal of having net-zero emissions in the city by 2020, and has devoted significant resources to influence improvements in commercial sector buildings, which generate a little over half of the city's greenhouse gas emissions (City Climate Leadership Awards, 2014). In 2010, Melbourne released the 1200 Buildings Program, which provides a platform for building owners and industry stakeholders to engage and collaborate on the retrofit of 1,200 commercial buildings (approximately 70 percent of the total). The goals of the program include: eliminating 383,000 tons of $CO_2$ emissions annually by 2020; reducing potable water consumption by 5 billion liters (1.32 billion gallons) annually; raising AUD $2 billion in private sector investment; creating green jobs; and positioning Melbourne as a leader in global climate change efforts (NYC Global Partners, 2011, 1). Since the beginning of the 1200 Buildings Program, 43 buildings owned by corporations, private business, government, and nonprofits have committed to undertaking these retrofits.

### Encouraging Renewable Energy

While energy efficiency is the low-hanging fruit of sustainability, it will not be enough to transform the fossil fueled economy; we also need to increase the amount of energy we use from renewable sources. Many cities have initiatives related to a specific source or sector. Increasing solar energy capacity has been a major focus for many large cities. For example, Boston launched its Renew Boston Solar program to encourage the installation of solar technology, maximize participation in state incentive programs, and map renewable energy systems. The overall goal is to increase solar energy system capacity to 25 MW by 2015. This was made possible through a partnership between the U.S. Department of Energy, the Massachusetts Clean Energy Center, local utility providers, and a range of other clean energy stakeholders (City of Boston, 2014).

In 2005, Austin Energy, a community-owned electricity supplier, won the U.S. Department of Energy's 2005 Wind Power Pioneer Award for its "leadership, demonstrated success and innovation in its wind power program" (US DOE, 2005). It runs one of the leading renewable energy programs in the nation (MacDonald, 2012). The program increased demand for renewable energy by providing new energy options and showing the importance of renewable energy sources when the local government adopted the option into its own operations.

In 2011, the government of Austin became the largest local government in the nation to power all of its facilities with 100 percent green energy when it enrolled all its electric accounts in GreenChoice (IRENA, 2014, 5). As of 2012, Texas had over 40 grid-scale wind farms with a capacity of 11,000 MW—more than 20 percent of the total installed wind capacity in the United States (IRENA, 2014, 4). Austin is also home to the 30 MW Webberville Solar project, a solar field that covers about 220 acres and produces enough energy to power 5,000 average homes per year; it is the largest project of its kind (MacDonald, 2012).

## Urban Air Quality Programs

To improve urban air quality, cities are attempting to reduce pollution by targeting two main sources of emissions: buildings and transportation.

### *Emissions from Buildings*

Combustion of heating fuels represents a significant source of local air pollution emissions, particularly in urban areas (NYC DOHMH, 2011).

New York City has the highest density of fine particulate matter ($PM_{2.5}$), or soot pollution, of any large U.S. city (City of New York, 2013, 39). The New York City Department of Health and Mental Hygiene projects that, every year, $PM_{2.5}$ pollution in New York City causes more than 3,000 deaths, 2,000 hospital admissions for lung and heart conditions, and approximately 6,000 emergency department visits for asthma in children and adults (NYC DOHMH, 2011). The city has targeted a number of different particulate sources such as idling automobiles and diesel-powered vehicles, including school buses and trucks. However, in New York City, building emissions account for a higher percentage of $PM_{2.5}$ pollution than transportation, and for this reason, New York focused on the burning of building heating oil under PlaNYC.

The city developed a multipronged policy approach to reduce emissions from heating oil, with a combination of laws, regulations, and voluntary efforts. First, they improved air quality monitoring at the neighborhood level with the 2008 implementation of the New York City Community Air Survey, the largest urban air monitoring study in the country (City of New York, 2013, 39). This monitoring quickly revealed that neighborhoods with more buildings with boilers that burned residual heating oils No. 4 and No. 6 (the dirtiest types of fuel oils) had higher levels of fine particles, sulfur dioxide, and nickel in the air (NYC DOHMH, 2013, 1). The city estimated that approximately 10,000 buildings, or 1 percent of total buildings, burned No. 4 and No. 6 heating oil, making them responsible for more air pollution than all of the city's cars and trucks combined; this made those buildings an obvious target for air pollution reduction (NYC DEP, 2011).

In 2010, New York City Council passed Local Law 43, which reduced the sulfur content of dirty No. 4 oil by half, and required all heating oil to contain at least 2 percent renewable biodiesel. In 2011, the city adopted regulations to phase out all No. 6 heating oil by 2015 and No. 4 heating oil by 2030. The city worked with state officials to pass a state law that reduced the sulfur content of No. 2 oil by 99 percent; low-sulfur heating fuels release fewer by-products and harmful emissions. It also partnered with Environmental Defense Fund (EDF) to launch the Clean Heat program to reduce $PM_{2.5}$ emissions further by providing information, technical assistance, and financing assistance and incentives to building owners. The goal was to help building owners phase out dirty fuels prior to regulatory deadlines to accelerate air quality benefits.

## *Vehicle Emissions*

The negative health effects of motor vehicle air pollution have been long established, but recently, scientists have examined street-level exposure and found a high-risk zone of about 500 to 1,500 feet (County of Los Angeles, 2013). Individuals living within that range of a heavily trafficked road face greater risks than those living at a greater distance from the road. The soot and fumes from cars, trucks and buses are linked to asthma, lung and heart disease, and cancer (American Cancer Society, 2013). For these reasons, many cities around the country are working to reduce emissions from the transportation sector.

Cities are frequently targeting municipal vehicle fleets, through either changing fuel sources or plugging into the city's electrical grid. San Francisco has one of the largest clean air municipal fuel fleets in the country: more than half of the city's municipal railway fleet is made of Zero-Emissions Vehicles (C40 Cities, 2011a). In 2005, the mayor issued Executive Directive 05–103, requiring that 70 percent of new vehicles use alternative fuel, and 90 percent of new light-duty purchases be alternative fuel or high-efficiency vehicles, and in 2006 an executive directive required fleet managers to transition to a 20 percent biodiesel blend (C40 Cities, 2011a).

Another way San Francisco is reducing emissions from vehicle traffic is by employing technology for smarter parking management. The SFpark program uses meters, sensors, and demand-responsive pricing to provide real-time parking information available online, via text and smartphone apps, to help people find parking, minimize traffic, and reduce idling, circling and double-parking (SFpark, 2014). This program was piloted in 7,000 metered spaces and 12,250 spaces in city-owned parking garages, funded primarily by the Department of Transportation's Urban Partnership Program, and made possible through collaboration with local businesses and communities (SFpark, 2014).

Portland is optimizing traffic lights to reduce idling and acceleration of vehicles, saving fuel and reducing carbon dioxide emissions. Timing parameters are specified to reflect traffic patterns at specific intersections, as well as specific times of the day and week. The city has done this at 135 intersections resulting in estimated savings of 1,750,000 gallons of gas annually (C40 Cities, 2011c).

Seattle is cutting vehicle emissions by targeting vessels that are sitting at port. "Simply by 'plugging in' to the city grid and turning off their engines, participating vessels are cutting annual $CO_2$ emissions by up to 29 percent annually, with financial savings of up to 26 percent per call" (C40 Cities, 2011d). Vessels that sit at port often are guilty of *hoteling*, continuously running diesel engines for onboard equipment. Through a collaboration between the Port of Seattle, major cruise lines, regulators, and industry, some of Seattle's vessels are voluntarily *cold ironing*, turning off their engines and plugging into the city grid, which eliminates emissions from the ship. This could be taken a step further, pairing these plugged-in vessels to local electricity generated from renewable energy sources at or near the port.

## Transportation Policies

To ensure long-term viability, cities are expanding and strengthening their existing public transportation networks so they are convenient and accessible, including bus, rail, ferry, and metro/subway systems. They are also working on improving fuel-efficient and low-emissions transportation systems, such as electric vehicles. Cities can also design and encourage active forms of transport, such as biking and walking. This also includes implementing intelligent traffic management systems to improve traffic planning and flow, which can reduce travel times and emissions.

## Public Transportation

Public transit affords greater mobility for more people, reduces congestion, and provides economic benefits (US DOT, 2014). Greater use of public transportation also reduces the number of cars on the road, curtailing emissions of harmful pollutants. While vehicle efficiency has increased, the global growth of the vehicle fleet has reduced it impact (UNDP and GEF, 2006, 6–7).

In the United States in 2007, the use of public transportation was calculated to reduce gas consumption by 1.4 billion gallons each year (Bailey, 2007). Transit travel can also be 26 to 79 times safer than auto travel (Litman, 2006). Public transportation can improve air quality and reduce greenhouse gas emissions; heavy rail transit like subways produce about 76 percent lower greenhouse gas emissions per mile than an average car (US DOT, 2014).

Public transportation can also support higher density land development, which reduces the distance and time people need to travel to reach their destination. In 2013, Americans took 10.7 billion trips on public transportation, which was the highest number in 57 years (APTA, 2014). From 1995 to 2014, public transit ridership increased 37.2 percent, which is higher than population growth and the rate of vehicle miles traveled (APTA, 2014). Recent studies show that Americans are buying fewer cars and getting fewer licenses. Driven by the millennial generation, who sometimes prefer urban spaces where they can walk and take public transit, many Americans do not see owning a car as an aspirational goal in the way the past few generations did. The car culture may well be fading – and to accommodate that change and retain young people, cities are improving and expanding alternative transportation systems.

According to WalkScore, the top 10 cities in the United States with the best access to public transit are New York, NY; San Francisco, CA; Boston, MA; Washington, DC; Philadelphia, PA; Chicago, IL; Seattle, WA; Baltimore, MD; Los Angeles, CA; and Portland, OR (Benfield, 2014). New York City's public transit and subway system is one of the most extensive in the world, and the majority of the city's commuters use public transit. In 2012, on an average weekday, the Metropolitan Transportation Authority (MTA) moved close to 8 million people through its subway, bus, and bus company services (MTA, 2013). NYC is expanding its system and building new subway lines in Manhattan, a rapid bus transit system, new ferry services, and car sharing. It is also directing new city growth to areas that are transit accessible, increasing residential capacity close to transit, and decreasing allowable densities in areas of the city where people depend on cars (City of New York, 2011, 20).

Although New York has one of the best public transit systems in the United States and the world, it is used at a lower rate than its counterparts in major Asian and European cities. Cities like London, Singapore, and Tokyo have recognized that providing more mass transit options creates a cleaner, healthier, more efficient urban environment.

## Case Study: Bogota Rapid Bus Transit System

Bogota, Colombia is an important case study in urban transportation. Bogota has a population of about 7.5 million people, but no city rail system. Prior to 2000, the only form of public transportation was an inefficient system of diesel buses. In 2000, the city began tackling its air pollution and congestion problems with the introduction of a bus rapid transit system called Trans-Milenio. By 2009, about 2,000 of the city's 18,000 buses were part of the bus rapid transit system (City Climate Leadership Awards, 2014). The system consists of a network of 54 miles and carries some 1.6 million passengers per day. Their pioneering rapid transit system more closely resembles an above-ground subway system than a collection of traditional bus routes. There are seven intersecting bus lines, enclosed stations entered by swiping a fare, and the buses themselves exude a "tram-like feel" (Rosenthal, 2009). The buses provide the benefits of public transportation, including improved traffic flows and reduced smog and GHG emissions, at only a fraction of the price and time that it takes to build a subway system.

The TransMilenio system has allowed Bogota to remove more than 7,000 small private buses from its roads, significantly reducing the resulting fuel emissions by over 350,000 tons annually since 2001 (City Climate Leadership Awards, 2014). As a result, the system has become the first large public transportation project approved by the United Nations to generate and sell Kyoto carbon credits. The credits have sold for between $100 million to $300 million to date and are expected to bring in approximately $25 million a year in the near future (Rosenthal, 2009; Urbanization Knowledge Partnership, 2014, 4).

Importantly, it has improved the quality of life for citizens of the city. Average trip times for TransMilenio users have fallen by 32 percent, city traffic fatalities have fallen by 92 percent, collisions by 79 percent, and injuries by 75 percent (Urbanization Knowledge Partnership, 2014, 4). Prior to 1998, bus service in Bogota was low-quality, dirty, and dangerous. Bus companies rented out routes to individual bus owners, which led to an overabundance of buses competing for passengers. This system suffered from very long commute times and was known to cause many accidents. In 1998, newly elected mayor Enrique Peñalosa wanted to shift the public bus system away from individual bus ownership to a highly complex and intricate system that would be one of the most efficient in the world (Ardila, 2005, 5).

Despite the great strides that the TransMilenio has made, it has its problems. TransMilenio may have become a victim of its own popularity and public opinion of the system has been on the decline since 2004 (Jaffe, 2012). The program has been so popular that expansion has not been able to keep up. Buses can be overcrowded and riders complain about the extremely high fares relative to the average income in the city. People complain that not only are the buses so crowded that they can't get on, but they miss their stops because they can't get off them quickly enough (Jaffe, 2012). While phase I was implemented on schedule in two years, phases II and III have fallen behind schedule. The original plan called for 170 km (105 miles) of lanes by 2011, but by the deadline only 84 km (52 miles) were completed (Jaffe, 2012). While these are significant setbacks, the system has transformed transportation in Bogota.

### Encouraging Active Transport

Active transport is powered by human motion, making it a zero-emission transportation option that also improves personal wellness. Currently, bicycles are the most popular active transport vehicles, and many urban areas are working to develop robust programs for urban bicycle transportation. Expanded bike lane and bike-share systems have been growing in popularity as ways to encourage active, sustainable transport that make cycling easier, safer, and more appealing. In 2013, there were more than 500 bike-share programs around the world; the largest are in Hangzhou

City, China and Paris, France (Guide to Greening Cities, 2014). These programs are typically funded through public-private partnerships that involve corporate sponsorships and some type of public subsidy.

In 2008, the first U.S. public bike-share program, Capital Bikeshare, launched in the Washington, DC, metro area with 100 bikes and 10 stations. The system grew quickly and now has over 1,800 bikes and 200 stations; more than 80 percent of trips taken were by Capital Bikeshare members, demonstrating the program's importance to the local transportation system. Two key factors in the success of this program were managing the public's expectations, as the program was slow to start and expand, and building in flexibility to accommodate changing ridership programs (Guide to Greening Cities, 2014).

New York City's Citi Bike program launched in 2012 with 6,000 bikes and 275 docking stations. To choose sites for the program, the city initiated an inclusive planning process with over 400 meetings with stakeholders, community boards, and members of the City Council (NYC DOT, 2014, 6) and 21 field demonstrations to introduce the program to the public (NYC DOT, 2014, 9). In the first 200 days of the program, Citi Bike users took 5.8 million trips, including more than 19,000 trips on a day in December when temperatures were below freezing (NYC DOT, 2013).

The transportation initiatives under PlaNYC were vital in making this bike-share program possible. To help the program succeed, in the first six years after PlaNYC was adopted, the city installed over 300 miles of bike lanes, including 20 miles of protected bike lanes, which are separated from car lanes by physical barriers. Ultimately, these efforts doubled the number of people who commute by bike and have increased bike safety and convenience (City of New York, 2013, 30).

The city of Boston recognizes the importance of bicycling for health; its Prescribe-a-Bike program allows doctors to give patients $5 bike-share memberships, which is a significant savings over the regular $85 membership (Gaitan, 2014).

In Copenhagen, Denmark, the city is developing a PLUSnet system for cyclists consisting of Green Routes, Bicycle Superhighways, and local routes. PLUSnet will ensure plenty of space, safe intersections, and regular maintenance so that cyclists can travel at their own pace safely and securely. The goal is to have three bike lanes in each direction for at least 80 percent of the biking routes (City of Copenhagen, 2011, 11). New shortcuts will also be built over water and railways and through squares that will greatly improve travel times and allow for safer travel (City of Copenhagen, 2011, 23).

## Electric Vehicle Infrastructure

Electric vehicles (EVs) can be an important element of a comprehensive sustainable transportation plan. Cities are increasingly purchasing electric vehicles for their fleets, replacing fossil-fueled vehicles with zero-emission cars. In addition to purchasing these vehicles directly, city governments can implement a number of policies to increase the uptake of electric vehicles. It is important to note many cities do not want to encourage more cars, regardless of their fuel source. The goal is not to add more cars to the road, but to increase the percentage of EVs. With that in mind, there is a lot that local governments can do to ready their communities for electric vehicles, much of that involves the charging infrastructure, rather than the cars themselves.

Electric vehicle charging stations must dovetail with parking regulations, as all charging occurs while the car is parked. City parking ordinances can address EV infrastructure issues by providing charging stations or pre-wiring so they can easily be installed later. Other issues that need to be addressed include on-street charging and parking, and the management of user rotation, access, and violations (WXY Architecture, NYSERDA and TCI, 2012, 12). For example, the city of Lacey, Washington, restricts all non-electric cars from parking in specially designated charging stalls. The local law adds parking enforcement to the zoning regulations required by the State of Washington (WXY Architecture et al., 2012, 12–13).

Zoning is a necessary part of electric vehicle deployment. City officials can use zoning ordinances to allow, incentivize, or even require EV infrastructure. In London, the city's development plan requires charging stations in all new construction, and 20 percent of new parking stalls must be allocated to electric vehicles (WXY Architecture et al., 2012, 10).

Vancouver, Canada, was the first city in North America to require electric vehicle connections in all new city development. In 2011, the city modified its building bylaws for new construction to require that charging stations be ready-wired for EV support in 20 percent of all multiunit

residential parking spaces and in 100 percent of single-family homes
(WXY Architecture et al., 2012, 17; City of Vancouver, 2012). The
city also decided that simple EV installations were safe and minor enough
that they no longer required any permit filing for these projects (WXY
Architecture et al., 2012, 20). Cities such as Houston, San Francisco, and
Los Angeles offer automatic and instantaneous online permitting for
standard charging station installations, reducing waiting times and administrative costs for the projects (WXY Architecture et al., 2012, 21).


## Congestion Charging

A common problem facing many cities is that there are simply too many
people moving at the same time in too small an area. Manhattan, for
example, has a resident population of 1.6 million, but serves approximately
4 million people every weekday and 2.9 million people each day of
the weekend (Moss and Qing, 2012, 1). Although only 4.6 percent of
New Yorkers commute to Manhattan by car, average commute times
continue to be among the worst in the United States. Like in the central
business districts of many other cities around the country, it is virtually
impossible to drive in midtown Manhattan during the day. Congestion
pricing could be a powerful tool for localities to reduce unnecessary
driving, promote environmentally sound practices and raise money for
transportation infrastructure.

No U.S. city has a comprehensive congestion charging system, due
primarily to low public support. Despite its lack of adoption in the
United States, congestion pricing is not a new idea. In 1952, Columbia
University professor William Vickery recommended it for the New York
City subway system, proposing that prices be increased during peak times
and on the busiest stretches of track (Columbia University, 1997). Whether
used on subways or roads, the increased prices would encourage people to
travel at different times or use alternative modes of transportation.

In 1975, Singapore became the first city to adopt congestion pricing
(Transportation Alternatives, 2013). The Singapore program was designed
to reduce rush-hour traffic into the central business district. Exemptions
were included for emergency vehicles (e.g., ambulances, fire trucks, etc.) as

well as high-occupancy vehicles carrying four or more passengers (Anas and Lindsey, 2011, 73). The program has expanded and evolved since 1975, and today it relies on technology similar to the E-ZPass electronic toll system, which, in the U.S. Northeast, was the world's first electronic road pricing system, charging tolls in accordance with the flow of traffic. While there has been no comprehensive cost–benefit analysis on the congestion pricing program in Singapore, the benefits are generally considered to outweigh the costs in the system and one report concludes, "Singapore's Congestion Zone has seen a 13% reduction of traffic during charging period. It has also led to a reduction of 24,700 cars driving during peak and a 22% rise of traffic speeds" (Transportation Alternatives, 2013).

In 2003, London Mayor Ken Livingstone implemented a fee for driving into London's central business district. The London system charges a flat fee (starting at £5 in 2005, rising steadily to £11.5 in 2013) to enter the specified zones. In London, cameras are set up at the entrance and exit of the taxed zones and images are taken of the license plates entering and exiting the zone. The pictures are then compared to a database of exemption, and users are issued fee notices, which can be paid online (Transport for London, 2014).

The charge was originally very controversial, but it has reduced congestion, emissions, and travel times (Transportation Alternatives, 2013). London has seen about a six percent increase in bus passengers during congestion fee hours since the beginning of the program. This congestion charge also funds London transportation infrastructure; all net revenues (£148 million in 2009–2010) are invested in improving the city's transit (Qureshi, 2013). Cost-benefit analyses found that the "combined benefits to motorists, public transport users, and the environment exceed system setup and operating costs" (Anas and Lindsey, 2011, 82).

## Water Management

Cities must address infrastructure issues to maintain a safe supply of water for domestic, commercial, and industrial use. Two examples from New York City illustrate the important way in which sustainability policy impacts fundamental water management decisions.

## Case Study: New York City's Water Supply

New York City's drinking water is among the best in the world, exceeding stringent federal and state water quality standards. New Yorkers get their water from three upstate reservoir systems that the city owns and operates: the Catskill, Delaware, and Croton watersheds. This extensive water system provides over 1 billion gallons of water daily to over 9 million people in New York City and the surrounding counties (City of New York, 2007, 78). The Catskill and Delaware watersheds, which together provide 90 percent of the city's water, are so pristine that their water does not need to be chemically filtered. This is a significant accomplishment; in fact, there are only four other major American cities that are not required to filter their drinking water: Boston, San Francisco, Seattle, and Portland.

To keep the sources of water clean, the city works hard to protect the watersheds from activities that can threaten their water quality. New York City actively engages in land acquisition when available and feasible, and has acquired more than 78,000 acres since 2002 (City of New York, 2007, 81). City ownership guarantees that crucial natural areas remain undeveloped, eliminating threats that could taint the water supply.

The city enforces an array of environmental regulations designed to protect water quality while also encouraging reasonable and responsible development in the watershed communities. New York City also invests in infrastructure—such as wastewater treatment facilities and septic systems— that shield the water supply, while working with its upstate partners to ensure comprehensive best practices for land use that curb pollution at the water's sources. While these efforts take significant investments of time and money, the alternative to maintaining these watersheds is far more costly. If the water quality deteriorated, the city would be forced to build a filtration plant that could cost as much as $10 billion to construct, which would cost roughly $1 billion a year in debt service and operation expenses. This would also cause a rate increase of at least 30 percent to New Yorkers (City of New York, 2007, 78).

Most of New York City's water supply is protected and filtered by the natural processes of upstate ecosystems. To environmental economists, this can be considered an *environmental service*. By calculating the price of a filtration plant and its annual operational costs, we can place a monetary value on the natural environment that already provides this filtration. This comes to

$1 billion per year minus the $100 million we spend annually to protect the upstate ecosystems. The remaining $900 million a year is savings that we lose if we don't protect these fragile environments. It's a graphic illustration of the point that what is good for the environment will often be good for our bank accounts, which is the essence of sustainability management.

Determining the value of such environmental services is only possible with a strong knowledge of how these ecosystems function. If our fundamental understanding of these natural processes is flawed or incomplete, we cannot figure out the financial benefits and costs of related projects. This reinforces the necessity of basic and applied science, which provide the foundation for critical public policy decisions, often involving substantial sums of public dollars. We can see that science is one of many critical inputs that managers and leaders need at their disposal to process complex problems and arrive at the best solution.

## Case Study: Green Infrastructure

Cities must collect and manage used water and stormwater, which is the runoff after a storm or flooding event that can contain trash, heavy metals, and other pollutants, and which is commonly discharged into nearby waterways. Cities are investing in local improvements to infrastructure and water management programs in efforts to reduce the negative environmental and public health risks posed by polluted stormwater as well as to comply with the Clean Water Act (NRDC, 2012, 2). One of the main problems with storm water is that most American cities, particularly those with older infrastructure, have combined sewer systems, handling both stormwater and sewage through the same pipes.

About 800 communities nationwide manage their stormwater through a combined sewer system (NRDC, 2012, 6). In combined systems, residential wastewater is combined with that from street sewers being piped to the local sewage treatment plant. Problems occur when heavy rain suddenly sends a high volume of water into street sewers. This can overwhelm treatment plants and push raw sewage into local waterways before it is treated. The traditional approach to dealing with the combined sewer overflow problem is to build tanks and other facilities to hold excess water during storms and then release it into the sewers once the storm has ended.

Increasingly, cities are turning to green options to manage this challenge. One option, termed green infrastructure, is an approach to water management that combines natural ecosystem processes with the built environment. Instead of using traditional pipes and tanks (called *gray infrastructure*) to manage water runoff, green infrastructure uses vegetation and soil to absorb rainwater where it falls, allowing it to be stored and managed naturally. According to NRDC: "Green infrastructure manages storm water onsite through installation of permeable pavement, green roofs, parks, roadside plantings, rain barrels, and other mechanisms that mimic natural hydrologic functions, such as infiltration into soil and evapotranspiration into the air, or otherwise capture runoff onsite for productive use" (NRDC, 2012, 2). Green infrastructure systems are not only important to help control stormwater runoff, but they are also beneficial to public health by reducing urban heat island effects, improving air quality, and contributing to a more livable urban environment (Daigger, 2011, 15).

The problem of combined sewer overflow remains one of the most difficult water quality issues facing New York City. In September 2010, the city released its Green Infrastructure Plan, which makes use of green infrastructure to augment traditional investment in gray infrastructure. These low-cost techniques reduce the impact of storms on the city's water treatment plants. They can also quickly reduce the flow of wastewater to treatment plants since it takes much less time to plant greenery or put out rain barrels than to site, design, build, and operate a holding tank. The city's 2010 plan estimates costs that are $1.5 billion less than the traditional gray strategy (NYC DEP, 2014). The plan called for a multi-agency taskforce to build partnerships and coordinate capital planning between the NYC Department of Environmental Protection (DEP) and a wide range of other city agencies.

A 2012 agreement between New York City and the state Department of Environmental Conservation (DEC) included many of the innovations proposed in the city's plan. The agreement modified the city's existing method of improving local water quality by calling for investment of approximately $187 million in green infrastructure projects by 2015 (NYC DEP, 2012, 20). The agreement calls for a total of $2.4 billion in public and private investment in green infrastructure over the next 20 years plus $2.9 billion in traditional gray infrastructure projects and upgrades (NYC DEP, 2012, 1). It also calls for cooperation with the DEC to reduce combined sewer overflows using a green/gray hybrid approach. The plan features city and state efforts as well as collaboration between the public and private sectors.

The agreement also promotes flexibility and accountability. The state and city have institutionalized a form of adaptive management that builds in milestones and performance measurement and allows for changes as data, technology and processes improve over time. According to the New York City Department of Environmental Protection: "The decentralized and diverse nature of green infrastructure demands non-standard approaches to capital planning and streamlined processes to meet aggressive targets" (NYC DEP, 2012, 23).

New York, of course is not the only locality active in this effort. Kansas City, Missouri, made improvements in its sewer systems, at a cost of $2.5 billion over the next 25 years to upgrade systems and incorporate green infrastructure into its water management program (EPA, 2010b). Cincinnati, Ohio, has a green infrastructure strategy that received support from regulators, environmentalists, and businesses. The Metropolitan Sewer District of Greater Cincinnati won the 2014 Water Prize from the United States Water Alliance in 2014. Its green infrastructure plan is expected to save taxpayers $200 million upfront and remove 1.78 billion gallons of combined sewer overflows annually from the city's Mill Creek (Simes, 2013).

Philadelphia's Green City, Clean Waters is a 25-year plan to enhance watersheds by using green infrastructure. The Philadelphia Water Department is committed to a balanced "land-water-infrastructure" approach by implementing land-based stormwater techniques and reconstructing aquatic habitats. Under the plan:

> Philadelphia will transform at least one-third of the impervious areas (think concrete and asphalt) served by its combined sewer system into 'greened acres'—spaces that use green infrastructure like roadside planting strips, rain gardens, trees and tree boxes, porous pavement, cisterns, and other features to infiltrate, or otherwise collect, the first inch of runoff from any storm. That amounts to keeping 80–90% of annual rainfall from these areas out of the city's over-burdened sewer system (Levine, 2011).

The plan includes $1.67 billion to be invested in greened acres, $345 million in sewage treatment plant capacity, and $420 million dedicated to a combination of green and gray infrastructure improvements (NRDC, 2011, 4). Philadelphia's program is unique because it is the first plan in the nation to invest more in green than gray infrastructure, make greater use of private investment, and include enforceable requirements for thousands of acres to be retrofitted with green infrastructure throughout the entire city (Levine, 2011). The program also constituted a legally enforceable update to the city's Combined Sewer Overflow Long Term Control Plan under the Clean Water Act (NRDC, 2011, 4).

Green infrastructure requires significant investment. Like energy-efficiency retrofits, stormwater retrofits also face financial challenges, but "policy frameworks can play a crucial role in attracting private investors to greener stormwater management efforts that focus on restoring hydrologic function in urbanized areas" (NRDC, 2012, 5). Previously in Philadelphia, the charge for municipal storm water services was based on the volume of drinking water used by the property, but since 2010, charges have been based on the size of the property and amount of impervious surface; this structure directly correlates fees to the volume of stormwater runoff that a lot produces (Philadelphia Water Department, 2014). Philadelphia established a parcel-based stormwater billing structure, which encourages installation of stormwater management practices onsite by providing a large credit (sometimes up to 100 percent) for non-residential and condominium owners who can show onsite management of the first inch of rain over their entire parcel (NRDC, 2012, 2).

## Waste Management

Garbage, despite its importance, may well be the least glamorous sustainability issue. There are no neat or clean ways of dealing with it. Few communities want a solid waste treatment facility in its backyard, so often waste generated in urban areas is sent elsewhere (sometimes hundreds of miles away) for processing and treatment, transforming local waste disposal challenges into a regional issue. Worldwide, we generate between 1.7 and 1.9 billion metric tons of municipal solid waste each year (UNEP, 2010, 6). This creates an opportunity for local managers to incorporate waste reduction, recycling, and composting measures in city planning. According to a survey of C40 member cities, "50% of all waste actions are related to waste treatment, 40% to waste reduction and 10% to waste collection" (Arup, 2014, 148). Effective waste management can save money and make urban settlements more sustainable.

New York City generates more than 14 million tons of waste per year, costing taxpayers more than $300 million for waste disposal (excluding collection), and releasing 2.2 million metric tons of carbon dioxide per year in the process (City of New York, 2013, 42). Most people in New York City live in apartments; space is scarce and often there is no garage to store recyclables and no garden to hold a compost heap. For these reasons, in 2006, the city adopted an ambitious long-term solid waste management plan to export all of the city's garbage, and divert 75 percent of solid waste from landfills by 2030. The strategy is to use barges and trains to carry the garbage away and to use waste reduction, recycling, composting, and waste-to-energy plants to avoid sending garbage to landfills. The plan will reduce annual greenhouse gas emissions by 192,000 tons and 58 million truck miles per year (Energy Conservation Steering Committee, 2008, 4). This plan will reduce greenhouse gas emissions as well as tipping fees and taxes at landfills.

New York City's strategy for reducing its use of landfills has three elements: (1) invest capital in waste-related infrastructure; (2) make it easier for the public to recycle and reduce waste; and (3) create incentives and engage the public in waste reduction and recycling. The City has made progress toward its 75 percent diversion goal. To reduce confusion over recycling rules, the city announced that all rigid plastics can be recycled and it deployed over 1,000 new recycling containers (City of New York, 2013, 43). It started an organic waste pilot program in 68 schools, in conjunction with an anaerobic digestion program with the Newton Creek wastewater treatment plant, and increased greenmarket collection of organic waste from residents (City of New York, 2013, 43).

San Francisco was the first city in the United States to launch a large-scale food composting program (C40 Cities, 2013a). Today, San Francisco has a very ambitious goal of achieving zero waste by 2020. By that time, it plans to send nothing to landfills or incinerators. The city uses a wide range of recycling initiatives, including:

- Separation of recycling waste into three streams;
- "Pay-as-you-throw" trash metering for businesses;
- Banning non-recyclable/compostable containers in restaurants;

- Eliminating plastic bags in stores; and
- Emphasizing recycling plans for special events (C40 Cities, 2012).

San Francisco is succeeding through a combination of strong waste management laws and regulations, public–private partnerships, and creating a recycling culture among its citizens (City Climate Leadership Awards, 2014). The city made recycling and composting convenient and easy for residents and businesses. San Francisco also provides grants to community-based organizations to increase recycling and composting at the grassroots level (C40 Cities, 2013a). San Francisco diverts 80 percent of its refuse from landfills, far more than New York.

## Community Design and Land Use

Sustainability is not just a series of programs to reduce waste and improve energy efficiency. Sustainability is about creating long-term growth and vibrancy. Community design to incorporate sustainability can revitalize neighborhoods. Land use and municipal zoning policies can better support community health, wellness, and equitable development. Sustainable community design can protect ecosystems, ensure health and safety are prioritized, support walkable neighborhoods, and increase economic vitality. Cities can redesign communities to increase the number of open spaces and parks, redevelop brownfields, encourage new development around public transit, and ensure that new buildings meet current resiliency standards.

### Brownfield Redevelopment

Brownfields are properties that contain a hazardous substance, pollutant, or contaminant, making the expansion, redevelopment, or reuse of that property complicated and difficult (EPA, 2014a). Brownfields can be as small as a corner lot or as large as an abandoned factory site. These sites often sit empty and idle, due to the complicated process of environmental remediation. The term *brownfields* is meant to contrast these potential building sites with more pristine *greenfield* sites in exurbia. An environmental goal is to concentrate development on brownfields in order to preserve the rural environment and take advantage of existing infrastructure.

Redevelopment of brownfields has been shown to reduce crime, increase property values, create jobs, and encourage private investment. Local governments can offer tax breaks, low-interest loans, expedited permits, or rezoning to allow residential or commercial uses. The EPA studied five communities that undertook brownfield redevelopment at 163 sites and compared the environmental performance of those sites to projects on greenfield sites. The results showed that the brownfield designs emitted between 32 and 57 percent less carbon dioxide and air pollutant emissions per capita relative to conventional greenfield developments, and between 43 and 60 percent less stormwater runoff compared to alternatives (EPA, 2011a, 2). By concentrating development in urban areas with mass transit, energy, water and sewage infrastructure in place, these developments averted the larger environmental impacts associated with development in exurban or rural greenfields.

The first brownfield policies were developed in the 1970s; but the program did not really have a significant impact until the 1990s. Christopher De Sousa from the University of Milwaukee observes that, "Since the mid-1990s, the redevelopment of brownfield sites has been a central imperative of government efforts in the U.S. as part of a general strategy of revitalizing urban cores and promoting smart growth" (De Sousa, 2005, 312).

Milwaukee's industrial past has left it with a large number of brownfields. Since 1990, the city has actively redeveloped these sites, making it a leader in brownfield remediation. The city has initiated 87 brownfield developments, generated $766.1 million of redevelopment investment along with 3,384 jobs (City of Milwaukee, 2014).

In neighboring Illinois, the Chicago Brownfields Initiative was established in 1993 to:

> acquire, assemble and rehabilitate properties, returning them to productive use. The Initiative links environmental restoration with economic development by cleaning up and redeveloping brownfields and by improving policies to promote private redevelopment of brownfields. The purpose of the Chicago Brownfields Initiative is to create jobs and generate tax revenues through redevelopment, thereby improving Chicago's environmental and economic health (City of Chicago, 2014).

Seattle has developed brownfields for new uses, such as to house office buildings and shopping centers (Carlton, 2011). In the South Lake Union district, 6.4 million square feet has been built on reclaimed properties since 2004 (Carlton, 2011). Seattle is an attractive place for brownfield redevelopment because it is a land-poor port city in need of room to expand.

New York City's PlaNYC set a goal of cleaning up all of the city's brownfields, and established a strategy based on economic development and community planning. Thus far the program has enrolled over 95 projects on more than 200 lots, most of which had been vacant for more than 20 years. Cleanup on these lots is projected to yield $3 billion in new private investment, create 3,100 permanent jobs, and provide over 1,400 units of affordable housing (City of New York, 2013, 20). The city also launched the Clean Soil Bank, to encourage the reuse of clean soil from brownfield site excavation, which is expected to save developers $5 million annually (City of New York, 2013, 21–22).

### Parks and Green Spaces

Parks and open spaces make a city more pleasant, reduce air pollution, mitigate the urban heat-island effect, and act as wetlands for climate resilience. Simply planting trees provides a number of environmental and health benefits, and can also help reduce crime and increase property value. In 2006, Los Angeles launched Million Trees LA, a partnership between businesses, community groups, and the public (Arup, 2014, 205). Austin, Texas, also has an urban forest plan, and a cost–benefit analysis showed that the urban forest provides millions of dollars a year in social, economic, and environmental benefits (Arup, 2014, 205).

New York City, in addition to its own goal to plant 1 million trees, aims for all New Yorkers to live within a 10-minute walk of a park or playground. Since the city does not have a lot of undeveloped land, the plan focused on using existing assets like schoolyards. The High Line, one of New York's newest parks, is a perfect example of repurposing land. The park was created from abandoned elevated rail tracks, and was built through a public–private partnership between the city and the nonprofit Friends of the High Line. It is now one of the most popular public spaces in New York City—attracting millions of tourists and residents alike to its airy, innovative green space with unique views of the city and the Hudson River.

Portland's Healthy Connected City initiative has a goal of "improving human and environmental health by creating safe and complete neighborhood centers linked by a network of city greenways that connect Portlanders with each other" (City of Portland, 2012, 73). This initiative combines elements of transportation, land use, infrastructure, human health, ecosystem health, and watersheds to determine how to best design a city (City of Portland, 2012, 80). It also encourages active transportation and integrates nature into neighborhoods, providing increased access to destinations across the city.

San Francisco's Pavements to Parks program—a collaboration between the planning department, public works department, transportation agency, and mayor's office—involves creating new street plazas and sidewalk platforms that replace parking spaces by reclaiming street space. San Francisco's streets make up more land area than its public parks, so the city saw an opportunity to convert underused land into pedestrian spaces (Pavement to Parks, 2014).

Cleveland, Ohio, started a program where community groups garden on unused land. Cleveland has about 18,000 empty lots and community and market gardening has grown substantially. The city has a working group on land use and planning that is leading these efforts, fostering partnership between government agencies and other stakeholders. The group was instrumental in passing two pieces of legislation around land and farming operations (Cleveland-Cuyahoga County, 2014).

## Resilient, Sustainable Cities

An overview of local sustainability isn't complete without a discussion about resiliency. The Rockefeller Foundation defines resiliency, or climate change adaptation as:

> the capacity of an individual, community, or institution to dynamically and effectively respond to shifting climate impact circumstances while continuing to function at an acceptable level. Simply put, it is the ability to

survive and recover from the effects of climate change. It includes the ability to understand potential impacts and to take appropriate action before, during, and after a particular consequence to minimize negative effects and maintain the ability to respond to changing conditions (2009, 1).

Resilience goes beyond surviving; it's about recovering and thriving against expected and unexpected changes. Resilience is a critical lens through which to consider climate change (Rockefeller and ARUP, 2014, 1). "The scale of urban risk is increasing due to the number of people living in cities. Risk is also increasingly unpredictable due to the complexity of city systems and the uncertainty associated with many hazards—notably climate change" (Rockefeller and ARUP, 2014, 3). Sustainability and climate change planning (both mitigation and adaptation) are highly connected.

While both climate action and sustainability plans address GHG emissions, sustainability plans address other issues such as air quality, public health, and social equity more thoroughly; they also use other indicators in addition to GHG emissions (ICLEI, 2009, 8). According to a 2012 survey, 68 percent of cities worldwide are developing climate adaptation plans (Carmin et al., 2012, 14).

In response to Superstorm Sandy in 2012, then-mayor Michael Bloomberg convened a Special Initiative for Rebuilding and Resiliency (SIRR) group to address the need for New York City to become more resilient. In June 2013, this group released a report called "A Stronger, More Resilient New York," with comprehensive and ambitious recommendations for rebuilding the communities impacted by Sandy and increasing the resilience of buildings and other critical infrastructure. The planning process for developing these recommendations involved a number of stakeholders, including city, state, and federal government agencies, public officials, businesses, community and faith-based organizations, environmental groups, labor organizations, and the general public. This $20 billion coastal protection plan laid out hundreds of specific actions that the city could take to protect from future storms, including:

- Building a network of dunes and floodwalls to protect the coastline;
- Planning to maintain and widen beaches;
- Creating redundancy to critical infrastructure such as subways and power grids;

- Updating zoning and construction codes to protect buildings;
- Creating an incentive program to encourage building owners to complete resiliency efforts;
- Reducing flood insurance premiums; and,
- Building a neighborhood called Seaport City to withstand major flooding (Urban Land Institute, 2013).

New York City is one of many urban areas focused on resiliency. In April 2014, an alliance between nine of the world's largest international organizations joined forces to create a new global collaboration for urban resilience, which was announced at the seventh World Urban Forum. These organizations include the UN Human Settlements Programme, the UN Office for Disaster Risk Reduction, the World Bank Group, the Global Facility for Disaster Reduction and Recovery, the Inter-American Development Bank, the Rockefeller Foundation, 100 Resilient Cities, C40 Cities, and ICLEI. The goal of this collaboration is to facilitate the flow of information and financial resources to help cities become more resilient to the disruptions posed by climate change, natural hazards, rapid urbanization, and other major shocks and stresses (UN Habitat, 2014).

### Sustainable Action

Unfortunately, smaller and poorer cities are less likely to develop and enact sustainability policies (Homsy and Warner, 2013, 1). Generally, the rate of sustainability policy adoption increases with a city's population (Homsy and Warner, 2013, 3). However, across the country you can find what we call *unlikely innovators*, small towns able to implement sustainable initiatives against the odds. They often are not recognized like major cities like New York, Seattle, and San Francisco, but their efforts and successes play a crucial role in transforming our nation's sustainability development.

Columbia, Wisconsin, with a population of about 5,000 was actually one of the first cities to convert all of its streetlights from incandescent bulbs to high-efficiency LED lights as a way to boost economic development; the city reduced electricity usage by 15.4 percent between 2007 and 2012 (Homsy and Warner, 2013, 2–4). The city of Homer, Alaska, was one of the first in the nation to make sustainability and energy/waste reduction a mandatory part of orientation for any municipal employee (Homsy and Warner, 2013, 6), and South Daytona, Florida, which is only three square miles in size, has undertaken grey-water reuse by buying millions of gallons of reclaimed sewage water from a neighboring municipality to use for landscape irrigation (Homsy and Warner, 2013, 5). The U.S. Chamber of Commerce and Siemens Corporation named Grand Rapids, Michigan, the most sustainable mid-size community in 2010; it was also recognized as a member of the EPA's Green Power Leadership Club for renewable energy efforts (Svara, Read, and Moulder, 2011, 18). There are many other examples of small-scale sustainability initiatives.

One article about these unlikely innovators summarized the factors that helped them make sustainability a priority. The researchers found that all these cities have entrepreneurial leaders who made it a priority to "reframe environmental issues in terms of cost savings or increased effi- ciency," and who started with the easiest and most sensible initiatives, while educating staff and the public. These entrepreneurial leaders focused on the connections between environmental protection and economic development (Homsy and Warner, 2013, 9).

Homsy and Warner identify six critical steps that city governments (large or small) should take to pursue a long-term plan that results in environmental, economic, and social sustainability:

1. Obtain a formal commitment and pursue a broad sustainability strategy.
2. Develop an engagement process to broaden community outreach.
3. Appoint a citizens' committee to engage the community.
4. Develop partnerships with key institutional, private sector, and nonprofit actors.
5. Make changes to break down silos and encourage coordinated action.
6. Measure performance to assess the sustainability effort (33–35).

In our view, these are the same features that make sustainability planning successful in large megacities. In 2014, C40 Cities and Arup, a consulting firm, released a quantitative report on the efforts that C40 member cities have taken to reduce GHG emissions and improve urban resilience. In just the C40 cities alone, 8,000 collective actions have been undertaken, from introducing cycling lanes to increasing urban mobility, and from reducing transport emissions to reducing carbon emissions from outdoor lighting. It also shows that ideas and best practices are flowing equally between developing and developed cities (Arup, 2014, 6).

The collective action of these cities is making an impact. Sustainable cities enable us to have hope that we can and will transition to a sustainable global economy. Local governments all over the United States continue to grind out small scale (but big impact) initiatives designed to make their regions more sustainable. Local level sustainability initiatives are examples of bottom-up innovation, and in our view they have helped overcome the absence of top-down strategy and resources that the U.S. federal government is not now able to provide.

# 6

# Sustainability Measurement and Metrics

## Introduction

The transition to a sustainable economy has begun and, like the process of industrialization itself, we are looking at a transformation process that will last for decades. To speed this transition, we need to create an environment where all organizations integrate sustainability principles into routine management decision-making. To accomplish that, we need to do a better job of measuring the sustainability of our organizations, cities, and nations. A clear sign of the growing importance of sustainability management is the impressive number of efforts to develop and utilize sustainability metrics to enable organizations to effectively measure their sustainability. However, there are a variety of different methods for measuring sustainability and reporting those efforts, and it seems that each company, organization, city, and country has a different method.

While the development of these indicators is critical and must be continued, it is time to begin the process of settling on sustainability indicators that *everyone can use and understand*. We need a generally accepted set of definitions and indicators for measuring sustainability. It should be mandatory for organizations to disclose a common and shared set of sustainability metrics and definitions to ensure that the required sustainability data is reliable, valid and comparable. Independent auditors will need to verify reported information and policy must hold organizations accountable for their performance. We should develop comparable measures for cities and states. If we are to develop a common set of metrics, we will need the U.S. federal government to take an active role to stimulate a discussion of metrics and decide on those that should be adopted. Along with agreement in the United States we will need to enter into discussions with the global community as well to ensure that all nations utilize the same benchmarks.

This chapter provides an overview of the current landscape of sustainability measurement and reporting. We begin with a discussion of sustainability metrics, followed by an introduction to the frameworks and indices that aggregate those metrics. We then explore the challenges with sustainability frameworks and reporting at the corporate level, and present an argument for the necessity of a set of standardized, generally accepted metrics. Next, we turn to the role of the public sector in sustainability measurement and metrics, beginning with an examination of mandated sustainability reporting as it exists in other countries, and how it compares to reporting in the United States. Finally, we look at the role of the U.S. federal government in measuring sustainability at the national level.

## What Are Sustainability Metrics?

As we discussed in Chapter 1, the term *sustainability* continues to resist a single, clear definition, yet its use and application has exploded in recent decades. Despite the lack of consensus over the term, the meaning has evolved from a vague concept to a set of precise definitions that attempt to present sustainability in quantitative terms and indicators (Moldan et al., 2012, 7). These quantitative definitions allow us to develop metrics and models for performance measurement and management. Metrics, or indicators, are the basic variables that are used to describe characteristics or states of a given entity or system. Among the broadest definitions, sustainability indicators are measures of resource and materials use, waste diversion, energy consumption, and efficiency, but they also track non-environmental factors like labor practices and corruption. This is because while some people interpret sustainability as *environmental* inputs and impacts, sustainability as a broader concept has expanded to include various social, governance, and economic factors as well.

This expansion of the definition is reflected in the widespread use of *environmental, social, and governance (ESG) metrics*. ESG metrics are often used interchangeably with sustainability indicators, especially by the corporate sector. Sustainability metrics can also be used to describe the *triple bottom line*, which features environmental, social, and economic factors, and are most typically used to describe governmental sustainability or sustainable development at the national or city levels. As one might expect, the sustainability metrics themselves are as varied as the definitions. In a recent research project undertaken at the Earth Institute, using the broad ESG framework as a definition of sustainability metrics, we found that there are close to 600 indicators measuring every imaginable facet of sustainability.

Looking a little more closely, we find that environmental indicators are what we call the physical dimensions of sustainability (e.g., greenhouse gas emissions per dollar of revenue or per unit, amount of wastewater produced, amount of freshwater utilized, percent of materials recycled, etc.). Social metrics measure organizations' performance in equality, justice, and other human aspects of operation; however, the definitions of social sustainability indicators are not very clear. The actual boundaries for these types of measures are quite vague when compared to environmental metrics, which tend to be more clearly defined and mostly, though not entirely, quantitative. In practice, social impacts are more difficult to observe and quantify than environmental impacts. For measures of social performance, quantitative methods are often applied to measuring only input (e.g., employee trainings, number of community-outreach activities, etc.), limiting their analytical use. Environmental performance involves both input and output, and thus can be measured more accurately. Governance indicators (not to be confused with data about the government or public sector) are the third type of sustainability metric. They measure things like how responsive a company is to its investors, the structure and function of a company's board, shareholders' rights, the disparity between a CEO's salary and the average employee's salary, overall transparency, and the prevalence of corruption, among other factors.

Governance indicators are the least quantitative of the three types, and can even include a company's mission statement or profile.

## Sustainability Frameworks and Indices

Sustainability indicators summarize a vast amount of information about complex and complicated environments into concise, policy-applicable and manageable information (Singh et al., 2012, 281). Because of the large universe of indicators, frameworks and composite indices have emerged to better organize and analyze these metrics. Sustainability indicators are either presented in a structured framework, which can be used to isolate and report on relevant indicators, or aggregated into a composite index or score. In general, sustainability *frameworks* provide a qualitative presentation and grouping of large numbers of indicators and can be more revealing and accurate than aggregated indices, while *indices* tend to be easy to use and more understandable by the general public. Frameworks, in contrast to indices, do not involve quantitative aggregation of data. Not surprisingly, the criteria for these types of frameworks and indices are as diverse as the concept of sustainability itself (Mayer, 2008, 279). We'll outline just a few here to showcase the scope of these measures and frameworks.

Since 1999, the Global Reporting Initiative (GRI), which is home to perhaps the most popular global framework, has been working to establish a credible set of sustainability indicators using four areas of performance and impact: economic, environmental, social, and governance. It provides general indicator guidelines as well as sector-specific guidance, both of which are refined and updated over time. GRI's reporting guidelines are now in their fourth iteration and specify 34 environmental indicators including energy, materials, impacts on biodiversity, and emissions. This reporting framework is currently used by almost 6,000 organizations across the globe and it gains more users and credibility every year (GRI, 2014). GRI aims to become the universal standard, regardless of an organization's size, sector, or location.

The Sustainability Accounting Standards Board (SASB) is a nonprofit engaged in the creation of sustainability accounting standards for use by publicly listed corporations. Investors, the general public, and the media can find sustainability disclosure material in annual reports, sustainability reports, and on corporate websites. The Sustainability Accounting Standards Board is developing sector-specific standards for reporting key sustainability impacts on existing financial reports in hope that this will allow all stakeholders to understand environmental, social and governance metrics and ensure reliable comparison. By focusing on industry-specific standards, they expect to be able to compare apples to apples. In 2010, Harvard University's David Wood, with Steve Lydenberg of Domini Social Investments and Jean Rogers of Arup, developed a methodology for determining industry-specific material issues and associated industry-tailored performance indicators. They applied their methodology to six industries, using indicators already in use by companies and analysts. The team focused on developing a process for determining key performance indicators, but stopped short of defining those specific metrics. They are in favor of accounting for industry-specific factors in any type of mandated sustainability reporting (Lydenberg, Rogers, and Wood, 2010). This methodology became the basis for the Sustainability Accounting Standards Board, which is currently developing standards in 10 sectors.

A recent development in the field of sustainability measurement is integrated reporting, which combines sustainability and other non-financial issues with financial information, ideally in a single report. Proponents of integrated reporting assert that such holistic thinking, which incorporates all sources of business value and risk, provides more accurate and efficient approaches to corporate reporting. In 2009, the International Integrated Reporting Council (IIRC), a coalition of regulators, investors, companies, standard setters, accounting professionals, and nongovernmental organizations (NGOs), was established to develop an international framework for integrated reporting. The framework was released in December of 2013 following a series of meetings, roundtables, and input from external stakeholders. It provides guiding principles and content elements to enable companies to develop an integrated report. The International Integrated Reporting Council (IIRC) launched a pilot program to test the framework, and includes over 100 businesses and 35 investor organizations (IIRC, 2014).

In the United States and across the globe, stock exchanges and financial firms have developed methodologies to track and score sustainability performance for their own sustainability indices. For example, many top-performing sustainability companies identified the S&P Dow Jones

Sustainability Indices as one of the most important sustainability rating systems that they report to annually. This collection of indices, launched in 1999, measures global and regional market indices, and was the first global collection to track financial performance of sustainability-driven companies (S&P Dow Jones and RobecoSAM, 2013, 1). Companies are selected for inclusion in one of these indices based on an assessment of economic, environmental, and social criteria. The indices are maintained by S&P Dow Jones Indices and RobecoSAM, an asset manager focused on sustainability investing. Their assessment methodology is based on media and stakeholder analyses, questionnaires completed by companies, other public documentation and reports, and direct communication with an organization. RobecoSAM invites over 3,000 public companies to report annually and includes only the top 10 percent in the indices. As of June 2013, the indices had approximately $8.8 billion in assets under management across a variety of products (S&P Dow Jones and RobecoSAM, 2013, 1, 3).

## The Challenges of Sustainability Measurement and Reporting

Ultimately, as is probably evident, sustainability officers spend a considerable amount of time and effort reporting to these many indices and rating and ranking organizations. A recent Ernst & Young/Green Biz Group survey sought to gauge the relative importance of these various reporting programs. They found that the Dow Jones Sustainability Index and CDP (formerly the Carbon Disclosure Project) are frequently cited as the most important, and *Newsweek*'s Green Rankings, though not included in the actual survey, was frequently a write-in by respondents. *Newsweek*'s Green Rankings was the only system from a mainstream media organization (Ernst & Young, 2012). Much of the data that companies report to these organizations is the same and there is considerable overlap in how it is used by reporting programs. Until a clear leader emerges from this pack of reporting agencies, or until a specific framework is mandated, companies must continue to engage with most of these rating organizations to compete with their peers.

While some of these reporting groups are rigorous and seek to provide comprehensive information about sustainability and ESG issues, most lack universal comparability, reliability, and materiality. Indeed, many of these efforts were not intended to achieve consistency, or to facilitate intra- or inter-industry comparability. Some groups, like the Global Reporting Initiative and CDP, are synergizing efforts, but there is still a long way to go before a universally accepted standard exists that replicates the applicability and universality of traditional financial indicators and generally accepted accounting principles (GAAP).

Organizations and individuals must wade through the array of ever-changing sustainability reporting and measurement standards, scorecards, and platforms to decide what to measure, how to assess information, how to differentiate between important and irrelevant information, what organization(s) to report to, and what reporting or benchmarking organizations they can depend on for reliable analyses. It has been widely argued that in many cases more is less, and abundant options may only serve to decrease productivity and confuse decision makers. The problem is more acute in sustainability measurement and reporting, when myriad choices and lack of consensus create confusion. Furthermore, these standards change over time, sometimes significantly in just a few years. When these benchmarking systems change, reporting can become a symbolic exercise rather than a tool for year-to-year analysis designed to influence decision making.

One of the most visible manifestations of the interest in sustainability measurement is the increase in corporate reporting. Going beyond simply reporting data to ranking or rating agencies, companies across the globe now voluntarily (or in some countries, by mandate) publish thousands of sustainability and corporate responsibility reports each year. However, activities and reporting efforts vary considerably across companies, industries, sectors, location, and time. Typically, these reports are not readily comparable. A reader of two sustainability reports can find completely different indicators reported in each, though both would claim to report on the sustainability performance of that given company. Because sustainability management is still a new field, reliable, consistently applied metrics for sustainability have not yet emerged. Even when organizations select the same indicators for their reports, they often use different units of measurement, different time frames, or different methodologies to calculate those metrics, which further complicates analysis and comparison.

The information gap also increases the difficulty of comparing metrics across different categories of effect; for example, it can be impossible to tell whether a product, process, or company that consumes less energy can be considered better or worse than one that uses more energy but produces fewer toxic by-products. Similar confusion arises when attempting to parse the effects of sustainability programs on a company's financial performance because different metrics of performance are used in different studies, increasing the difficulty of direct comparison. Comparing two sustainability reports can be like comparing apples to oranges. Consensus has not even been reached regarding the terminology for such reporting. Reports utilize terms such as "environmental, social, and governance goals," "corporate social responsibility," "sustainability development and practices," "socially responsible investing," "environmental governance," "green operations," "corporate sustainability performance," "corporate environmental strategy," and so on, to describe programs implemented to enhance sustainability.

Sustainability reports vary widely in scope and scale because sustainability means different things depending on who you ask and what you want. This lack of consistency leaves public and private decision makers at a distinct disadvantage. While these reports may look comprehensive, they can be overwhelming, or at worst misleading, to those unfamiliar with the details of the measurement and reporting methodology for that specific company. It is difficult for the average reader of these reports to make sense of the information, and to know whether a given organization is reporting on the organization's most important sustainability issues or whether the report is simply greenwashing for public relations purposes.

Are companies cherry-picking data to report what makes them look better while excluding information that might call into question some of their practices or business value? Are organizations only reporting information that is easily accessible or inexpensive to collect? How were the indicators selected, and did decision makers have a sophisticated understanding of the materiality of those sustainability issues? Do the individuals developing these reports, and the people making decisions based upon this performance, understand the issues that are most relevant to the organization and to the health of the environment? Reading a typical sustainability report often provides few answers to these and similar questions.

These problems demonstrate the need for a set of mandated, generally accepted sustainability metrics. The many sustainability metric and framework initiatives have advanced the science of sustainability measurement, but we are not yet close to a set of adequate and accepted indicators (Dahl, 2012,

15). None have emerged from the literature as a standard. Parris and Kates point out that "to date, there are no indicator sets that are universally accepted, backed by compelling theory, rigorous data collection and analysis, and influential in policy" (2003, 581). They provide three reasons for this: "(1) the ambiguity of sustainable development; (2) the plurality of purpose in characterizing and measuring sustainable development; and (3) the confusion of terminology, data, and methods of measurement" (2003, 581).

We need metrics that measure performance and progress, yet, today much of the work on sustainability metrics focuses on *disclosure* or *reporting* of environmental impact and risk. This is particularly true when it comes to private sector sustainability reporting. Just because a company reports their emissions, energy use, and waste does not necessarily mean they are implementing programs to reduce their environmental footprint or improve their sustainability performance. Arthur Lyon Dahl calls this a focus on the "hardware," which he describes as:

> the measurable status of and trends in environmental, social and economic parameters (pollution levels, energy consumption, poverty, education, etc.) rather than the processes of decision-making and control (the "software") that determine whether sustainability is really taken into account in decision-making. Adding indicators of processes and the dynamics of change would help to discriminate between conscious progress towards a sustainable system and incidental improvements or correlations that result, perhaps, from rising levels of economic prosperity (2012, 15).

Furthermore, the collection and reporting of these metrics is voluntary, self-completed, and inadequately audited, and there is no penalty for deceptive, incomplete, or incompetent reporting.

## The Need for Standard, Generally Accepted Metrics

These challenges highlight the need for standards to be established to alleviate some of this confusion and to establish credible measures of sustainability within organizations or jurisdictions. Reliable metrics that measure sustainability performance are needed for organizations, cities, managers, policymakers, consumers, and investors to adequately assess growth drivers and connect sustainability to strategic goals, expenditures and investments. Performance metrics and measurement systems are critical to successful management strategies; without them, it is impossible to determine what is working and what is not. To once again paraphrase Peter Drucker, to be able to manage something, whether it's a process or organization, you must be able to measure it. Without measurements you cannot tell if management activities are making the situation better or worse. An organization needs to measure and benchmark its programs to know whether an activity is improving and advancing towards its goals. Before you can measure something, you need to define it, but sustainability has loose boundaries; its definition varies depending on the organization, jurisdiction, and context. There is simply no clear set of measures that defines precisely what and how an organization or place should measure its sustainability.

Sustainability metrics, like traditional financial and management indicators, provide decision makers with information to quantify, measure, and benchmark environmental performance of a given entity, be it a multinational corporation, a small business, a government agency, or a city. Definitive metrics enable organizations to set and meet goals, manage change, and make investments in order to make their operations more sustainable. Measuring sustainability and disclosing an organization's impact on the environment helps make the intangible benefits and risks related to these issues more concrete. Standardized metrics help decision makers distinguish information that is relevant from that which is secondary or irrelevant. In addition, a common set of metrics will not only allow organizations to track their own performance, but will also allow for comparison to entities in similar situations. The vague boundaries and definitions of sustainability means managers may be bombarded with information, or may receive very little at all. We need to know: What is the most appropriate, crucial information that managers at all types of organizations should receive, understand, and utilize?

Just as we have generally accepted accounting principles and clear definitions of financial indicators, we need physical measures of organizational performance: sustainability metrics. These measures should ultimately be part of the private sector's overall organizational performance measures, as important as market share, return on equity, and profit and loss. Perhaps in some way, monetized to influence the computation of return on investment and profits. In the public and nonprofit sectors, the organization's performance measures might be different, but of equal importance; sustainability metrics would be reported along with data on committed crimes, graduation rates, medical treatment outcomes, emergency response times, and other indicators of public sector performance. They should also be included in the normal organizational process and output measures such as labor productivity, efficiency, value of goods and services delivered, employment, personnel turnover, and so on. The physical dimensions of sustainability must be defined as a key and routinized element of organizational management. In addition to organizational indicators, we need indicators that can chart local, state and national progress towards a sustainable economy.

While the need for mandated universal indicators may be clear, the selection of those indicators is not. Some argue for industry-generic indicators that could apply to all organizations and could be supplemented with sector-specific metrics. Others argue that indicators must be industry-specific to be relevant and truly comparable. Many frameworks of indicators have been proposed, but there are no clearly established rules.

We expect that a core set of roughly a dozen common sustainability metrics will emerge as a *nationally recognized standard* that comprehensively measures the key indicators of sustainability for any given organization or locality (city or state) in the United States. While there are industry-specific and place-based metrics that aid in more detailed analysis and understanding, we expect that there are some indicators that cut across all organizations and locations. We also believe that physical sustainability indicators are the most universal type of environmental metrics and will ultimately comprise generally accepted sustainability indicators. The current inclusion of social and governance issues within the definitions of sustainability metrics will fall away as convergence occurs on widely accepted sustainability indicators. Social and governance metrics are inherently culturally specific, politically relative, and geographically based. Even though national consensus on these two types of indicators could potentially be achieved in the United States, they will not translate easily to other countries and will vary considerably across regions. These are also more likely to change over time as cultural and political norms and institutions change. We suggest that it is only the physical dimensions of environmental sustainability that will achieve national and, ultimately, global consensus. These environmental indicators are universal and will comprise the recognized sustainability standards.

In addition to a common set of metrics, we need a standardized process for data collection, verification, and audit. We need a measurement *system*, not simply a set of measures. The added cost of verification and audit, however, can be justified for only a few of the indicators. In the absence of a commonly accepted core group of metrics, it is difficult for policymakers to mandate disclosure of an open-ended range of indicators. The first job for government must be to move the sustainability field towards a common standard—something that the U.S. federal government has done before, when it arbitrated the development of generally accepted accounting principles (GAAP).

## The Role of the Public Sector

The public sector is a key player in advancing and supporting sustainability metrics, measurement, and reporting. It can play a role in mandating and monitoring various forms of sustainability reporting, in guiding the development of specific information that private business, as well as public and nonprofit organizations, ought to measure and communicate externally. Government must also establish and maintain national indicators of sustainability, including measures of green jobs or the green economy.

### *Mandated Corporate Sustainability Reporting*

In the United States, sustainability reporting is not required, despite the efforts of many organizations to evaluate environmental, social and governance issues. Internationally, however, over a dozen countries require some type of mandatory sustainability reporting.

The move toward required disclosure of sustainability metrics increases the importance of environmental issues, giving more power to sustainability officers; managers of environmental, health, and safety issues; and managers in corporate social responsibility (CSR) and government relations. It can even bring them to parity with chief compliance officers, chief operations officers, and chief financial officers. When this occurs, sustainability is inevitably more directly linked to core business decisions and values. When sustainability becomes part of regulatory compliance, increased funding and management attention is dedicated to it. It can also benefit from the support of more established processes and teams in the financial and compliance functions.

This is not to diminish the importance of motivated companies whose commitment to sustainability precedes government regulation. Mandated disclosure sets rules and establishes a level playing field, allowing established leaders and innovators to clearly demonstrate their competitive advantage. There will also always be companies who will not act until mandates are established. Instituting mandatory indicators could overcome a company's reluctance to disclose performance and would ensure comparability (Searcy, 2012, 251). Regulations set the minimum bar that can help organizations improve performance as they seek to improve their reported metrics over time. Required reporting is a prerequisite to any serious effort at improving performance.

Mandated reporting can also lead to innovative measurement and assessment tools as organizations and regulators adapt to new requirements for transparency and assurance. Even for organizations who already voluntarily publish sustainability reports, their procedures for data collection, measurement, and assessment will likely need to be refined to meet standardized verification rules. They may need to create new tools, programs, and processes to meet the expectations set by government regulation.

Countries around the globe, including many developing countries, are beginning to experiment with legislation that requires sustainability reporting and disclosures of environmental risks. A 2013 report by the Global Reporting Initiative, the United Nations Environment Programme (UNEP), KPMG Climate Change & Sustainability Services, and the Centre for Corporate Governance in Africa examined the growth of mandatory reporting measures globally. They found that in 2006, 58 percent of policies were mandatory (the rest were voluntary efforts for public disclosure of sustainability information), but in 2013, 72 percent of the 180 policies across 45 countries were mandatory (2013, 8). This represents a significant trend in the field. They also note this trend is likely to continue: "As reporting organizations voice their concerns about the various frameworks they may use or need to comply with, there will be increasing calls for the alignment and harmonization of frameworks" (2013, 9).

Many of these laws pertain only to specific environmental issues, such as climate change, or apply only to state-owned enterprises or specific industries, like the mining or financial sectors. For example, countries that specifically target state-owned companies for reporting include Brazil, China, France, India, Russia, South Africa, Spain, and Sweden (GRI et al., 2013, 17). Still, other regulations are more far-reaching.

## France

France is considered a leader in corporate sustainability reporting. Since 2001, France has required public companies to report on social and environmental impacts in their annual reports. In 2010, it passed a new law, Grenelle II, expanding the requirement to include new types of entities. It now extends beyond listed companies on French stock exchanges to *subsidiaries* of foreign companies that are listed in France and *unlisted* companies with subsidiaries *located* in France. This new requirement is significant in that it is not limited to domestic companies, and could therefore have serious impacts on many international companies that operate in France. The regulations, which will be phased in by company size, also require that companies have their data verified by an independent third party auditor (Ernst & Young, 2012, 1–2). This new law is particularly strong, requiring disclosure of up to 42 environmental social and governance indicators.

## China

In China, the number of sustainability reports grew considerably after recent government policies were enacted to increase sustainability reporting and disclosure. The 2007 Environmental Information Disclosure Act requires public disclosure of compliance with regulations, requiring reporting of any serious environmental pollution releases or failure to comply with requirements. In addition to this mandatory component, the act encourages companies to voluntarily disclose environmental information, including emission and pollution levels, reduction targets, resource use, investment in environmental technologies, and other related programs. The government provides incentives for compliance with the voluntary programs, including priority for grants (GRI et al., 2013, 57).

China's stock exchanges, in partnership with government agency initiatives, also encourage, and in some cases require disclosure of environmental and corporate social responsibility information. This includes the Shenzhen Stock Exchange, the Shanghai Stock Exchange, the China Banking Regulatory Commission, the State Assets Supervision and Administration Commission, and the China National Textile and Apparel Council. In 2008, China adopted the Green Securities Policy, which sought to link environmental and financial policies, and was co-developed by the Ministry of Environmental Protection and the China Securities Regulatory Commission. It requires Chinese-listed companies in 14 highly polluting industries that trade on the Shenzhen Stock Exchange and the Shanghai Stock Exchange to report certain environmental information to the public (Wang and Bernell, 2013, 343–344). As a result, in 2012, over 1,600 sustainability reports were published, a 20-fold increase over 2007. However, there is still very little auditing of these reports (only 5 percent were assured by third parties) and the quality of the reports remains low, often with little or insufficient quantitative data on issues like greenhouse gas emissions and energy efficiency (GRI et al., 2013, 27–28). Despite these formal requirements, pollution levels throughout China continue to grow, and there is clearly a large gap between policy intent and actual implementation.

## India

In India, the Ministry of Corporate Affairs announced Voluntary Guidelines on Corporate Social Responsibility. These were revised in 2011 to become the National Voluntary Guidelines on Social, Environmental, and Economical Responsibilities of Business. While the efforts themselves are voluntary, the guidelines provide broad principles for businesses to follow. They are complemented by the Securities and Exchange Board of India's 2012 requirement that the 100 top companies prepare business responsibility reports requiring responses to each of the voluntary guidelines. Requirements for other companies will be phased in over time. Also in 2012, India passed its first law on sustainability reporting, the 2012 Companies Bill, which requires companies to develop corporate social responsibility policies and to spend two percent of the previous three years' average net profit on implementing those policies (German Society for International Cooperation et al., 2012, 26–27). This funding requirement is a unique approach to environmental improvement.

## South Africa

We see additional evidence of reporting requirements throughout the world. South Africa has emerged as a leader in integrated reporting, which incorporates sustainability and other non-financial issues with financial information in a single report. In 2002, South Africa first required, through the King Code on Corporate Governance, that all companies report annually on social, transformation, ethical, safety, health, and environmental management policies and practices, and in 2009, updated its regulation to require companies to produce an integrated report with this information (GRI et al., 2013, 35).

## The European Union

The European Union (EU) has also been active in sustainability reporting, as it is incorporated into their broader corporate social responsibility disclosure requirements and rules. For example, the 2003 EU Modernisation Directive required that European companies include non-financial information in their annual reports if it is "necessary for an understanding of the company's development, performance or position" (GRI et al., 2013, 51). The directive leaves the decision of materiality up to the company, and does not go so far as to mandate non-financial information disclosure across the board. In 2013, however, legislation was proposed that would require all large companies in the EU to disclose policies, risks, and results relating to environmental, social, and governance issues. If a company did not believe an area was material to them, they would be required to specifically explain why it was not reporting on that issue (GRI et al., 2013, 30). The European Commission, recognizing the need to do more on sustainability reporting, adopted two reports in February 2013, highlighting transparency in sustainability reporting, "Corporate Social Responsibility: accountable, transparent and responsible business behaviour and sustainable growth" and "Corporate Social Responsibility: promoting society's interests and a route to sustainable and inclusive recovery" (European Commission, 2014b). These are strong indications of continued high-level government support for sustainability reporting across the European Union.

## Denmark

Denmark's sustainability and Corporate Social Responsibility (CSR) reporting is voluntary, but large companies and state-owned businesses must disclose their views on corporate responsibility in their annual reports. If they do not have a sustainability policy, they must explicitly say so. This law, while not an outright requirement to disclose specific sustainability initiatives, can serve to encourage organizations without sustainability programs to establish them (GRI et al., 2013, 29). In addition to the Corporate Social Responsibility policy mandate, in 1996, Denmark established a green accounting scheme that was mandatory for large businesses and heavy polluters to require public disclosure of environmental impacts (e.g., material input, emissions, and waste) (GRI et al., 2013, 29). Subsequent analyses of Denmark's green accounts found that the public had little confidence in the published reports, and so, while about half of the compliant firms achieved environmental improvements, they were failing to effectively communicate those results (Jorgensen and Holgaard, 2004, 9). The law was later strengthened to focus on more holistic accounting, increased detailed and quantified information, and improved communication. Revisions of the law also required forward-thinking disclosures, such as environmental policies and pollution-prevention programs. It is not simply enough to report their impacts; Denmark wants its companies to show leadership and commitment to sustainability principles at the top levels of management (Jorgensen and Holgaard, 2004, 14–17).

## The United Kingdom

Reporting on greenhouse gas emissions is one of the most common sustainability metrics, although this is only one aspect of the global sustainability challenge. For example, in June 2012, the UK Department for Environment announced that it was requiring all companies listed on the Main Market of the London Stock Exchange to report their greenhouse gas emissions in their annual reports beginning October 1, 2013. The UK is the first country to require greenhouse gas emissions reporting for all companies, regardless of size or industry. Methodologies for calculation must be included and any missing information must be noted with an explanation of why it could not be obtained. The measure is required to include "at least one ratio which expresses the quoted company's annual emissions in relation to a quantifiable factor associated with the company's activities," commonly referred to as carbon intensity (UK Government, 2013).

*Trends and Impacts*

While these efforts vary from country to country, it is possible to detect four broad trends:

1. Efforts are evolving over time to provide more quantified, verified information for shareholders. Every iteration strengthens the disclosure requirements to demonstrate that sustainability is being integrated into core management decision making.
2. Policies are collaborative efforts between different public agencies and stock exchanges, using a variety of tools at the country's disposal.
3. Many efforts are still industry-specific.
4. Policies typically mandate general disclosure of environmental impact, but the state of this field is not yet at the point where countries are specifying a set of indicators that are universally mandated.

Most of the focus is on corporate behavior, although we see some efforts to improve the sustainability of government operations and a growing use of comprehensive urban sustainability plans. These plans, such as PlaNYC 2030, require periodic reporting of progress toward specific sustainability goals.

What is the impact of these efforts? In 2012, George Serafeim, of Harvard Business School, and Ioannis Ioannou, of London Business School, looked at data from 16 countries that had adopted some level of mandatory corporate sustainability reporting and compared those to 42 countries that had not. They found that companies that waited to disclose until there were legal requirements to do so, had significant declines in energy use, water consumption, and waste (5). They also found that mandated corporate sustainability reporting affects management practices, and that the impact is greatest in countries with systems for stronger enforcement and more frequent disclosure assurance (Iaonnou and Serafeim, 2012, 28). They also predict that integrated reporting would have an even greater effect. Integrated reports bring environmental issues up to the same level as financial disclosures and, according to Serafeim, the process "forces companies to explain the relationship between financial and nonfinancial measures and how managing these nonfinancial issues contributes to the long-term profitability of the company" (Blanding, 2011).

When compared to Europe, the United States lags behind on mandated sustainability reporting. In the United States, businesses themselves have led the effort to encourage action by federal regulators. In 2010, the Securities and Exchange Commission (SEC) provided guidance on disclosing climate change risk in existing disclosure requirements. This does not constitute a new requirement, but was issued to provide clarity and ensure that the rules are followed consistently (SEC, 2010). The guidance, which covers three areas: (1) regulatory risks, (2) indirect effects of regulation or business trends, and (3) physical impacts, was in response to business pressure to clarify climate risk information in corporate disclosures. According to Ceres, a network of investors, companies, and public interest groups committed to sustainability, over 100 institutional investors representing over $7.6 trillion supported a petition to the SEC requesting that it issue this guidance (Ceres, 2014, 1).

Another way that the United States has addressed the issue of corporate sustainability reporting is through its "Green Guides," which are an effort by the Federal Trade Commission (FTC) to discourage greenwashing by helping companies properly market environmental products, ensuring that sustainability claims do not mislead or confuse consumers (FTC, 2014). The guides were originally developed in 1992 and were updated as recently as 2012. The most recent update included revisions of existing guides, plus new sections on carbon offsets, toxicity claims, green certifications and seals, and renewable energy and material claims (FTC, 2012). These efforts are aligned with the mission of the Federal Trade Commission, which was established to prevent deceptive business practices and enhance informed consumer choice; however, the guides do not set forth rules or regulations issued by the Federal Trade Commission. These are meant to assist companies as they develop their marketing materials, not to mandate specific information about environmental impact. They are designed to describe the types of claims that the Commission would find deceptive under the Federal Trade Commission Act. The act empowers the Commission to take enforcement action against a company, which can include prohibiting the deceptive advertising and fines (FTC, 2012). While the Green Guides are a step in the right direction, they do not come close to what other leading countries are doing in this field.

## *A U.S. National Commission on Sustainability Metrics*

Required sustainability reporting is a critical step towards advancing sustainable practices, but before the U.S. passes a mandate, there needs to be a consensus on what reports should include. We believe the logical next step for the U.S. is federally led action to help determine the metrics that organizations would be required to disclose. Like the decades-long process that resulted in generally accepted accounting principles(GAAP), we believe the process to establish a set of mandated generally accepted sustainability metrics—including standard methods of collection, reporting, and verification—will take years, if not decades. First, businesses, stakeholder groups, and academics must agree on a recommended set of core sustainability metrics, and those metrics must be selected based on the current state of environmental, earth, and management sciences. Second, the federal government must develop policy tools and regulations for compliance, monitoring, and enforcement of mandatory sustainability reporting.

The federal government can serve a role not only in mandating and monitoring the reporting of sustainability metrics, but first can serve as the forum to bring together interested stakeholders to develop consensus around a set of generally accepted metrics. To ensure their adoption and widespread use, the federal government can use its convening power to generate momentum for a standardized set of metrics. The absence of such an authoritative moderator of the discussion stunts the drive to develop robust, universal sustainability metrics.

The federal government, through the Department of Commerce, for example, could establish a national commission on sustainability metrics. The commission would include a variety of federal agencies, including the Environmental Protection Agency, Department of Energy, Department of Labor, Department of Defense, Office of Management and Budget, Securities and Exchange Commission, and the Office of Science and Technology Policy, and would serve to bring together a coalition of leading experts from top universities, nonprofit organizations, advocacy groups, think tanks, and industries to lead a coordinated national effort to develop and build consensus around a set of mandated, generally accepted sustainability metrics. Such a commission would bring together the top minds in the field for information sharing, collaborative research, and outreach relating to the importance of this critical field. The federal government has a unique ability to assemble top leaders in the field to communicate and coordinate their activities across disciplinary, organizational, and geographic boundaries.

The commission would be an authoritative and potentially objective moderator of the discussion on sustainability metrics. Academia, corporations, think tanks, environmental interest groups, and others would be key stakeholders in developing metrics, but none can have the final word. The U.S. federal government has this key role to play. Analyses developed by experts would form the basis for recommendations to a national commission, but this commission's report would subsequently propose legislation that could serve as the *final authority* on sustainability metrics. The final output of such a commission would be to report on the state of sustainability metrics today and recommend a set of nationally mandated metrics, a defined reporting framework and requirements, and a detailed plan to implement the collection, auditing, and reporting of these indicators. The commission would advise on and develop proposed legislation, policy tools, and regulations to create and enforce mandatory measurement and reporting of generally accepted sustainability metrics.

### *Measuring the Green Economy*

Another role for the U.S. federal government in sustainability measurement is the development of local, state, and national sustainability indicators. It will be important to aggregate the various efforts at the individual, corporate, and city levels to have a comprehensive understanding of environmental performance on a national level. One example of a national sustainability metric was the Labor Department's effort to measure and report on green jobs.

Unfortunately, this very important project was suspended in the spring of 2013 due to the budget reductions mandated by the sequestration process. This effort should be restored immediately, and other aggregate measures of sustainability at the macro level need to be developed and implemented.

Why is it so important to measure green jobs? Green jobs can be used as one proxy measure for the green economy, and we believe that the green economy is the key to a sustainable future. Again, measuring our sustainability performance at the national level can help us understand how we are progressing and spur action to make changes. However, as we have seen, it is difficult to measure sustainability and the green economy because related issues cut across all industries and sectors. The United Nations Environment Programme (UNEP) developed a definition of a green economy as "one that results in improved human well-being and social equity, while significantly reducing environmental risks and ecological scarcities" (UNEP, 2014). The green economy includes jobs that "protect ecosystems and biodiversity; reduce energy, materials, and water consumption through high efficiency strategies; de-carbonize the economy; and minimize or altogether avoid generation of all forms of waste and pollution" (UNEP, 2008, 3).

However, not all green jobs are equal in their environmental impact and questions arise about where thresholds exist to define green jobs. Where the bar is set substantially changes the size and scope of the green economy. Some businesses only spend part of their time on green practices or products, making it especially difficult to measure. Similarly, some individuals work on green projects as only a portion of their responsibilities. Some industries and activities that help green the economy are harder to define and capture than easily identifiable ones such as energy auditing or solar manufacturing. For example, many of the new technologies and process shifts that will yield environmental benefits will occur in existing companies and industries, and so are difficult to separate out when attempting to measure the green economy or the jobs associated with that work (UNEP, 2008, 36). How are these counted when looking at the green economy? Additionally, differences in opinion exist over whether or not to include *process jobs* that make a business greener regardless of whether the total output is environmentally friendly (Pollack, 2012, 5). For all of these reasons, isolating and counting green jobs is problematic, yet necessary to make informed short- and long-term policy and business decisions.

In our view, one of the most important measures of the green economy is green employment. As noted earlier, the U.S. Bureau of Labor Statistics (BLS) began measuring green jobs in 2010. This green jobs initiative was an effort to gather data on "(1) the number of and trend over time in green jobs, (2) the industrial, occupational, and geographic distribution of the jobs, and (3) the wages of the workers in these jobs" (BLS, 2012b). Without a standard industry definition, the BLS developed a definition of green jobs based on the interpretations of academics, business leaders, and government actors. It defined green jobs as either: "(A) Jobs in businesses that produce goods or provide services that benefit the environment or conserve natural resources, or (B) Jobs in which workers' duties involve making their establishment's production processes more environmentally friendly or use fewer natural resources" (BLS, 2012b). Across sectors, 333 industries have been identified through BLS as being potential producers of green goods and services (BLS, 2012c).

According to the first BLS survey data, in 2010, 3.1 million jobs in the U.S. were associated with the production of green goods and services, accounting for 2.4 percent of total U.S. employment in that year. Of the total, 2.3 million jobs were in the private sector, and 860,300 in the public sector (BLS, 2012d, 1). Using then current BLS data, the Economic Policy Institute noted that 1 in 20 federal jobs was a green job, and 1 in 50 private-sector jobs met the same requirements (Pollack, 2012, 5).

The most recent report by the Bureau of Labor Statistics on green goods and services was released in September 2012 and is based on data from 2010 and 2011. Underscoring the idea of "shades of green" jobs, the Bureau further subdivides its green jobs into "all-green" jobs, meaning their core purpose is producing a green good or providing a green service. The report notes that roughly three-fifths (or 1.9 million) of the 3.1 million green jobs in 2010 were in establishments that received all of their revenue from green goods and services; See Figure 6.1 (BLS, 2012d, 1).

These data indicate that we are moving toward a green economy. The 2010 data serves as a benchmark from which we can measure our progress, but we can only do so if the Bureau of Labor Statistics resumes its green jobs initiative. The federal government is the only entity capable of collecting this type of data on a national level, and until we find other robust measures for nationwide sustainability, green jobs will remain a key component of measuring our green economy. The federal government must continue

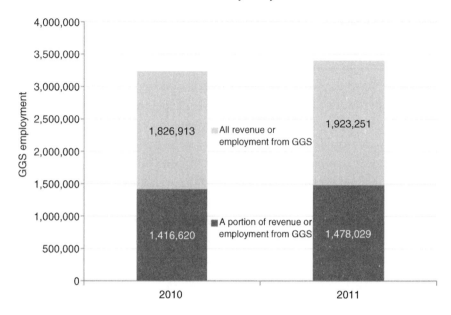

**Figure 6.1   Green-Goods-and-Services (GGS) Employment Level by Green Activity, 2010–2011 Annual Averages**
*Source:* U.S. Bureau of Labor Statistics. "Employment in green good and services, 2011." United States Department of Labor. April 1, 2013. http://www.bls.gov/opub/ted/2013/ted_20130401.htm

to play this critical role, and expand its initiatives as our understanding of the green economy continues to expand.

## Metrics as Momentum for Change

We believe convergence on a set of generally accepted sustainability metrics will drive momentum towards a change in organizational focus from simply reporting, disclosure, and transparency to uncovering real opportunity, competitive advantage, and financial and non-financial benefits of sustainability. As sustainability becomes clearer and more accessible to a greater number of users, its uptake will expand. A federal effort to develop generally accepted standards can uncover decision making tools and models that can be made available to a variety of stakeholders who are eager to incorporate the physical dimensions of sustainability into their management practices.

Deciding what indicators to track and to report is a critical step in engaging organizations, particularly in the private sector, in the transition to a sustainable economy. With consensus on metrics, the U.S. government can then mandate disclosure, drawing upon the many examples of other nations that now require sustainability reporting.

Complex sustainability challenges do not follow political borders or corporate boundaries. They cut across ecological and organizational systems, and so to truly understand our impacts, we must look at our performance on a higher level. It is not enough to know how well Walmart performed in comparison to Target this year. We need to know how their collective impacts are improving or damaging the country's sustainability performance overall. We must understand how the individual actions of companies, nonprofits, and governments in the United States are aggregated at a national level.

The federal government has critical roles to play in each of these processes. Top U.S. corporations and major U.S. cities already understand the importance of sustainability management, and as this momentum continues to build, we believe the U.S. federal government will emerge as a strong force in building a green economy that uses data-driven metrics to advance its sustainability goals. We fully expect to see the United States emerge as a leader in sustainability measurement.

# 7 | The Politics of Sustainability

## Introduction

It can sometimes be a struggle to understand why environmentalism and sustainability are such hot-button political issues. It is difficult to understand why safe air, water, and land should be a subject of political controversy, but this story is not new. In the 1970s, during the early environmental movement, public managers, policy experts, and students of environmental politics were working to understand the root causes of the environmental problem and trying to help the newly formed Environmental Protection Agency (EPA) as it tried to create policies and programs to address the problem. People involved in this work wanted to understand why rivers were on fire, toxics were oozing out of the ground, and the air was sometimes orange. The environment was not seen as an issue of ideology any more than cancer treatment was considered a partisan issue.

It became apparent quickly that the polluters were the makers of automobiles, steel, and gasoline, and they did not want government telling them how to run their businesses. They saw environmental regulation as an inconvenient impediment to production and profit. Many were unconcerned about the environmental impact of their businesses and assumed that the planet was big enough to absorb pretty much anything. In response, a growing group of environmental activists came to demonize these businesspeople as evildoers bent on poisoning people and the planet. By the end of the 1970s all of this had hardened into an ideological battle— the economy versus the environment—resulting in the environmental politics we have seen for the past several decades. The perceived trade-off between a clean environment and economic growth persists to a large extent to this day.

Fast forward to today, and we see environmental protection as a political issue co-existing with a growing concern for something we call sustainability. With the human population topping 7 billion and economic activity on a massive global scale, we are starting to see the emergence of global-level environmental challenges. Climate change is the most obvious of these challenges, but it is not the only problem. Our oceans, ecological systems, food supply, and drinking water are all threatened by the unforeseen impacts of human technology. At one end of the spectrum there are some corporate leaders and politicians who pretend that there are not any real problems. They argue that these issues are the inventions of a few pesky scientists and environmental activists. On the other end are the staunchest environmentalists who act as if we can simply shut economic production down and return to nature to live off the land. Both extremes are wrong; the environmental problems are real, but it's impossible to go back to nature. Looking beyond these radical perspectives, the politics of sustainability and public opinion about environmental issues remain critical to policymaking and sustainability management.

In this chapter, we will examine the increasing partisanship in Washington and its impact on sustainability policy. We will discuss the emergence of the Tea Party, and the deregulation agenda that helped it gain veto power over the Congressional agenda. Then, we will discuss the influence of lobbyists and the media on politics and discuss the difference between local and national politics. Next, we'll examine public opinion on sustainability, and finally, conclude with an analysis of the key drivers of sustainability policy and the future of sustainability politics.

## Increasing Partisanship in Washington

We are living through an era of deep although not unprecedented partisanship in Washington. Congressional gridlock has become an assumption, and most Americans have little faith that the federal government can do much of anything. We have certainly been here before. Remember, this is a nation that fought a long and bloody civil war. In the 19th century there were even instances of fistfights on the floor of Congress. However, from the end of World War II until the early 1990s we saw many instances of bipartisan cooperation. The environmental legislation of the 1970s and 1980s included a number of examples of bipartisan deal making. However, with the Republican takeover of the House of Representatives led by Newt Gingrich in 1994, and the subsequent government shutdowns of 1995 and 1996, we entered the current period of hyperpartisanship. How did we get here?

As the country has turned more and more against government, the Democrats have essentially adopted the policy perspective of the Reagan administration and the Republicans have continued to move as far as possible away from the idea that government has a legitimate role to play in civil society. The national political center has moved dramatically to the right. Thomas E. Mann and Raffaela Wakeman of the Brookings Institution concisely highlight this point, "It's no secret that floor dynamics in the House of Representatives are heavily influenced by sharp ideological differences between the parties and a very high level of unity within each party . . . party polarization first surfaced dramatically in the 104th Congress, and now the most 'conservative' Democrat is consistently more liberal than the most 'liberal' Republican" (2013). The problem for both parties is that the world is not getting simpler: environmental sustainability, the global economy, the aspirations of impoverished people, the communications capacity of the Internet, terrorism, and the growing technology of destruction can create and possibly help solve a set of vexing problems. The partisan dynamic in Washington is no friend to sustainability. In fact, no new piece of major environmental legislation has been enacted since the 1990 amendments to the Clean Air Act.

The increase in partisanship in Washington, DC, can be seen in issues like immigration reform, health care, deficit reduction, climate change, and the environment. It is impossible to deny the growing partisan divide that has profoundly influenced a U.S. climate and sustainability debate that seems to grow more polarized every year, even as climate science has become more definitive and environmental destruction more obvious. This persistent gap suggests that climate change and environmental protection have become ideological issues—much like gun control, taxes, or regulation—that define what it means to be a Republican or Democrat (Nisbet, 2009, 14). Somehow, environmental sustainability has been defined as a Democratic issue, despite the fact that breathing clean air and drinking clean water affect both sides of the aisle.

## The Do-Nothing Congress

The intense politicization of nearly all policy issues has made even routine congressional activities nearly impossible. The Republican preoccupation with reducing taxes and the size of government and eliminating the Affordable Care Act seems to have pushed out other issues, leaving no real opportunity for legitimate bipartisan policy conversations. Contemporary Congress seems unwilling or unable to engage in policymaking, resulting in a series of crippling struggles. In the fall of 2013, there was a government shutdown that lasted more than two weeks. Republicans, especially, use political weaponry to slow progress of any kind: They have used the debt ceiling for political leverage, putting the country's debt rating in jeopardy; they constantly threaten to filibuster in the Senate; and they have delayed the approval of presidential appointees. Democrats have also refused to compromise, often preferring appeals to their base constituency at the expense of progress. Moderates are a rare breed in today's Congress, which increases the distance between Republicans and Democrats. These are all indications of the degree of dysfunction in the federal government over the past several years.

Senator Claire McCaskill (D-MO) noted the lack of willing dealmakers: "You've got an atrophy of the middle, a cannibalization of the middle, and people are worried about their right flank if they're Republicans, some Democrats are worried about their left flank if they're Democrats, and the way this place works is by people hanging out in the middle and forging compromise" (qtd. in Welna, 2013). The political middle, which is generally where most Americans land on the political spectrum, has very few members left in Congress, and those few who remain have difficulty finding allies. It should come as no surprise that Congress has become increasingly unproductive. In December 2013, at the close of the first year of the 113th Congress, the Pew Center looked at how many substantive laws had been enacted (excluding ceremonial legislation like post-office renamings), and found that only 55 laws had been passed. This number is low even when compared to the 63 laws passed in 2011, the first year of the 112th Congress, which was already one of the least productive in recent history (Desilver, 2013).

## The Tea Party and the Deregulation Agenda

The hyperpartisanship that has emerged in this country over the last decade is perhaps best epitomized by the rise of the Tea Party. The Tea Party emerged after the 2008 elections, which put control of the White House and both houses of Congress into Democratic hands. While it lacks an official agenda, it is known for its staunch support of a reduction of the national debt and a smaller federal government, which includes lower taxes and deep federal spending cuts. It has come to represent the most conservative of conservatives, and most Tea Partiers identify themselves as Republicans. Many Tea Party candidates were elected to office in the 2010 and 2012 elections, uprooting more moderate Republicans in Congress and resulting in a more extreme right wing. Maryland House Democrat Chris Van Hollen attributed the lack of Congressional productivity to "deep divisions within the House GOP majority. 'The fight is between what used to be the mainstream Republicans in the House and the Tea Party Republicans in the House, and the Tea Party keeps winning'" (qtd. in Welna, 2013). The Tea Party movement is a natural extension of the Reagan revolution of the 1980s, where government was identified as a problem to be solved rather than a place where solutions to public problems might be shaped. Reagan's approach echoed the 1964 speech of Barry Goldwater, who in accepting the Republican nomination for President declared: "Extremism in the defense of liberty is no vice . . . moderation in the pursuit of justice is no virtue" (Washington Post, 1998).

Both Goldwater and Reagan would be considered moderate by contemporary conservative standards. Both were deal makers and today,

Reagan's fraternizing with Democratic leader Tip O'Neill would be considered socialist, rather than social. By delegitimizing government and its capacities, conservatives have made it impossible to conduct a serious analysis of the role of government in developing renewables and the conditions under which public and private sector partnership might make sense. Government is not perfect. It wastes resources and focuses far too much on process than results, especially in Washington. But the right-wing mantra that government is a beast that must be starved has only served to distract the public from real problems such as:

- The role of interest groups in policy making and the subtle corruption of 21st century influence peddling.
- Government agencies that move too slowly and are poorly managed.
- Deceptive elected officials who care more about winning the next election than speaking the truth.

In the contemporary anti-tax, starve-the-beast, ideology-driven budgetary environment there is little chance we can develop effective and sophisticated regulations and a meaningful public-private partnership.

### Deregulation at All Costs

There seems to be no place in the Tea Party ideology for a sophisticated relationship between government and the private sector in pursuit of sustainable economic growth. In this view, government agents can only be power-grabbing, bumbling, communist bureaucrats, and regulation is never a good idea. On the one hand, it's true that regulation costs money, and some business leaders seem to have a reflex that causes them to oppose regulation whenever it is proposed. On the other hand, it's true that lawlessness and an absence of rules can be quite expensive. Although many of the costs of regulation are borne by individual businesses and their customers, the costs of a lack of regulation fall on the shoulders of all of us. In fact, most businesses do not believe in blanket opposition to all regulation because they understand that reasonable law helps ensure that everyone plays by the same rules. The anti-regulation attitude creates a powerful and dangerous political dynamic when it is coupled with the Republican Party's current anti-tax, anti-government ideology.

The danger of the Republican right wing's zeal against government and regulation is that it inhibits our ability to deal with the complexity and interconnectedness of modern life and the modern economy. The BP Deepwater Horizon oil spill in the Gulf of Mexico, the Fukushima nuclear power plant accident in Japan, and the damage to the environment caused by hydrofracking in Ohio and Pennsylvania are all the results of inadequate regulation—not too much government, but too little. The U.S. Department of Interior failed to adequately police deep-sea oil drilling in the Gulf of Mexico. The Japanese government did not require the Tokyo Electric Power Company to guard the Fukushima plant against the threat of a tsunami. And more disasters are likely to emerge. The virtually unregulated extraction of natural gas in Pennsylvania and Ohio has resulted in preventable accidents and unnecessary damage. The chemicals in the fracking fluid are considered proprietary trade secrets, and without regulation it is impossible to determine or control what effect they will have on the ground and water where they are deposited. The damage caused by unregulated business not only brings harm to our planet, but also damages the economy and communities as well. The lack of adequate regulation of mortgages led to people buying and losing homes they couldn't afford and the lack of regulation on Wall Street led to a financial crash. Regulation is an important tool of economic development, but it must be properly designed and enforced to be effective.

Conservatives say that government is too ignorant of business practices to adequately police them. By that argument only criminals are qualified to serve as police. In the conservative view, regulations destroy initiative and hold businesses back from reaching their true potential. To some degree this is true, but when economic growth is slower and more cautious, it can also be more sustainable. It is true that you can regulate an activity to such a degree that you destroy it. You can also deregulate an activity to the point that modern business operates as ineffectively as it would the Wild West. Neither approach makes sense.

The anti-regulation movement is particularly pernicious because it prevents us from doing what we really need to do, which is to get better at developing and implementing effective regulation. Thanks to technology, the economic and social environment we live in is changing rapidly. We need to do a better job of understanding this environment and developing reasonable rules to govern economic competition within it. In any mining operation there are best management practices and there are also quick and dirty shortcuts. Like the citizens and wildlife that could be harmed, the companies that act responsibly are penalized in the absence of government rules and enforcement. Careless operators that damage the environment are rewarded by the lack of rules.

## The Costs and Benefits of Regulation

We know that a clean environment has many more economic benefits than costs. First, there are reduced expenditures for health care. Second, clean air and water have economic value that is difficult to quantify, but areas with toxic orange air and burning water cease to be productive when residents move away. Third are the benefits of technological innovation undertaken to comply with regulation. In seeking to meet new standards, engineers are given the resources to develop engines that pollute less or air conditioners that use less electricity. All of these factors stimulate rather than stunt economic growth.

Since 1997 the Office of Management and Budget (OMB) has reported that the benefits of all federal regulations have far exceeded their costs. OMB submits a report each year to comply with the Regulatory-Right-to-Know Act. According to a draft 2013 report, the benefits of federal regulation over the 10-year period ending September 2012 totaled "between $193 billion and $800 billion, while the estimated annual costs are in the aggregate between $57 billion and $84 billion. These ranges are reported in 2001 dollars and reflect uncertainty in the benefits and costs of each rule at the time that it was evaluated" (OMB, 2013b, 3). Figure 7.1 provides a summary of these data for the decade between FY 2004 and FY 2013.

In an excellent summary of OMB's report, Katie Greenshaw of OMB Watch noted the prominence of air pollution rules in the federal regulatory analysis. According to that summary, "the highest costs and benefits come from the U.S. Environmental Protection Agency's (EPA) air pollution rules. Specifically, the Clean Air Fine Particle Implementation Rule has the highest costs and benefits of any rule . . . The benefits, which far exceed the costs, include prevention of premature deaths, heart attacks,

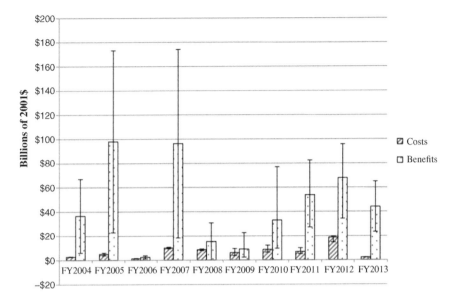

**Figure 7.1    Total Annual Costs and Benefits of Major Rules, by Fiscal Year**

*Source:* Office of Management and Budget. "2014 Draft Report to Congress on the Benefits and Costs of Federal Regulations and Unfunded Mandates on State, Local, and Tribal Entities." Office of Information and Regulatory Affairs. 2014. Page 21, Figure 1-1.

and respiratory illness among Americans" (Greenshaw, 2011). Greenshaw further observed that "Although many House Republicans claim that regulations are too costly and negatively impact jobs, this report presents findings consistent with recent independent research from the Economic Policy Institute (EPI) concluding that the benefits of regulation greatly exceed the costs. The EPI research also indicates that 'regulations do not tend to significantly impede job creation'" (Greenshaw, 2011).

It is hard to believe that we are reduced to making arguments on the necessity of regulation. It would be a much better use of our time and energy to focus our attention on developing *more effective* regulations. We need to learn more about the planet's conditions and the impact of our activities on productive ecosystems. It's true that regulations come with costs, but so does everything of value. It costs time and money when a driver stops at a red light, but the cost is lower than the cost of a road system without rules. Stopping is cheaper than crashing. The problem is that the benefits measured by OMB come to all of us, but some of the costs come to the kind of people who donate money to political campaigns.

## The Influence of Money, Lobbyists, and the Media

The ability of powerful economic interests to control America's political agenda is not news, and the degree to which facts and science are willfully denied seems to be getting worse. In 2010, the *Citizens United* Supreme Court ruling concluded that the government cannot limit corporate spending on political campaigns, cementing corporations' ability to influence American politics, essentially introducing super PACs (political action committees) into the political game. While the actual influence of campaign finance is not clear and difficult to trace, it is hard to deny that corporate money is flooding politics today. Some studies indicate that spending bans do not change election outcomes, nor do they have an effect on the success of parties in determining control of state legislatures (Raja & Schaffner, 2014). However, some studies provide evidence of corporate influence on election outcomes while others say that it depends on the circumstance (Powell, 2013). The argument comes down to a belief in the logic that unlimited donations to super PACs could skew the agendas of candidates in favor of very wealthy individuals or corporations that supported them. Super PACs cannot make contributions to specific candidates or parties, but they can spend all they want on things like ads, mailers, and other tools to influence how people vote. Some argue that this might not matter in a presidential race, where spending is already high, but it will impact hot-button issues (such as fracking) or congressional races where an extra $5 million could have a more distorted impact (Stewart et al., 2012). This degree of influence by the wealthy class doesn't happen in places like France, where it is illegal for corporations and special interest groups to make contributions to candidates, or in Germany, where campaigns are primarily government-funded (Simmons, 2014).

However, since the Supreme Court has overturned much of the legislation that regulates campaign contributions, and since super PACs have proliferated rapidly, there is a growing concern over the influence corporations and wealthy individuals have on elections. In the *McCutcheon* decision in April 2014, the Supreme Court further removed limits to contributions to federal political campaigns, opening the door for the wealthiest few in America to have the most influential voices. This case was brought by an Alabama businessman who wanted to contribute more than the allotted cap in order to encourage the adoption of conservative principles. Supreme Court Justice Stephen Breyer noted that this ruling would allow "a single individual to contribute millions of dollars to a political party or to a candidate's campaign" (Liptak, 2014). There is no consensus on the impact of this type of financing, due to the fact that these changes are still new and difficult to study. While politics always reflect economic power, the costs of modern political campaigning and the deregulation of campaign finance have created an even more one-sided political dialogue than before, especially when it comes to the environment.

### The Climate Change Denial Machine

The influence of lobbyists is especially apparent when looking at climate change and renewable energy. The fossil fuel industry has caused much of the political division on climate change through aggressive action to promote skepticism among the public. The industry, typically through conservative think tanks, has funded opposing scientific opinions, economic reports, and public relations campaigns. Riley E. Dunlap and Aaron M. McCright describe the strategy well: "[T]he conservative movement/fossil fuels complex quickly adopted the strategy of 'manufacturing' uncertainty and doubt (perfected by the tobacco industry) as its preferred strategy for promoting skepticism regarding ACC [anthropogenic climate change]" (2011, 146). They provide a clear explanation for how the fossil fuel industry (e.g., Peabody Coal, Exxon-Mobil, and the American Petroleum Institute), corporate America (including the U.S. Chamber of Commerce and the National Mining Association) and conservative foundations (Koch-controlled foundations, the John D. Olin Foundation, and others) use conservative think tanks (e.g., American Enterprise Institute, Cato Institute, etc.) and front groups (e.g., Global Climate Coalition, Center for Energy, and Economic Development) to feed misinformation to the public. This gets repeated and amplified by an echo chamber of politicians, the media, and blogs who spread the message over and over again (Dunlap and McCright, 2011, 147). These think tanks and front groups gain credibility with the public and media by funding contrarian scientists who are treated as legitimate experts on the issue, without consideration of the relevance or quality of the work. Their studies are traditionally not peer-reviewed (peer-review is a hallmark of sound science), and often developed by scientists who may be credentialed but are not experts in the field of climate science.

Just how widespread is the misinformation campaign? In 2005, Chris Mooney of *Mother Jones* found 40 ExxonMobil-funded organizations that either sought to undermine mainstream scientific findings on climate change or maintained affiliations with a small group of skeptic scientists (Mooney, 2005). The coal industry and wealthy billionaires like the Koch brothers have similar influence, funding think tanks and PACs that serve to influence public opinion about the facts as well as Congressional action (or inaction) in Washington and at state levels. In 1998, in anticipation of an attempt to ratify the Kyoto Protocol, several members of the denial machine, including the Marshall Institute, ExxonMobil, and the American Petroleum Institute, proposed a $5 million campaign to prevent policymakers from taking action by convincing the public that climate science is riddled with controversy and uncertainty by training up to 20 "respected climate scientists" on media relations (Begley, 2007). This is a well-funded, well-organized machine that continues to take aggressive action against climate change mitigation efforts in any form. Industries are increasingly using the foundations to conceal their own donations, rather than making publicly traceable contributions. One effort to quantify this movement found that conservative foundations providing funding to the denial movement use foundations as pass-through mechanisms to conceal their identities. It found that "140 foundations funneled $558 million to almost 100 climate denial organizations from 2003 to 2010. Meanwhile the traceable cash flow from more traditional sources, such as Koch Industries and ExxonMobil, has disappeared" (Fischer, 2013). The study concluded that only a fraction of sources of the hundreds of millions of dollars supporting the denial movement can be identified, while approximately 75 percent of revenue from these organizations is unidentifiable (Fischer, 2013).

While climate denial continues, the science is settled. Over 450 lead authors, with input from another 800 contributing authors, and another 2,500 expert reviewers developed the Fourth Assessment Report of the Intergovernmental Panel on Climate Change (IPCC) in 2007. The IPCC reports represent the most comprehensive synthesis of climate science (Union of Concerned Scientists, 2007). An IPCC report released in March 2014 confirmed the conclusions it had made in 2007 and earlier, and highlighted with renewed levels of certainty the risks we face for a changing climate.

A March 2014 study by geochemist James Lawrence Powell found that out of all 10,855 climate studies published in peer-reviewed journals during 2013, only 2 explicitly rejected anthropogenic global warming. Only 0.02 percent of published research denies outright the existence of man-made climate change (Atkin, 2014). Climate Progress, a blog from the Center for American Progress that provides information on climate science, solutions, and politics, points out that these figures are completely disconnected from the non-scientific debate about climate change in Congress:

> Politicians tasked with making crucial decisions on national energy policy and air pollution have a propensity for ignoring the science. Approximately 56 percent, or at least 130 members, of the current Republican caucus in the House of Representatives deny the basic tenets of climate science. Sixty-six percent, or at least 30 members, of the Senate Republican caucus also deny the reality of climate change (Atkin, 2014).

What's ironic is that before climate science became the target of ideology, it was the American right wing that developed market-based methods of moving away from fossil fuels. One of their most creative methods was a form of regulation called cap and trade, designed to raise the price of fossil fuels in order to speed the day that renewable energy could compete with fossil fuels on price. However, in recent years, the Tea Party gained power, the climate deniers gained legitimacy, cap and trade was renamed "cap and tax," and climate policy disappeared from America's federal political agenda.

### The Impact of a Noisy Media

If the science is still in question, how can you take action? There is a scientific consensus on many environmental issues, particularly on climate science. Conservative members of the House of Representatives have been unwilling to engage in a discussion of the challenges of sustainability. Influential lobbyists push for a debate about the validity of climate science, which distracts attention from policy discussions. The media, always hungry for stories of government controversy and conspiracy, exacerbates the issue. In our view, the media, in attempts to offer *balanced* stories, give politically motivated climate change deniers too much airtime. Always reporting both perspectives equally does a disservice to the public and policymakers by giving a small handful of climate change contrarians significant attention—and legitimacy—despite the fact that nearly all climate scientists agree that climate change is underway and that it is caused by human activity. When they share equal airtime it sends the message that the science is more uncertain than it is.

Another problem that arises from this is that it can turn scientists into policy advocates. While scientists may be quite careful about the way they present scientific findings, they might be less careful about presenting policy solutions. Scientists, after all, are not policy experts. When the American right wing and the political assaults funded by their rich bene-factors constantly call science into question, they prove to be a distraction to those interested in moving the planet to a path of sustainable economic growth. It is turning analysts into advocates and advocates into hysterics. Again, the media doesn't help the problem. The recent IPCC report focused a great deal of attention on solutions, but media accounts of the report focused on the possibility of food shortages and emphasized extreme catastrophe that is, in our view, unlikely. The result is a conflict-laden, unproductive policy process.

It is important to note that the American public shares a growing belief that the media exaggerates the impact of climate change. Steven F. Hayward, from the Pacific Research Institute, suggests that survey findings imply that the public has become jaded about environmentalism due to extensive "greening" (2011, 250). Observers have described this as *apocalypse fatigue* resulting from the public's growing skepticism of the flood of media and marketing content touting weak environmental claims. This fatigue, in part because of greenwashing, can be a problem not just for companies engaging in the marketing practices, but for the field of sustainability as a whole. Hayward points to a *New York Times* article that attributes "green noise" to consumers feeling apathetic, hostile, and suspicious to green claims (Williams, 2008). There is a serious risk of the public becoming tired of and overwhelmed by sustainability. Williams points out:

> the news media issues dire reports about disappearing polar bears; Web sites feature Brad Pitt arriving at a movie premiere in his hydrogen-powered BMW . . . An environmentally conscientious consumer is left

to wonder: are low-energy compact fluorescent bulbs better than standard incandescents, even if they contain traces of mercury? Which salad is more earth-friendly, the one made with organic mixed greens trucked from thousands of miles away, or the one with lettuce raised on nearby industrial farms? . . . If even well-intentioned activists are feeling overwhelmed, the average S.U.V. driver must be tuning out (2008).

We need the media to highlight issues of sustainability, but it becomes dangerous when exaggerated claims cause Americans to tune out. In the 2014 Gallup environment poll, 42 percent observed that media reports of climate change were exaggerated, 33 percent said that the seriousness of the issue was underestimated, and 23 percent thought that reports were generally correct (Jones, 2014). While it is not clear if this is a commentary on the news media or on the issue itself, it reinforces the impression that Americans are not too worried about climate change. And other sustainability issues face the same problem. We need an engaged and informed public, and the media plays an important role in bringing information to the people. But they should not use extremes to terrify people into action, or bombard people with information that seems to overwhelm most audiences instead of inspiring them.

## All Politics are Local

As we have noted throughout the book, local sustainability policies are pushing political and traditional boundaries; municipalities are emerging as innovators and leaders while efforts at the federal level languish. Why do we see this over and over again? As the late Speaker of the House of Representatives, Tip O'Neill, used to say, "All politics are local." After watching the U.S. Congress over the past several years, one has to be grateful for a federal political structure that provides state, county, and local governments with the power to act. While global issues such as climate change are ignored by our national government and international structures fail to provide feasible solutions, a wide range of sustainability issues have entered the political agenda and are being acted on by local governments. What is it about municipalities that make the politics of sustainability so different?

For one, the issues of environmental quality, public health, and resource scarcity are understood and deeply felt at the local level. People directly experience traffic jams and pollution alert days, and they can easily see the gradual shrinkage of open and undeveloped land in their hometowns and neighborhoods. While there are always opponents to local sustainability efforts, the opposition is based on operational rather than ideological issues. In New York City, Upper East Side residents oppose the nearby marine waste transfer station due to fears of traffic, pollution, and other potential impacts—not out of opposition to advanced waste management processes. Several decades ago, similar issues were raised when a sewage treatment plant was built in west Harlem. In exchange for allowing the plant to be built, the community was able to modify the structure's design so a state park could be built on top.

Unlike the work that goes on in Washington, what happens at the local level has immediate and often dramatic impact. If the subway breaks down, people walk. If the water main breaks, people can't bathe. The work of local government tends to be less influenced by ideology and more influenced by performance. One of former mayor Michael Bloomberg's most important innovations in PlaNYC 2030 was defining sustainability in broad terms and equating it with the quality of life experienced by the public. For example, PlaNYC 2030 set the goal of ensuring that every New Yorker lived within a 10-minute walk of a park. The green space is important in environmental terms because it absorbs rainwater and reduces the heat-island effect, but the most visible benefit to the average New Yorker is proximity to a park. The problems of congestion, flooding, and access to parks are well recognized, and not usually subject to the type of ideological warfare typical in our nation's capital.

The support for the sustainability agenda is deep and increasingly becoming a routine and expected part of local government. There are a number of obvious indicators that sustainability issues have become inte-grated into the American political culture. Local governments are simply responding to the public's demands, a trend that continued during the depths of the recession and shows a good level of staying power. People seem to really like the idea of breathing fresh air, drinking clean water, and eating nontoxic food.

The facts of population growth, economic growth, environmental degra-dation, and human reliance on the natural world make sustainability politics, technology, and management inevitable. The political pressure of our increas-ingly crowded planet is already found in local politics in America, where it is often called the *not-in-my-backyard* (NIMBY) syndrome. Development of our most valuable land is an increasingly contentious political process. Communities in large cities expect to be compensated for the negative impacts of new development. The politics around hydraulic fracturing for natural gas in small towns in New York State's Southern Tier indicate that the anti-development political impulse is not limited to large cities. More positive manifestations of sustainability politics can be seen in the widespread public support of programs like bike lanes, greenmarkets, and recycling.

In contrast, the politics of climate change are more complicated. Climate has never been an easy issue for the American political system. We do much better with problems that have a geographic home, can be seen and felt, and have an immediate visible impact. On the one hand, toxic waste, oil spills, and hydraulic fracturing can be seen and their impact is immediate. On the other hand, by its very nature, the climate problem is a tough political issue for our system to address. The causes of the climate problem are everywhere; they can't be located like a point source of pollution or a toxic-waste dump. The impacts of climate change are largely in the future, and they cannot be seen or smelled. The American political system, based as it is on places as well as people, will pay more attention to problems that have specific, as opposed to general, effects. As a global problem with widespread negative consequences, climate change brings problems that do not necessarily hit close to home. However, events like Hurricane Sandy are starting to change this. After the storm, a Siena College Research Institute poll found that "by an overwhelming 69–24 percent margin, voters say recent severe storms demonstrate global climate change rather than representing isolated weather events" (Greenberg, 2012, 1).

When it comes down to it, sustainability politics can be most visible at the local level as communities work to preserve the quality of their water, air, and way of life. The force of this political current should not be underestimated. It combines the political salience of economic growth with the emotional power of protecting our children's future. Ultimately, local sustainability policies depend on community interest and action, which come down to public interest in issues that directly impact voters.

## Public Opinion on Sustainability

So what do people really think about environmental sustainability? How have viewpoints and agendas changed over time? Americans' opinions on environmental issues surfaced in the 1960s as these issues were becoming more obvious and threatening. Public concern for environmental issues was high in 1970, but declined throughout that decade. In the 1980s this trend reversed; our concern grew as we collectively discovered more environmental problems, but it leveled off in the mid-1990s (Dunlap and Scarce, 1991, 652; Pulia, 2008, 2). Because events like Hurricane Sandy make climate change less abstract and more visible for Americans, awareness and concern for global sustainability issues seems to now be increasing again. Today, there is widespread public support for protecting the environment and ensuring sustainability.

## *Public Opinion Polling*

To understand where Americans stand on these issues, policymakers, politicians, the media, and business leaders rely on public opinion polling. Opinion polls are important resources to help policymakers better understand factors that shape public sentiment. A number of studies examine the historical influence of public opinion on policymaking, and many state that environmental policy is strongly affected by it (Hays, Esler and Hays, 1996). One study found that public opinion's influence on policy increases with public awareness and concern. This correlation holds true even in the face of activities by interest organizations and political parties (Burstein, 2003, 29). Another study found that shifts in public opinion correlate to changes in government attention, which implies that the government is attentive to the public (Pulia, 2008, 9). Not surprisingly, politicians take a keen interest in what their electorate thinks.

However, polls may not always be true representations of what the public really believes. We must consider the accuracy of public opinion data. What do the numbers actually represent? Brace and his colleagues argue that it's necessary to consider factors like social composition, demographic characteristics, and the institutional design of policies when measuring public opinion on issues (Brace et al., 2002, 184). These factors can alter public opinion in some way. The kinds of polls that are conducted also depend on who has the money, personnel, and formal organization to carry them out (Sparrow, 2008, 588). It can be surprisingly easy for politicians— or anyone—to manipulate polls for their own needs.

Sometimes the way the question is framed may not accurately capture public views. It is important to understand the method in which questions are asked, since this can have a significant impact on the results of a study. A team from Stanford University (Yeager et al.) tested variations of the same questions in three different subject groups in order to effectively measure the *most important problem* that Americans consider the country or world is facing (2011, 126–136). Their study found that applying different methods when asking about Americans' priorities resulted in different outcomes. When asked the traditionally phrased question (*What is the most important problem the world is facing?*), respondents seldom mentioned global warming or the environment. But these were the most frequent responses when subjects were asked to identify *the most serious problem the world will face in the future if nothing is done to stop it*. The authors recommend that future surveys pose this question in a variety of ways, because how the questions are phrased can elicit different responses in public opinion polls. It's also important to be aware of the fact that poll questions can also change year to year (adjusting for changes in culture, technology, science, politics, etc.), making comparisons across time difficult.

While we must be careful about how we interpret public opinion polls, and look closely at their design, they nonetheless remain a critical resource for policymakers—one of the few that allow us to take the pulse of the American public's attitudes about given problems and activities.

## How Americans View Sustainability

Let us return to the question: What does the American public think about sustainability? According to research gathered from public opinion polls conducted by various organizations such as Pew Research Center, Gallup, and ABC news, the American public ranks the environment, specifically global warming, as a low priority compared to other issues (Hayward, 2011, 243). An analysis of the Pew Research Center's annual survey found that consistently from 2007 to 2013, the economy, jobs, terrorism, and the budget deficit rank at the top of Americans' national priorities, while energy ranks in the middle, and the environment ranks at the bottom with illegal immigration, global trade, and global warming (ecoAmerica, 2013, 10). In Pew's 2014 survey, 80 percent of those polled rated strengthening the nation's economy as a top priority for the president and Congress, while 49 percent rated protecting the environment as a top priority, and 29 percent selected dealing with global warming, making it the second-lowest of the 20 items, just above dealing with global trade issues, which was the top pick for 28 percent (Doherty, Tyson and Dimock, 2014, 1). Despite occasional increases from year to year, issues like energy, the environment, and global warming remain on the low end of concerns compared to other national priorities.

While most Americans may prioritize the economy, this does not mean that the public is willing to trade a clean environment for economic growth. The Pew poll does not pit one against the other; in the case above, survey respondents were ranking a long list of priorities. Many polls are designed with questions where Americans are asked to choose between the environment and economy, and as we have noted before, these are false choices, as sustainability is a requirement of long-term economic growth. In the annual Gallup environment poll, respondents must trade off environmental quality against economic growth. Since we think that economic growth depends on environmental quality, we find the question misleading. Despite the false premise, until recently, Americans have historically believed that protecting the environment should be given a higher priority than economic growth. According to polling data from throughout the 1980s and 1990s, well over 60 percent of the American public favored protecting the environment even if it harmed the economy, and less than 30 percent favored economic growth that might damage the environment (Swift, 2014). The gap between these numbers closed during the George W. Bush administration, and during the Great Recession the focus on economic growth at all costs grew, reaching a peak in 2009 when 54 percent favored that over the environment and only 36 percent favored environment over economic growth. In recent years, the traditional pattern has resumed, and in 2014, 50 percent prioritized environmental protection over economic growth and only 40 percent favored economic growth over environmental protection (Swift, 2014).

When polls do not pit the economy and environment against one another, they can find that support for environmental issues is higher than originally suspected. Unfortunately, even when polls show evidence of broad support for environmental goals, that support can be shallow, and not necessarily substantial enough to lead to action or to persuade certain groups of people "to give up things they enjoy or need—cheap gasoline, jobs in industries like coal mining or logging—in order to advance environmental needs" (Yglesias, 2014). So even if polls say that a majority is in favor of "protecting the environment," that support might not be as strong as it seems (Shellenberger and Nordhaus, 2004, 11).

### How Americans View Climate Change

As you might expect, one of the most commonly polled sustainability issues over the last decade is climate change. It is pervasive in public discourse because it has become a mainstream, almost definitional environmental issue (Burns, 2008, 8). According to a Gallup poll in March 2014, 60 percent of Americans say there is already scientific consensus for climate change (Dugan, 2014). The majority of Americans (65 percent in 2014) believe that the effects of global warming are happening or will begin to happen during their lifetimes, yet at the same time, only 36 percent (as of 2014), believe that "it will pose a serious threat to their way of life during their lifetimes" (Jones, 2014). The scientific community appears to have had some success in communicating the consensus that global warming is occurring, but there is a gap between perceived existence and perceived threat.

Climate change reached the top of the international agenda in 2007 and 2008 following former vice president Al Gore and the Intergovernmental Panel on Climate Change (IPCC) receiving the 2007 Nobel Peace Prize for their work in raising awareness about the threat of climate change, and public support for action. Then in 2008 and 2009, a series of events quickly led to a decline in belief in climate change. A study led by Anthony Leiserowitz at Yale University attributes this decline to several potential causes: the poor state of the economy, a new administration in Congress, abnormal weather, and distrust of scientists.

First, the House of Representatives' climate bill stalled in the Senate while President Obama remained focused on his fight for health care reform (Leiserowitz, et al. 2013, 2). Second, there was a media frenzy surrounding what came to be known as *Climategate*, in which deceptive emails between British and American scientists were released to the public. Adding to the public's skepticism of climate scientists' claims, the scientists who authored the IPCC's 2007 Fourth Assessment report faced allegations that they had been pressured to suppress certain articles, a claim the IPCC denied. While several minor mistakes were later identified in the report, an independent review of the IPCC process found that the errors did not undermine the conclusions of the report. Additionally, December 2009 brought record cold temperatures and snowfall in the eastern half of the U.S., leading to some climate skeptics and deniers to assert that climate change was a hoax (a claim repeated during the *polar vortex* winter in early 2014). In fact, a 2014 study published in *Nature* found that the polar vortex—the unusual freezing temperatures that much of the U.S. experienced—may actually be linked to decreases in Arctic sea ice cover from global warming (Schultz, 2014). Finally, the global recession appeared to influence the public's views: "As concerns about one risk increase (e.g., the economy), concerns about other risks tend to decrease. Thus, soaring public worries about jobs and the state of the economy may have contributed to the decline in public concerns about climate change and other issues" (Leiserowitz, et. al. 2013, 4). Following this plunge, the U.S. public's belief in climate change has gradually begun to climb back up, but still remains low compared to other nations.

According to the Pew Research Center, since the low point in 2009, the percentage of Americans saying there is solid evidence of global warming has steadily increased to 69 percent in 2013. For comparison, 2009's low was 57 percent and the high, in 2006, was 77 percent. The same trend line is found in those who say that the rise in the earth's temperature is attributable to human activity. That high, from 2006 through 2008, was 47 percent. This number ticked down to 34 percent in 2009 before rising back to 42 percent in 2012 and 2013 (Dimock, Doherty, Christian, 2013, 3). However, poll responses always seems to account for how individuals are affected by the issue. The general public may not understand how a certain environmental concern directly affects them; for example, opinion polls show that people view the effects of climate change on their personal lives differently than its effects on wider society (Lorenzoni and Pidgeon, 2006, 80). People care about issues that they can see and feel. If problems are so abstract that people can't make that connection, it is difficult to capture their attention.

## U.S. Public Opinion and Political Ideology

According to most U.S. public opinion polls, political ideology is the most consistent predictor of environmental opinion, with Democrats and liberals showing greater concern for the environment than their Republican and conservative counterparts (Konisky, 2008, 144). Gallup's analysts consider the evolution of hyperpartisan politics to be the driver of the trend to prioritize environment over economy or vice versa. According to the Gallup Poll Social Series survey, before George W. Bush's presidency, both Republicans and Democrats prioritized environmental protection over economic growth; in 2000, 60 percent of Republicans and 75 percent of Democrats prioritized environmental protection over economic growth in response to Gallup's standard trade-off question. By 2011, the percentage of Republicans who were environmental advocates had declined to 19 percent, recovering to 32 percent in 2014. Similarly, Democrats favoring economic growth at the cost of environmental damage peaked at 44 percent in 2009, but by 2014 had declined to 27 percent. The number of Democrats prioritizing the environment over economic growth grew from 55 percent in 2013 to 66 percent in 2014 (Swift, 2014). Clearly, we are seeing a result that combines objective economic conditions with partisan politics. The shock of job loss and economic insecurity dominated American politics from 2008 until 2011, but by 2014 we saw the political impact of the Great Recession begin to fade.

We can see the politicization of the climate issue even more clearly when looking at the poll by political party. "In 2009, 35% of Republicans, 53% of independents and 75% of Democrats said there was solid evidence of rising temperatures on earth. Today, half of Republicans (50%), 62% of independents and 88% of Democrats say this" according to Pew's October 2013 survey. However, less than a quarter of Republicans (24 percent), less than half of independents (43 percent), and only two-thirds of Democrats (66 percent) say that there is solid evidence that global warming exists and is the result of human behavior (Pew Research Center, 2014).

An analysis of other environmental issues can also illustrate the party split. A March 2013 survey displayed broad public support (66 percent) for the building of the Keystone XL pipeline (Dimock, Doherty, Christian, 2013, 1). However, a sharp divide on the issue by political parties was apparent. Participants were asked whether they "favor or oppose building the Keystone XL pipeline that would transport oil from Canada's oil sands region through the Midwest to refineries in Texas?" Republicans overwhelmingly favor the construction of the pipeline with 82 percent supporting, compared to 70 percent of independents, and about half of Democrats (54 percent) (Dimock, Doherty, Christian, 2013, 8).

A similar September 2013 Pew survey assessed EPA regulations, and found that nearly two-thirds of the public favor stricter emissions limits on power plants; again we saw a significant difference by party: 74 percent of Democrats, 67 percent of independents, and 52 percent of Republicans were in favor of restrictions (Dimock and Doherty, 2013, 2). In 2011, during Congressional hearings regarding loosening standards of the Clean Air Act, the American Lung Association released a bipartisan survey examining the public views of the EPA's updating and enforcing clean air standards (American Lung Association, 2011). Based on the survey's findings, three out of four voters supported EPA efforts to set stricter standards on specific air pollutants and fuel efficiency. In addition, 68 percent thought Congress should not stop the EPA from updating the Clean Air Act standards, and 69 percent believed that EPA scientists rather than Congressional members should be the ones setting pollution standards. "The survey demonstrates that when it comes to protecting EPA's ability to update and enforce clean air standards, Independents and moderate voters are more in line with Democrats and liberals" (American Lung Association, 2011). These findings indicate the broad public support for the regulation of air quality—an issue closer to people's everyday lives than climate change. Gallup's 2014 survey also found that Americans care about the quality of the environment and focus more on immediate environmental insults (like air pollution) than on issues like climate, which they consider a long-term threat. Bipartisan support can be found for having clean air to breathe, clean water to drink, and an environment free of toxics.


### Opinions on Government's Role in Sustainability

The 2014 Gallup poll also asked respondents about the government's role in environmental performance over time. It found that Americans are not sure if the environment's quality is getting better or worse: 50 percent think it is getting worse and 42 percent think it is getting better (Riffkin, 2014). Back in 2008, 68 percent thought the environment was getting worse and 26 percent thought it was getting better. The next year, with newly elected and still-hopeful President Obama in office, the number of people who thought the environment was getting worse dropped by 17 percent and the number of people who thought it was getting better increased by 15 percent. In 2007, before Obama was elected, only 9 percent of all Democrats thought the environment was getting better, but by 2009 that had grown to 39 percent. While the views of Democrats shifted dramatically, the percentage of Republican environmental optimists remained in the 40 percent range for most of the past decade.

This means that some of the responses to this question recorded perceptions of the government's performance in improving and protecting the environment. In our view, this question does not provide a clear read on people's perceptions of the nation's overall environmental quality because it is measuring a management dynamic: *Is the situation getting better or worse?* People are telling the pollsters whether they believe that government is making the situation better or worse.

When you look at polls question by question, the overall impression may be that the public is just confused, but there is a compelling logic here. Let's think of all of these survey questions as elements of a multiple-indicator measure of American environmentalism. Here's what the polls tell us: People know that the planet is under threat, and they are willing to address the most urgent threats—especially if they directly experience them. In that respect, climate change is a tough issue. It is caused everywhere and its impacts are subtle and largely in the future. Drinking water in Charleston, West Virginia, air pollution in Los Angeles, California, and toxics in New York City's waterways can be seen, smelled, and felt. Americans understand those issues. They understand the threat posed by climate change, but they consider the threats posed by poisoned land, air, and water to be a higher priority.

Americans think that it is government's job to keep the environment clean enough to protect their health and the health of their loved ones. Some think that government is doing a good job in delivering that protection; some do not. But overall, Americans believe that many other public policy issues are more urgent. They understand and want to see action on environmental issues. It may well be that Americans have judged that government is making sufficient and steady progress in protecting the environment. In that sense, the issue works like crime or education. These issues have great latent potential, but only become a high priority when government is perceived as not doing enough.

## The Future of Sustainability Politics

The environmental issue is now part of the overall issue of economic development and growth. Logic tells us that non-sustainable economic growth leads to economic decline. The politics of sustainability are about protecting the planet so we can continue to benefit from the resources and wealth it provides for us. The evolution of the sustainability issue is not well understood by many in the political world, but that is starting to change. Before we conclude this chapter, we'll take a brief look at the key drivers of sustainability policy. How do issues of sustainability get on the political agenda and where do we go from here?

### *The Role of Citizens*

We know that public policy is much more likely to be politically durable if it touches on an issue that is salient to the broad public (Patashnik, 2003, 205). And we have seen that issues that are close to people's everyday lives can achieve this more easily. Sustainability rises in importance when it is transformed from an environmental issue into one of integrating economics and overall quality of life. Environmental issues that are supported only by environmentalists are unlikely to achieve political momentum and effect change. We also know that policymakers are more likely to *take action* on an issue when the public as a whole, outside the community of environmental specialists, takes an interest (Burns, 2008, 8). Making sustainability a high-profile issue by showcasing that it is critical to our economic growth and tied to our overall well-being can give issues of environmental sustainability greater legitimacy and political support. According to Steven Burns: "Given an infinite number of issues and a limited amount of time, policymakers have more reason to work on high-profile matters and have less to gain politically from their efforts on lesser-known issues" (Burns, 2008, 10).

An engaged citizen base is an important driver of public policy. Advocacy groups can influence the policy process, particularly in the agenda-setting stage (Johnson et al., 2010, 2284). Many achievements in the environmental arena dealing with clean air, water, and toxic sites, happened in the wake of grassroots mobilization and public support (Loewentheil, 2013). Sustainability is connected to people's daily lives—protecting families' health, advancing the source of their economic well-being, and providing a better quality of living. Sometimes, this can happen after the passage of environmental legislation. An active public may not support an issue until they recognize the benefits of a given policy. Huber and Stephens find that reform policies that quickly receive support do so because citizens enjoyed the benefits—the policies themselves changed the preferences of the public (2001, 29).

## The Role of Policy Design and Implementation

The implementation of any given policy is inherently political, which is important given that policies often continue to be defined during this process (Lockwood, 2013, 1340). It is important for a policy to be designed with enough flexibility to evolve to meet the needs of changeable circumstances. Policymaking is an iterative process and program design is incredibly important in ensuring that later stages of implementation can adjust to new information, knowledge, and technology while adhering to the original goals of the policy. It is possible for a policy to become so rooted in our culture and political practice that it becomes essentially irreversible; it is even possible with environmental reform, such as with the Clean Air Act of 1970 (Patashnik, 2003, 211). The Clean Air Act has stood the test of time, despite efforts to limit its scope, challenge its legitimacy, and reduce funding for its enforcement. It is now being used to address climate change in ways that the writers of the legislation couldn't have possibly predicted. Even so, it was written in such a way that it can be utilized to address this new problem. Because acceptance of a policy or passage of a law is simply the first step, making changes to support its survival is an important process. Many scholars cite the importance of a *policy feedback* effect among politically important groups or even among the public in order to enable its existence in the long term (Lockwood, 2013, 1341; Patashnik, 2008). The job is not done once legislation is passed, and the coalitions of stakeholders cannot drop support after the president signs a bill.

## *The Role of Science*

Finally, we must address the role of science in decision making, policy, and politics. Science and sustainability policymaking ought to go hand in hand. Science should inform what gets on the sustainability political agenda, what laws are needed and how laws are implemented. Policy should be based on information about the world around us. Scientific evidence can play a large role in decision-making, particularly as science identifies new risks; however, implications for policy are rarely clear cut, and scientific evidence can be a source of political conflict (Rayner, 2006, 4; Sarewitz, 2004, 393). We see this most clearly with climate change but it cuts across all issues. The more knowledge we have, the more questions arise, and the more information becomes available for interested parties to choose from. Science is inherently tied to uncertainty of varying levels. We cannot avoid that, but we should use the best knowledge we can obtain to make informed decisions. Unfortunately, we have seen that opposing scientific views on a single issue can have the effect of canceling each other out (Rayner, 2006, 5). Science is consistently subject to being politicized, which can lead to gridlock on policy reform, sustainability or otherwise, but in the end it's not about the science. The controversy only exists because of the underlying conflict over values and interests (Sarewitz, 2004, 397).

Ultimately, our lifestyles are an expression of our values. Those values find expression in our use of energy and in the coastal locations of our cities and homes. Efforts to change those values directly will tend to fail. While crises and catastrophes might change attitudes and behavior for a time, political propaganda that calls the science fake can also influence public opinion. For many people, it is preferable to doubt environmental science because if it is true they will need to sacrifice their comfortable ways of life. As long as the issue is framed as a stark trade-off, people will resist its premises. It is a political non-starter to argue that we must turn off the lights and get out of our cars or we will all be flooded out by sea-level rise. Politicians must reframe the issue, highlighting how our economy and lifestyles depend on a sustainable planet, and they must do it soon.

## Toward a New Politics of Sustainability

Sustainability integrates economic development with environmental protection. The old politics of environmental protection and the old politics of economic development are combined. Infrastructure that might be built by government to facilitate development is now assessed for its impact on water and energy consumption and its ecological impact. Environmental regulations are designed not simply to preserve resources, but to ensure they are available for human use. The political dynamics of this transition from environmentalism to sustainability is still underway. The old political paradigm of choosing between environment and economic growth is breaking down, but it still influences decision makers and politics. Our prediction is that this old way of thinking will continue to wither away.

# 8 | Conclusion

This book has focused on the role of government and public policy in hastening the transition to a sustainable economy based on renewable resources. The idea is to examine the ways in which government can influence private sector organizations to manage their operations sustainably. We began Chapter 1 by defining sustainability management. Then, we discussed the evolution of the environmental movement along with the incorporation of the sustainability perspective into our jobs, homes, and social norms. Chapter 2 introduced the role of the public sector in sustainability policy, and outlined a variety of policy tools and regulations that the government can use to ensure that the transition to a renewable economy is well managed. We looked at the government's role in everything from funding basic science and infrastructure, to providing financial incentives, to building effective public–private partnerships.

In the heart of the book, we provided an overview of sustainability policy tools available at the federal, state, and local levels. In Chapter 3, we reviewed federal market-based tools such as the Production Tax Credit (PTC) for renewables and effective environmental regulation such as the Clean Air Act. We also discussed regulatory failures like the BP oil spill and criticized the federal government for its continued support of the fossil fuel industry through the oil depletion allowance. We reviewed a select group of policies around the world to understand what might be feasible here in the U.S. We discussed carbon taxes in Finland and high-speed rail systems in China. In Chapter 4, we focused on initiatives at the state level—the level that David Osborne once termed the "laboratories of democracy." We not only examined state energy policies such as regional cap and trade and renewable portfolio standards, but also described transportation, wastewater infrastructure initiatives, and climate adaptation programs. In Chapter 5, we observed that cities are at the cutting edge of sustainability initiatives, and are experimenting with energy initiatives, air quality programs, community design, and climate resiliency projects. We provided examples such as innovative active transport systems in Hangzhou, China, brownfield redevelopment in Milwaukee, Wisconsin, and a range of initiatives under New York City's PlaNYC long-term sustainability plan.

In Chapter 6 we shifted our focus and detailed the status of efforts to develop standard sustainability metrics. We analyzed the current status of sustainability reporting as well as at the laws that mandate reporting in other nations. We called upon the U.S. government to develop a national commission on sustainability metrics. Without measurement you cannot tell if your management efforts are making the situation better or worse. Without agreed-upon sustainability metrics there can be no sustainability management and no effective sustainability policy.

Chapter 7 provides our broad overview of the politics of sustainability. We discussed the increasing partisanship in Washington, the deregulation agenda, and the impact of lobbyists, money, public opinion, and the media on sustainability. Finally, we speculated on the future of sustainability politics, and how an engaged citizen base, flexible policy design, and informed science can have a positive impact, especially at the local level.

However, we are focused not only on government's role in influencing private organizations, but on that of families and individuals as well. This concluding chapter steps back and takes a big-picture view of the change process now underway, moving the U.S. toward a sustainable, renewable resource–based economy. We provide some concluding thoughts on the process of changing consumption, technology, and political processes.

# The Role of Consumption and Lifestyle in the Transition to Sustainability

As we make the long transition to a sustainable and renewable economy and culture, a key question is centered on individual responsibility and personal lifestyle. In the end, our individual behavior as consumers has created the sustainability crisis, but the causes of this crisis are far from simple. First, there are many people in dire poverty who would love to have the problem of overconsumption. Second, there are a number of choices that may seem individual, but in fact are highly constrained by the production and infrastructure systems available to us. For most of us, getting back to the land and living at one with nature is not a realistic option. Our livelihoods and lifestyles are found in cities. Nevertheless, we will need to *become the change we wish to see*, to paraphrase Mahatma Gandhi. Individual choice will influence political, institutional, and economic systems, and those systems in turn will influence individual choices and behavior. Sustainability requires individual- and system-level change, and both are highly interdependent. So, how do we stimulate this change?

The leading edge of the dialogue about the global sustainability crisis is climate policy. In U.S. politics, concern about global warming has become a political fault line. Polling indicates that independent voters understand the reality of climate science, but climate science deniers dominate the right-wing base that controls many Republican primary races. Those that do not see a climate crisis tend to also disbelieve the global sustainability crisis.

On the environmental side of the divide, we see a diverse coalition, but a common thread in the discussion is that problems can only be solved when we put ourselves on a consumption diet and stop our super-sized, resource-intensive lifestyles. A second but related thread views the problem of extreme poverty in the world as a direct result of overconsumption in the developed world. We should therefore feel guilty when we consume, and if we would only consume less, the world's poor would get to consume more and the sustainability crisis would go away.

For some environmentalists, the sustainability crisis is a moral issue, particularly when it is combined with the growing degree of income inequality here in the U.S. This is not an argument for an era of superficial, unexamined, conspicuous-consumption lifestyles of the rich and famous glamorized by reality TV. We are asking only that people take a hard look at the interconnection between the economic, political, energy, and environmental systems that we depend on. Put simply, while today's version of economic development damages the environment, when economic growth ends, the working poor are the first to lose their jobs and their families are the first to suffer. Rich people have plenty to buffer them from the impacts of economic contraction but those without wealth have no margin for error. Our economic and political systems are dependent on economic growth. But economic growth can be decoupled from environmental destruction. The answer is not to reduce consumption, but to change it. On an individual level, sustainability relies on different patterns of consumption, not reduced consumption.

Some consumption requires material goods—particularly food, clothing, shelter, and transportation. The production, consumption, and disposal of those material goods are based on a series of unsustainable processes:

- One-time use of natural resources such as fossil fuels.
- Planned obsolescence of cars, electronics, and clothing.
- The use of toxic substances in production.
- Thoughtless, destructive waste management.
- Polluting production processes.

At the same time, an increasing number of jobs and a greater proportion of wealth are now generated in less resource-intensive occupations: web design, communications, finance, education, research, health care, hospitality, events management, social service delivery, and so on. Fewer of us work at factories and farms making things. Some of these production functions have been exported to the developing world, but many more of them have been automated and require less human labor than they once needed. Farming, construction, manufacturing, and even shipping and distribution are increasingly automated. This automation requires energy, but if energy could be renewable, and production and consumption could be less destructive, it is possible to imagine a larger economy with a smaller impact on the planet's interconnected ecosystems.

While we can imagine it, that doesn't mean we know how to do it. The emerging field of sustainability management is at the center of an effort to learn how to add the physical dimensions of sustainability to routine organizational management. The objectives of sustainability management are a response to today's unsustainable economy. These goals include:

- Reduced use of nonrenewable energy and materials in production.
- Efforts to reuse and recycle the materials that are used in production.
- Reductions in the volume and toxicity of waste from production and consumption.

The key question is how do we get from here to there? How do we make the transition to a renewable, sustainable economy? In our view, trying to make people feel guilty for their consumption is a losing strategy. No one wants to sit hungry and bored in a cold, dark place. A positive vision of a sustainable lifestyle includes entertainment, education, creativity, exciting ideas, stimulating social interactions, healthy and flavorful food and drink, exploration, and fun. While we need to pay attention to the environmental impact of our lifestyle, we need to understand that it will take a long time to develop sustainable consumption and economic growth.

We do not yet understand the planet's physical and natural systems enough to understand all of the impacts we have on them. We can't develop truly sustainable lifestyles until we develop a better understanding of the planet.

As we gain the knowledge needed to assess the environmental impacts of our economic life, and develop the technologies needed for renewable production, we must also develop the public policies and organizational management practices needed to put this knowledge to work. Our government, nonprofit, and for-profit organizations need to learn how to incorporate sustainability factors into routine and strategic decisions and actions. This will be a long and painstaking process. Similar to the change from an agricultural economy to an industrial one, the sustainability economy will be the end result of the post-industrial era that is now underway. Left on its own, this process will develop slowly and we will continue to damage ecosystems and change our climate. That is why we need to do all we can to accelerate the rate of change.

While technology and organizations must evolve, so must culture, social norms, and values. At the foundation of the transition we will need the idea of a sustainable lifestyle to be one that is not built on an artificial and irrelevant sense of moral superiority, but on the exciting and rewarding benefits it brings. We don't pretend to know what shape that might take, but we think it will involve active, engaged social interaction, experiential and virtual learning, and reduced emphasis on conspicuous consumption. Today, the popular media often defines the good life as having many homes, fancy cars, lavish parties, and wealth without work. The appeal of that lifestyle will probably never disappear, but it can be made to look ridiculous and out of step.

One should not understate the impact of social change, and evolving social norms. Racial equality, gender equality, gay rights, and global multi-culturalism are growing forces in American life. A rich, but less resource-intensive lifestyle could follow a similar path. The way people live can change quickly in response to new technologies, ideas, and even images.

While fear will always be a great motivator—as will its close relation, guilt—in a crowded, complex, and interconnected global society, it can also be dangerous and destabilizing. Fear that our children will inherit a dying planet is inescapable, but in our view, positivity about a renewable economy is a more sound political strategy than promoting fear about our current path. A sustainable, urban lifestyle may well be emerging with smaller personal spaces, more frequent use of public spaces, bikes, parks, high tech media, and constant attention to one's environmental footprint. We don't know if it can compete with the dream of a 4,000-square-foot climate-controlled suburban home, SUVs, speedboats, and a lifestyle of relentless luxury.

Government and the leadership of elected officials are needed to paint this positive image of a sustainable lifestyle. We see American federalism already beginning this process. A number of mayors have begun this process. Sustainability planning has become an integral element of urban economic development around the world.


## The Political Change Process that Brings Us to Sustainability

Rich people, poor people, Tea Partiers, Republicans, Democrats, old people, young people, Americans, people from other countries—we all are united in the biological necessities of being human. We all need food, air, and water that are not contaminated with toxic substances. The political support for environmental protection is derived from this fundamental fact, along with the equally fundamental awareness that all of these resources are at risk on a crowded and increasingly interconnected planet.

In a piece analyzing Gallup's polling on America's attitudes toward the environment, Cohen observed that:

Those under 30 favor environmental protection over economic growth by 60% to 30%. In contrast, those over 65 years old favor economic growth over environmental protection by 50% to 39%. Since there is no evidence that someone ages out of environmentalism, it is likely that environmentalism will become a stronger force in American politics in the next several decades (2014).

While there are aspects of Gallup's approach to measuring environmental attitudes that need improvement, they remain one of the best sources of longitudinal (comparing today to the past) data on American attitudes. With the exception of during the Great Recession, Americans have consistently valued environmental protection over economic growth. Even during the Great Recession, young people continued to support environmental protection over economic growth.

Nevertheless, Gallup's data is countered by more in-depth academic research that indicates that growing materialism and faith in technology has resulted in declining environmentalism among young Americans. Laura Wray-Lake, Constance A. Flanagan, and D. Wayne Osgood published a superb study in 2010 of the environmental attitudes of young people. The very careful and rigorous surveys that this article is based on were focused on measuring specific attitudes and behaviors over time, and indicate that young people do not act the way that scholars think environmentalists should behave. They don't conserve energy or express pro-environmental views as much as they might. We do not doubt their research or question Gallup's seemingly contradictory findings because a close look at the data indicates that the surveys are measuring different things. However, all of these data support our view that today's young people are more aware of sustainability than young people were 50 years ago, and these issues help frame their view of how the world works. Their views of the environment may be inconsistent and difficult to explain, but young people are deeply aware of the issue.

The authors of this book come from two different generations. As a millennial, Alison Miller understands the complicated awareness and choices she and her peers face when considering the environment. The most striking characteristic of millennials, for Bill Eimicke and Steve Cohen, who grew up in the 1970s is how well formulated and complex their views are. Americans born after 1970 have grown up in the *environmental era*. They have been witnesses to an effort to protect the planet against the assaults of modern economic development. They've heard their parents and grandparents describe the development of open spaces in their hometowns and in places they've visited. Congested roads, environmentally induced illness, and images of endangered species have always been part of the world they understand. Our growing awareness of nutrition, health, and exercise is part of a wider understanding of the interconnection between the environment and individual wellness, and these perceptions have created a change in our culture.

Environmentalism is less a political perspective than a way of understanding how the world works. One can compare it to the changing views of gender, race, homosexuality, and what we have come to term *parenting*. When Eimicke and Cohen were growing up, being a parent described a stage of one's life cycle. It was a status. Today parenting is a verb describing the actions involved in raising your children. While racism, sexism, xenophobia, and homophobia remain strong forces in American society, they are less tolerated than they once were. Social and cultural changes during the last half-century have created a profound change in how we live and how we interact with each other. This, in turn, has had a deep impact on politics and public policy. The drive for a renewable economy housed on a sustainable and not-deteriorating planet is a key part of the cultural shift we are describing.

In our view, these social changes create a nearly irresistible force for political change. It may take decades to manifest itself, and the forces opposing these views can often remain in power through the use of economic and military power, but the current of history and social change are difficult to overcome. That is because these social trends are based on technological changes that have transformed our lives and are incredibly seductive.

The technology of transportation, information, and communication has helped create a global, interconnected economy. The way many people in the developed world live today would have seemed dream-like to people a century ago. Americans born in 1900 lived through changes that resulted in a world they could barely imagine at the start of the 20th century. Ideas, images, goods, services, and everything humans can imagine are transmitted and shipped throughout the world. These technologies bring enormous benefits, but also carry significant costs. Traditional community life is endangered, as is a sense of place, replaced by a homogeneous world culture. And of course, the natural resource base of the world economy is also threatened by the wanton destruction of relentless, non-renewable material production.

While few people think about the transformation underway, it forms the backdrop for our worldview. For young Americans, the influence of these new facts is greater, since it is all they have ever known. All have been exposed to the view of a single fragile earth photographed from outer space. Most were not exposed to the casual, unthinking racial and social biases America began to confront in the second half of the 20th century. Today everyone knows people from different places with different life-styles. One needs to willfully go off the grid and disconnect from the Internet to grow up isolated and parochial—although we recognize that the web also empowers fact-free, delusional discussion. Nevertheless, TV images of family life have changed from *The Adventures of Ozzie and Harriet* to *The Cosby Show* to *Modern Family*. This is happening at the same time when distinct identities and communities are struggling to survive and absorb the unifying but sometimes empty values created by the global economy.

These technological, social, and economic changes influence politics and public policy. While there are many feedback loops and interactive effects, the basic chain of causality is this: Technological change results in economic change that, in turn, causes social change. Social change forms the boundaries for political legitimacy and the political agenda and creates the context for political change.

In the final analysis, people in the developed world like their lifestyles and do not want to lose them. The notion of progress and improvement is being replaced by the more conservative sentiment to retain or sustain what we have. If we achieve some success in transitioning to a renewable economy, we may see a return to the ideology of improvement. The politics of sustainability will have an ideological component—no different from other political dialogues—but the facts of global interconnectivity are increasingly hardwired into our culture and values. The importance of environmental quality and sustainability is an inescapable part of our shared understanding of how the world works. The political manifestation of that understanding has begun, even though its specific trajectory is difficult to predict.

We do know that people like to breathe, drink water, and eat. Preserving the resources needed to ensure sustenance is a requirement of all political processes and governing regimes. You can't have a tea party without clean water to brew tea.

This volume provides clear evidence that the technological, social, cultural, economic, and political transition to a sustainable economy has begun. We hope that we have provided some ideas of the role that government can play in facilitating and speeding up that transition. In our view, sustainability is not a question of *if*, but *when*. In our view, the transition process can be gentle and gradual or brutal and abrupt. We vote for gentle.

# References

Adamson, Kerry-Ann. "Executive Summary: Renewable Energy for Military Applications." *Pike Research*. 2012. Accessed on January 22, 2014. http://lgdata.s3-website-us-east-1.amazonaws.com/

Advanced Research and Projects Agency-Energy. "ARPA-E History." Accessed April 24, 2014a. http://www.arpa-e.energy.gov/?q=arpa-e-site-page/arpa-e-history

Advanced Research and Projects Agency-Energy. "ARPA-E Projects Attract More Than $625 Million In Private Funding." February 25, 2014b. Accessed April 24, 2014. http://energy.gov/articles/arpa-e-projects-attract-more-625-million-private-funding

American Association for the Advancement of Science. "Guide to R&D Funding Data – Historical Data." June 2013. Accessed March 14, 2014. http://www.aaas.org/

American Cancer Society. "Diesel Exhaust." February 19, 2013. Accessed June 13, 2014. http://www.cancer.org

American Council for an Energy-Efficient Economy. "Building Codes." Accessed March 25, 2014a. http://www.aceee.org/sector/state-policy/building-codes

American Council for an Energy-Efficient Economy. "Energy Efficiency Resource Standards (EERS)." Accessed March 12, 2014b. http://www.aceee.org/topics/eers

American Council for an Energy-Efficient Economy. "On-Bill Financing for Energy Efficiency Improvements." April 2012. Accessed April 28, 2014. http://www.aceee.org/

American Council for an Energy-Efficient Economy. "States Energy Efficiency Resource Standards (EERS)." Policy Brief. February 2014c. Accessed April 28, 2014. http://www.aceee.org/

The American Institute of Architects. "Local Leaders in Sustainability, Green Building Policy in a Changing Economic Environment." 2009. Washington, DC.

American Legislative Exchange Council. "Electricity Freedom Act." 2012. Accessed April 28, 2014. http://www.alec.org/

American Legislative Exchange Council. "Updating Net Metering Policies Resolution." 2014. Accessed April 28, 2014. http://www.alec.org/

The American Lung Association. "American Lung Association Bipartisan Poll Shows Strong Public Support for Lifesaving Clean Air Act." February 16, 2011. Accessed March 14, 2014. http://www.lung.org

American Public Transportation Association. "Record 10.7 Billion Trips Taken On U.S. Public Transportation in 2013." *Transit News*. March 10, 2014. Accessed April 22, 2014. http://www.apta.com/

American Water Works Association. "Infrastructure Financing." 2014. Accessed April 28, 2014. http://www.awwa.org/

Anas, Alex and Robin Lindsey. "Reducing urban road transportation externalities: road pricing in theory and in practice. 2011. *Review of Environmental Economics and Policy*. Vol. 5. No. 1. 66–88.

Anderson, Soren T., Ian Parry, James M. Sallee, and Carolyn Fischer. "Automobile Fuel Economy Standards Impacts: Impacts, Efficiency, and Alternatives." *Resources for the Future*. 2010. Washington, DC.

Ardila, Arturo. "Study of Urban Public Transport Conditions in BOGOTA." Public-Private Infrastructure Advisory Facility (PPIAF). April 15, 2005. Accessed June 16, 2014. www.ppiaf.org

Arup and C40 Cities. "Climate Action in Megacities 2.0 (CAM 2.0)." Volume 2.0. February 2014.

Atkin, Emily. "This One Simple Graphic Explains The Difference Between Climate Science And Climate Politics." *Climate Progress*. March 27, 2014. Accessed March 29, 2014. http://thinkprogress.org

Azapagic, A. and S. Perdan. "Indicators of Sustainable Development for Industry: A General Framework." *Process Safety and Environmental Protection*. 2000. Vol. 78. Issue 4. 243–261.

Bacchus, Jamy. "Title 24: Saving Homeowners Money, Reducing Pollution and Creating Jobs. What's Not to Like?" NRDC Switchboard. March 9, 2012. Accessed April 28, 2014. http://switchboard.nrdc.org/blogs/

Bai, Xuemei and Ryan RJ McAllister, R. Matthew Beaty and Bruce Taylor. "Urban Policy and Governance in a Global Environment: Complex Systems, Scale Mismatches and Public Participation." *Current Opinion in Environmental Sustainability*. 2010. Vol. 2. 129–135.

Bailey, Linda. "Public Transportation and Petroleum Savings in the U.S.: Reducing Dependence on Oil." ICF International. 2007.

Bakken, Gordon Morris. "The Creation of Law in a Democratic Society." Democracy Papers. Accessed August 4, 2014. http://www.ait.org.tw/infousa/zhtw/docs/demopaper/dmpaper5.html

Ball, Jeffrey. "Ending Energy Subsidies: Environmental No-Brainer, Political No-Winner." *The New Republic*. December 18, 2013. Accessed April 25, 2014. http://www.newrepublic.com/

Ball, Jeffrey. "Obama's Meaningless 'All of the Above' Energy Strategy is Infuriating Both Environmentalists and Fossil Fuelers." *The New Republic*. January 30, 2014. Accessed April 25, 2014. http://www.newrepublic.com/

Banks, John P, and others. "Assessing the Role of Distributed Power System in the US Power Sector." *The Brookings Institution Energy Security Initiative*. October 2011. Accessed March 14, 2014. http://www.brookings.edu/

Barringer, Felicity. "An Unclear Course on Emissions Policy." *New York Times*. May 29, 2011. Accessed April 28, 2014. http://www.nytimes.com/

Bassett, Ellen and Vivek Shandas. "Innovation and Climate Action Planning: Perspectives From Municipal Plans." *Journal of the American Planning Association*. 2010. Vol. 76. 4. 435–450.

Beattie, Andrew. "Financial History: The Rise of Modern Accounting." Investopedia. February 26, 2009. http://www.investopedia.com/

Begley, Sharon. "Global Warming Deniers Well Funded." *Newsweek*. August 12, 2007. Accessed April 2, 2014. http://www.newsweek.com/

Benfield, Kaid. "The top 10 US cities for public transportation." NRDC Switchboard. January 28, 2014. Accessed April 18, 2014. http://switchboard.nrdc.org

Bernanke, Ben S. "Promoting Research and Development: The Government's Role." At the Conference on "New Building Blocks for Jobs and Economic Growth." Board of the Governors of the Federal Reserve System. May 16, 2011. Accessed April 10, 2014. Washington, D.C. http://www.federalreserve.gov/

Betsill, Michele and Harriet Bulkeley. "Looking Back and Thinking Ahead: A Decade of Cities and Climate Change Research." *Local Environment.* 2007. Vol. 12. 5. 447–456.

Biedenkopf, Katja. "Emissions Trading, A Transatlantic Journey for an Idea?" *KFG Working Paper Series.* 2012. The Transformative Power of Europe. No. 45. 1–29.

Bifera, Lucas. "California Marks First Anniversary of Cap-and-Trade." *The Energy Collective.* November 14, 2013. Accessed April 28, 2014. http://theenergycollective.com/

Blanding, Michael. "Corporate Sustainability Reporting: It's Effective." *Harvard Business School.* May 23, 2011. Accessed February 18, 2014. http://www.hbs.edu/

Blumenthal, Les and Erika Bolstad. "U.S. agency let oil industry write offshore drilling rules." *McClatchy Newspapers.* May 10, 2010. Accessed May 1, 2014. http://www.mcclatchydc.com/

Boston Redevelopment Authority. "A Citizen's Guide to Development Review under Article 80 of the Boston Zoning Code." April 2014. City of Boston. http://www.bostonredevelopmentauthority.org/

Boston Redevelopment Authority. "Climate Change Preparedness and Resiliency." Last updated November 14, 2013. Accessed April 15, 2014. City of Boston. http://www.bostonredevelopmentauthority.org/

Bosworth, Brendon. "California's carbon market may succeed where others have failed." *High Country News.* April 15, 2013. Accessed April 28, 2014. https://www.hcn.org/

Brace, Paul, Kellie Sims-Butler, Kevin Arceneaux, and Martin Johnson. "Public Opinion in the American States: New Perspectives Using National Survey Data." *American Journal of Political Science.* 2002. Vol. 46. No. 1. 173–189.

Bradsher, Keith. "Speedy Trains Transform China." *The New York Times.* September 23, 2013. Accessed February 25, 2014. http://www.nytimes.com/

Brokaw, Leslie. "Five Ways That Sustainability Commitment is Up—Dramatically." *MIT Sloan Management Review*. November 27, 2011. Accessed April 9, 2014.

Brown, Lucas Merrill, Hanafi, Alex, and Annie Petsonk. "The EU Emissions Trading System: Results and Lessons Learned." Environmental Defense Fund. 2012. Accessed February 28, 2014. http://www.edf.org/

Bulkeley, Harriet and Michele Betsill. "Rethinking Sustainable Cities: Multilevel Governance and the 'Urban' Politics of Climate Change." *Environmental Politics*. 2005. Vol. 14. No. 1. 42–63.

Burns, Steven. "Environmental Policy and Politics: Trends in Public Debate." *Natural Resources & Environment*. 2008. Vol. 23. No. 2. 8–12.

Burstein, Paul. "The impact of public opinion on public policy: a review and agenda." *Political Research Quarterly*. 2003. Vol. 56. 29–40.

Burtraw, Dallas and Matt Woerman. "US Status on Climate Change Mitigation." *Resources for the Future*. Discussion Paper. 2012. Washington, DC.

C40 Cities Climate Leadership Group. "A World-Leading Low Emissions Transport System with Zero-Emission Vehicles." November 4, 2011a. http://www.c40.org/

C40 Cities Climate Leadership Group. "C40 Cities." Accessed July 1, 2014. http://www.c40.org/cities

C40 Cities Climate Leadership Group. "Expert Voices: Melanie Nutter, Director of San Francisco Department of the Environment." November 21, 2013a. http://c40.org/blog_posts/

C40 Cities Climate Leadership Group. "LED Traffic Lights Reduce Energy Use in Chicago by 85%." November 3, 2011b. http://www.c40.org/

C40 Cities Climate Leadership Group. "Optimizing Traffic Signal Timing Significantly Reduces the Consumption of Fuel." November 4, 2011c. http://www.c40.org/

C40 Cities Climate Leadership Group. "Port of Seattle Cuts Vessel Emissions by 29 percent Annually and Saves 26 percent on Energy Costs per Call." November 4, 2011d. http://www.c40.org/

C40 Cities Climate Leadership Group. "Seattle Sets the Standards for Green Buildings." November 4, 2011e. Accessed April 15, 2014. http://www.c40.org/

C40 Cities Climate Leadership Group. "Zero Waste Program." December 16, 2012. http://www.c40.org/

Cadmus Group, Inc. and Northwest Energy Efficiency Alliance. "Washington Residential Energy Code Compliance." Report #E13–251. March 27, 2013.

California Air Resources Board. "California Air Resources Board Approves Advanced Clean Car Rules." News Release #12–05. January 27, 2012. Accessed April 30, 2014. http://www.arb.ca.gov/

California Energy Commission. "Low Carbon Fuel Standard." 2014. Accessed April 28, 2014. http://www.energy.ca.gov/

The California Majority Report. "Germanyâ€™s Solar Feed-in-Tariff not Right for U.S., says German Industry Veteran." 2013. Accessed March 12, 2014. http://camajorityreport.com/

Caperton, Richard. "Good Government Investments in Renewable Energy." *Center for American Progress.* January 2012. 1–12.

Carlton, Jim. "Brownfields Bloom in Seattle." *The Wall Street Journal.* July 25, 2011. Accessed April 11, 2014. http://online.wsj.com/

Carmin, JoAnn, Nikhil Nadkarni, and Christopher Rhie. "Progress and Challenges in Urban Climate Adaptation Planning: Results of a Global Survey." ICLEI Local Governments for Sustainability and Massachusetts Institute of Technology. 2012. Cambridge, MA: MIT.

Center for Clean Air Policy and Center for Neighborhood Technology. "High Speed Rail and Greenhouse Gas Emissions in the U.S." January 2006. Accessed on March 10, 2014. http://www.cnt.org/

Center for Climate and Energy Solutions. "California Cap-and-Trade Program Summary." January 2014a. Accessed April 28, 2014. http://www.c2es.org/docUploads/calif-cap-trade-01-14.pdf

Center for Climate and Energy Solutions. "Colorado Passes Tax Incentives to Support Electric Vehicle Adoption." Accessed April 28, 2014b. http://www.c2es.org/us-states-regions/news/2013/colorado-passes-tax-incentives-support-electric-vehicle-adoption

Center for Climate and Energy Solutions. "Nebraska to Support Wind Farm Development with Tax Incentives." Accessed April 28, 2014c. http://www.c2es.org/us-states-regions/news/2013/nebraska-support-wind-farm-development-tax-incentives

Center for Climate and Energy Solutions. "Transportation and Climate Initiative in the Northeast and Mid-Atlantic U.S." Accessed April 30, 2014d. http://www.c2es.org/us-states-regions/news/2010/transportation-climate-initiative-northeast-mid-atlantic-us

Ceres. "Reducing Systemic Risks: The Securities & Exchange Commission and Climate Change." February 2014. Accessed February 28, 2014. www.ceres.org/

City Climate Leadership Awards. "Celebrating Leadership: 2013 C40 & Siemens City Climate Leadership Award Winners. Accessed March 31, 2014. http://cityclimateleadershipawards.com/celebrating-leadership-2013-c40-siemens-city-climate-leadership-award-winners/

City of Boston. "Renew Boston Solar." 2014. http://www.cityofboston.gov/

City of Chicago. Bureau of Environmental Management. "Chicago Brownfields Initiative." Accessed on April 14, 2014. http://www.cityofchicago.org/city/en/depts/dgs/supp_info/chicago_brownfieldsinitiative.html

City of Copenhagen. Technical and Environmental Administration Traffic Department. "Good, Better, Best: The City of Copenhagen's Bicycle Strategy 2011–2025." 2011.

City of Los Angeles. Office of the Mayor. "Mayor Villaraigosa Announces Completion of Largest LED Street Light Replacement Program." June 18, 2012. http://bsl.lacity.org/

City of Milwaukee. Department of City Development. "Brownfield Redevelopment." Accessed July 1, 2014. http://www.cityofchicago.org/city/en/depts/dgs/supp_info/chicago_brownfieldsinitiative.html City%20of%20Milwaukee.%20Department%20of%20City%20Development.%20%E2%80%9CBrownfield%20Redevelopment.%E2%80%9D

City of New York. "Mayor Bloomberg Announces New Measures to Allow Home and Property Owners Rebuilding After Hurricane Sandy to Meet Updated Flood Standards." January 31, 2013. Accessed April 11, 2014. http://www1.nyc.gov/office-of-the-mayor/

City of New York. PlaNYC. "A Greener, Greater New York." April 22, 2007. New York City Mayor's Office of Long Term Planning and Sustainability. http://www.nyc.gov/

City of New York. PlaNYC. "Greener, Greater Buildings Plan." 2014. New York City Mayor's Office of Long Term Planning and Sustainability. http://www.nyc.gov/

City of New York. PlaNYC. "PlaNYC 2030: A Greener, Greater New York." April 2011. New York City Mayor's Office of Long Term Planning and Sustainability. http://www.nyc.gov/

City of New York. PlaNYC. "PlaNYC Progress Report 2013." 2013. New York City Mayor's Office of Long Term Planning and Sustainability. http://www.nyc.gov/

City of Portland. "Global Warming Reduction Strategy." November 1993. http://www.portlandoregon.gov/

City of Portland. "The Portland Plan." April 2012. Accessed April 16, 2014. http://www.portlandonline.com/portlandplan/

City of Seattle. "Seattle's Comprehensive Plan." Accessed June 16, 2014. http://www.seattle.gov/dpd/cityplanning/completeprojectslist/comprehensiveplan/whatwhy/

Cleveland-Cuyahoga County. Food Policy Coalition. "Land Use & Planning." Accessed April 18, 2014. http://cccfoodpolicy.org/working-group/land-use-planning

Cohen, Steve. "A Strategic Framework for Devolving Responsibility and Functions from Government to the Private Sector." *Public Administration Review*. 2001. Vol. 61. No. 4. 432–440.

Cohen, Steven. *Sustainability Management: Lessons from and for New York City, America, and the Planet*. New York: Columbia University Press, 2011.

Cohen, Steven. "Understanding How Americans View the Environment." *The Huffington Post*. March 24, 2014. http://www.huffingtonpost.org

Columbia University. "William Vickrey (1914–1996)." Columbia University Record. October 10, 1997. Accessed June 16, 2014. http://econ.columbia.edu

Columbia Water Center. "Joint Columbia Water Center and USWP Webinar: 'Making the Grade: How to Fix America's Failing Water Infrastructure.'" April 1, 2014. Accessed April 1, 2014. http://water.columbia.edu/

Conant, Jeff. "Planning for Climate Disaster: Resilient Communities Respond." *Race, Poverty & the Environment*. 2012. Vol. 19. No. 2. 31–33.

Conniff, Richard. "The Political History of Cap and Trade." *Smithsonian Magazine*. August 2009. Accessed April 19, 2014. http://www.smithsonianmag.com/

Convery, Frank. "Budget 2013 – Three Cheers For the Carbon Tax." *Public Policy.ie*. September, 21, 2012. Accessed March 12, 2014. http://www.publicpolicy.ie/

Corfee-Morlot, Jan and Lamia Kamal-Chaoui, Michael G. Donovan, Ian Cochran, Alexis Robert and Pierre-Jonathan Teasdale. "Cities, Climate Change and Multilevel Governance." *OECD Environmental Working Papers*. 2009. Vol. 14.

Cory, Karlynn and Blair Swezey. "Renewable Portfolio Standards in the States: Balancing Goals and Implementation Strategies." National Renewable Energy Laboratory. December 2007. Accessed April 28, 2014. http://www.nrel.gov/

County of Los Angeles Public Health. "Air Quality Recommendations for Local Jurisdictions." Last Revised January 22, 2013. Accessed April 18, 2014. http://publichealth.lacounty.gov/

Cutter, Bowman, M. Rhead Enion, Ann Carlson, and Cara Horowitz. "Rules of the Game: Examining Market Manipulation, Gaming and Enforcement in California's Cap-and-Trade Program." UCLA School of Law, Emmett Center on Climate Change and the Environment. 2011. Accessed April 28, 2014. http://law.ucla.edu/

Dahl, Arthur Lyon. "Achievements and gaps in indicators for sustainability." *Ecological Indicators*. 2012. Vol. 17. 14–19.

Daigger, Glen T. "Sustainable Urban Water and Resource Management." The Bridge. Linking Engineering and Society. National Academy of Engineering of the National Academies. Spring 2011.

Database of State Incentives for Renewables & Efficiency. "Minnesota Incentives/Policies for Renewables & Efficiency." June 4, 2013a. Accessed April 28, 2014. http://www.dsireusa.org/

Database of State Incentives for Renewables & Efficiency. "New York Incentives/Policies for Renewables & Efficiency." Last Reviewed January 14, 2013b. Accessed May 1, 2014. http://www.dsireusa.org/

Database of State Incentives for Renewables & Efficiency. "Renewable Portfolio Standard Policies." March 2013c. Accessed April 28, 2014. http://www.dsireusa.org/

Database of State Incentives for Renewables & Efficiency. "West Virginia Incentives/Policies for Renewables & Efficiency." Last updated November 19, 2012. Accessed April 28, 2014. http://dsireusa.org/

Database of State Incentives for Renewables & Efficiency. "PACE Financing." Accessed April 30, 2014. http://www.dsireusa.org/solar/solarpolicyguide/?id=26

De Sousa, Christopher. "Policy Performance and Brownfield Redevelopment in Milwaukee, Wisconsin." *The Professional Geographer*. 2005. Vol. 57. No. 2. 312–327.

Desilver, Drew. "Congress Ends Least-Productive Year in Recent History." *Pew Research Center*. December 23, 2013. Accessed March 27, 2014. http://www.pewresearch.org

Dierwechter, Yonn. "Metropolitan Geographies of US Climate Action: Cities, Suburbs, and the Local Divide in Global Responsibilities." *Journal of Environmental Policy & Planning*. 2010. Vol. 12. No. 1. 59–82.

Dimock, Michael and Carroll Doherty. "Continued Support for Keystone XL Pipeline: What Energy Boom? Half Unaware of Rise in U.S. Production." *Pew Research Center*. September 26, 2013. Accessed March 21, 2014. http://www.pewresearch.org

Dimock, Michael, Carroll Doherty, and Leah Christian. "Keystone XL Pipeline Draws Broad Support: Continuing Partisan Divide in Views of Global Warming." *Pew Research Center*. April 2, 2013. Accessed March 20, 2014. http://www.pewresearch.org

Doherty, Carroll, Alec Tyson, and Michael Dimock. "Deficit Reduction Declines as Policy Priority: Just Half of Democrats Rate Deficit as 'Top Priority.'" *Pew Research Center*. January 27, 2014. Accessed March 20, 2014. http://www.pewresearch.org

Dubner, Stephen. "How Much Does Campaign Spending Influence the Election? A Freakonomics Quorum." *Freakonomics RSS*. January 17, 2012. http://freakonomics.com/2012/01/17/how-much-does-campaign-spending-influence-the-election-a-freakonomics-quorum/

Dugan, Andrew. "Americans Most Likely to Say Global Warming Is Exaggerated." *Gallup*. March 17, 2014. Accessed March 20, 2014. http://www.gallup.com

Dunlap, Riley E. and Aaron M. McCright. "Organized Climate Change Denial." In Dryzek, J.S., Norgaard, R.B., Schlosberg, D. (Eds). The Oxford Handbook of Climate Change and Society. *Oxford University Press*, Oxford, UK. 144–160.

Dunlap, Riley E. and Rik Scarce. "Poll Trends: Environmental Problems and Protection." *The Public Opinion Quarterly*. 1991. Vol. 55. No. 4. 651–672.

Earth Institute Environmental Science and Policy Workshop Group. "The Future of PlaNYC: Innovations in Sustainability." Spring 2013.

Columbia University, School of International and Public Affairs, Master of Public Administration.

Eaton, Collin. "New US Wind Power Installations Plummet." *Fuel Fix*. March 26, 2014. Accessed April 19, 2014. http://www.fuelfix .com/

ecoAmerica. "New Facts, Old Myths: Environmental Polling Trends." 2013. Accessed on March 13, 2014. http://ecoamerica.org/

Elsner, Gabe. "The Campaign Against Net Metering: ALEC and Utility Interests' Next Attack on Clean Energy Surfaces in Arizona." *Huffington Post*. November 29, 2013. Accessed April 28, 2014. http://www .huffingtonpost.com/

The Economist. "Can China Clean up Fast Enough?" August 10, 2013. Accessed April 11, 2014. http://www.economist.com/

The Economist. "The Invisible Green Hand." July 4, 2002. Accessed April 17, 2014. http://www.economist.com/

Energy Conservation Steering Committee. "Long-term Plan to Reduce Energy Consumption and Greenhouse Gas Emissions of Municipal Buildings and Operations." July 2008.

Energy Information Administration. "California's First Greenhouse Gas Emissions Auction Sells Near Minimum Price." United States Department of Energy. December 21, 2012a. Accessed March 15, 2014. http://www.eia.gov/

Energy Information Administration. "Feed-in tariff: A policy tool encouraging deployment of renewable electricity technologies." United States Department of Energy. May 20, 2013. Accessed April 28, 2014. http:// www.eia.gov/

Energy Information Administration. "Participation In Electric Net-Metering Programs Increased Sharply In Recent Years." United States Department of Energy. May 15, 2012b. Accessed March 15, 2014. http://www.eia.gov/

Energy Solutions Forum. "2014 NY State of the State: Energy and Climate." January 9, 2014. Accessed April 28, 2014. http://www .energysolutionsforum.com/

Environment Northeast. "Economic Benefits of RGGI." June 2013. Accessed April 28, 2014. http://www.envne.org/public/resources/ ENE_RGGI_Economic_Benefits_20130607.pdf

Environmental Defense Fund. "Acid Rain: The Power of Markets to Help the Planet." Accessed April 19, 2014a. http://www.edf.org/approach/markets/acid-rain

Environmental Defense Fund. "California: A climate launch pad." Accessed March 24, 2014b. http://www.edf.org/climate/california-climate-launch-pad

Environmental Law Institute. "Estimating U.S. Government Subsidies to Energy Sources: 2002–2008." 2009. Washington, DC. www.eli.org

Environmental Leader. "Sustainability is Key, 42% of Companies Say." *Environmental Leader & Energy Management News*. October 29, 2012. Accessed April 9, 2014. http://www.environmentalleader.com/

Environmental Leader. "Sustainability Initiatives Cut Costs by 6–10%." *Environmental Leader & Energy Management News*. June 9, 2009. Accessed April 9, 2014. http://www.environmentalleader.com/

Environmental Protection Agency. "Acid Rain and Related Programs: 2009 Highlights." Last updated December 20, 2010a. Accessed March 14, 2014. http://www.epa.gov/

Environmental Protection Agency. "Air and Water Quality Impacts of Brownfields Redevelopment A Study of Five Communities." 2011a. Office of Brownfields and Land Revitalization. http://www.epa.gov/

Environmental Protection Agency. "Brownfields and Land Revitalization." Last updated February 20, 2014a. Accessed March 4, 2014. http://www.epa.gov/brownfields/

Environmental Protection Agency. "Cap and Trade: Acid Rain Program Results." Accessed April 19, 2014b. http://www.epa.gov/

Environmental Protection Agency. "Clean Energy-Environment Guide to Action, Policies, Best Practices, and Action Steps for States." April 2006. Accessed April 28, 2014. http://www.epa.gov/

Environmental Protection Agency. "Combined Heat and Power Partnership (CHP)." Last updated April 2009. Accessed April 28, 2014. http://www.epa.gov/

Environmental Protection Agency. "Kansas City, Mo., to Spend $2.5 Billion to Cut Sewer Overflows." May 18, 2010b. http://www.epa.gov

Environmental Protection Agency. "Public Benefit Funds." Last updated June 7, 2013a. Accessed May 1, 2014. http://www.epa.gov/

Environmental Protection Agency. "Second Prospective Study—1990 to 2020." February 2011b. Accessed April 25, 2014. http://www.epa.gov/

Environmental Protection Agency. "Transportation and Climate." Last updated September 30, 2013b. Accessed April 28, 2014. http://www.epa.gov/

Environmental Protection Agency. "Tribal Green Building Codes: Existing Green Building Codes." Accessed March 25, 2014c. http://www.epa.gov/region9/greenbuilding/codes/existing.html

Epstein, Lee. "The essential elements of green cities." NRDC Switchboard. April 3, 2013. Accessed March 31, 2014. http://switchboard.nrdc.org/

Ernst & Young with the GreenBiz Group. "Six Growing Trends in Corporate Sustainability." *GreenBiz Group*. 2012. Accessed February 12, 2014. http://www.greenbiz.com/

European Commission. "Auctioning." March 12, 2014a. Accessed March 12, 2014a. http://ec.europa.eu/clima/policies/ets/cap/auctioning/index_en.htm

European Commission. "Non-Financial Reporting." Last Updated January 30, 2014b. Accessed February 19, 2014. http://ec.europa.eu/internal_market/accounting/non-financial_reporting/index_en.htm

Eurostar. "London-Paris and London-Brussels Flights Generate Ten Times More Carbon Dioxide Emissions Than Eurostar." October 2, 2006. Accessed March 1, 2014. http://www.eurostar.com/

The EV Project. "Overview." 2013. Accessed April 23, 2014. http://theevproject.com/

Federal Housing Finance Agency. "FHFA Statement on Certain Energy Retrofit Loan Programs." July 6, 2010. Accessed May 1, 2014. http://www.fhfa.gov/

Federal Railroad Administration. "FY 2014 Budget & Five-Year Reauthorization Proposal." April 10, 2013. Accessed March 14, 2014. United States Department of Transportation. http://www.fra.dot.gov/

Federal Trade Commission. "FTC Issues Revised 'Green Guides.'" October 1, 2012. Accessed February 28, 2014. www.ftc.gov/

Federal Trade Commission. "Green Guides." Accessed February 28, 2014. http://www.ftc.gov/news-events/media-resources/truth-advertising/green-guides

Feiock, Richard C. and Simon A. Andrew. "Introduction: Understanding the Relationships Between Nonprofit Organizations and Local Governments." *International Journal of Public Administration*. 2006. Vol. 29. 759–767.

Fischer, Douglas and The Daily Climate. "'Dark Money' Funds Climate Change Denial Effort." *Scientific American*. December 23, 2013. Accessed April 2, 2014. http://www.scientificamerican.com/

Fresh Energy. "Legislative Agenda." 2014. Accessed April 28, 2014. http://fresh-energy.org/

Friedrich, Kat. "Residential PACE Energy Programs Pursue Innovative Approaches." *Renewable Energy World.com*. September 6, 2013. Accessed April 28, 2014. http://www.renewableenergyworld.com

Funkhouser, David. "Con Ed Agrees to Climate Change Plan." *Columbia University State of the Plane Blog*. February 24, 2014. Accessed April 28, 2014. http://blogs.ei.columbia.edu/

Gaitan, Catalina. "New City Program lets Doctors 'Prescribe' Bike-Sharing Memberships." *The Boston Globe*. March 27, 2014. Accessed April 22, 2014. http://www.bostonglobe.com/

Gallagher, Kelly Sims. "Why & How Governments Support Renewable Energy." *Daedalus, the Journal of the American Academy of Arts & Sciences*. 2013. Vol. 142. No. 1. 59–77.

Gallopoulos, Nicholas E. "Industrial Ecology: An Overview." *Progress in Industrial Ecology: An International Journal*. 2006. Vol. 3. No. 1–2. 10–27.

Gallucci, Maria. "Northeast Markets Eyed for Oil Sands as Clean Fuels Standard Fades." *Inside Climate News*. March 29, 2012. Accessed April 28, 2014. http://insideclimatenews.org/

Geary, Caitlin. "Sustainable Connections: Linking Sustainability and Economic Development Strategies." National League of Cities. Center for Research and Innovation. 2011.

Georgetown Climate Center. "Governors from Eight States Pledge to put 3.3 Million Zero-Emission Vehicles on the Road by 2025." Georgetown Law. October 28, 2013. Accessed April 30, 2014. http://www.georgetownclimate.org/

Georgetown Climate Center. "Understanding Freight Movement in the Northeast." March 27, 2012. Accessed April 30, 2014. http://www.georgetownclimate.org/

German Society for International Cooperation, The Global Reporting Initiative, Through Arbitrage Research Institute. "Sustainability Reporting: Practices and Trends in India 2012." May 2012. Accessed February 19, 2014. http://www.giz.de/

Gero, Gary. "California's Cap-and-Trade Program—More Than Just a Solution for California." *Huffington Post*. November 18, 2013. Accessed April 28, 2014. http://www.huffingtonpost.com/

Glatt, Sandy. "Public Benefit Funds: Increasing Renewable Energy & Industrial Energy Efficiency Opportunities." United States Department of Energy. March 2010.

The Global Reporting Initiative. "Sustainability Disclosure Database." Accessed February 28, 2014. database.globalreporting.org

The Global Reporting Initiative, the United Nations Environment Programme, KPMG, and the Centre for Corporate Governance in Africa. "Carrots and Sticks: Sustainability Reporting Policies Worldwide – Today's Best Practice, Tomorrow's Trends." 2013. Accessed February 18, 2014. https://www.globalreporting.org/

Goldenberg, Suzanne and Ed Pilkington. "ALEC calls for penalties on 'free-rider' homeowners in assault on clean energy." *The Guardian*. December 4, 2013. Accessed May 1, 2014. http://www.theguardian.com/

Granade, Hannah Choi, Jon Creyts, Anton Derkach, Philip Farese, Scott Nyquist and Ken Ostrowski. "Unlocking Energy Efficiency in the U.S. Economy." McKinsey & Company. July 2009. Accessed April 28, 2014. http://www.mckinsey.com/

Greenberg, Steven. "Voters: Cuomo, Obama, Bloomberg, MTA & FEMA Do Good Job Dealing with Sandy; ConEd Mixed Review; LIPA Panned." *Siena College Research Institute*. December 2, 2013. Accessed April 6, 2014. http://www.siena.edu/

Greenshaw, Katie. "OMB Annual Report Shows Regulations' Benefits Exceed Costs." *Center for Effective Government*. 2011. Accessed March 31, 2014. http://www.foreffectivegov.org

Greenstone, Michael. "The Importance of Research and Development for US Competiveness and a Clean Energy Future." *MIT Center for Energy and Environmental Policy Research*. June 2011.

Greenworks Philadelphia. Alex Dews and Sarah Wu, Mayor's Office of Sustainability. "2013 Progress Report." 2013.

Guide to Greening Cities. "Prioritizing Healthy Transportation: Bike Share in Washington, D.C." Accessed July 1, 2014. http://guidetogreening cities.org/content/prioritizing-healthy-transportation-bike-share-washington-dc

Haanaes, Knut, Martin Reeves, Ingrid Von Streng Velken, Michael Audretsch, David Kiron, and Nina Kruschwitz. "Sustainability Nears a Tipping Point." *MIT Sloan Management Review and The Boston Consulting Group*. Research Report. 2012. Vol. 53. No. 2. 1–17.

Hargreaves, Steve. "Big Oil's $4 Billion Tax Break In Doubt." *CNNMoney*. April 29, 2011. Accessed April 19, 2014. http://www.money.cnn.com/

Hays, Scott P., Michael Esler, and Carol E. Hays. "Environmental Commitment among the States." *Publius: The Journal of Federalism*. 1996. Vol. 26. 41–58.

Hayward, Steven F. "2011 Almanac of Environmental Trends." *Pacific Research Institute*. 2011. 242–250.

Heeter, Jenny and Lori Bird. "Including Alternative Resources in State Renewable Portfolio Standards: Current Design and Implementation Experience." National Renewable Energy Laboratory. Technical Report NREL/TP-6A20–55979. 2012.

Henderson, Philip. "On-Bill Financing Overview and Key Considerations for Program Design." Natural Resources Defense Council. July 2013. Accessed April 28, 2014. http://www.nrdc.org/

Hendricks, Bracken and Ben Bovarnick. "Banking on Clean Energy: State Leadership in Financing a Greener Future." Center for American Progress. January 17, 2014. Accessed April 28, 2014. http://www.americanprogress.org/

Hibbard, Paul, Susan F. Tierney, Andrea M. Okie, and Pavel G. Darling. "The Economic Impacts of the Regional Greenhouse Gas Initiative on Ten Northeast and Mid-Atlantic States." The Analysis Group. 2011. Accessed April 28, 2014. http://www.analysisgroup.com/

Hoffmann, Andrew J. "Sociology: The growing climate divide." *Nature Climate Change*. 2011. Vol. 1. 195–196.

Homsy, George and Mildred Warner. "Defying the Odds: Sustainability in Small and Rural Places." 2013. ICMA Center for Sustainable Communities. National Association of Development Organizations (NADO) Research Foundation.

Horowitz, Noah. "New California building code to slash energy bills by billions." *GreenBiz.com*. May 31, 2012. Accessed April 28, 2014. http://www.greenbiz.com

Hsia-Kiung, Katherine, Emily Reyna, and Timothy O'Connor. "California Carbon Market Watch: A Comprehensive Analysis of the Golden

State's Cap-and-Trade Program/Year One: 2012–2013." Environmental Defense Fund. 2014. Accessed April 28, 2014. https://www.edf.org/

Huber, Evelyne and John D. Stephens. "Development and Crisis of the Welfare State, Parties and Policies in Global Markets." *University of Chicago Press*. 2001.

Hull, Dana. "Ninth Circuit upholds California's Low Carbon Fuel Standard." *San Jose Mercury News*. September 18, 2013. Accessed April 28, 2014. http://www.mercurynews.com/

ICLEI Local Governments for Sustainability. "Sustainability Planning Toolkit." December 2009. Accessed April 7, 2014. http://www.icleiusa.org/

Institute for Building Efficiency. "Feed-In Tariffs: A Brief History." August 2010. Accessed March 13, 2014. http://www.institutebe.com/

Institute for Energy Research. "PTC Extension Passes; Layoffs and Cancellations Continue." January 16, 2013. Accessed on April 25, 2014. http://www.instituteforenergyresearch.org/

International City/Council Management Association. "Local Government Sustainability Policies and Programs, 2010." 2010. 1–4.

International Council on Clean Transportation. "Global Comparison of Light-Duty Vehicle Fuel Economy/GHG Emissions Standards." June 2012. Accessed April 28, 2014. http://www.theicct.org/

International Energy Agency. "Joint report by IEA, OPEC, OECD and World Bank on fossil-fuel and other energy subsidies: An update of the G20 Pittsburgh and Toronto Commitments." 2011.

International Energy Agency. "Tracking Clean Energy Progress: Energy Technology Perspectives 2012 Excerpt as IEA Input to the Clean Energy Ministerial." 2012.

The International Integrated Reporting Council. "Integrated Reporting." Accessed February 28, 2014. https://www.theiirc.org/

International Renewable Energy Agency. ICLEI Local Governments for Sustainability. "Stimulating Renewable Energy through Public and Private Procurement." Accessed April 24, 2014. http://www.irena .org/Publications/RE_Policy_Cities_CaseStudies/IRENA%20cities% 20case%204%20Austin.pdf

Ioannou, Ioannis and George Serafeim. "The Consequences of Mandatory Corporate Sustainability Reporting: Working Paper." *Harvard Business School*. October 26, 2012. Accessed February 18, 2014. http://www .hbs.edu/

Isodore, Chris. "Exxon Mobil Profit Is Just Short of Record." *CNNMoney*. February 1, 2013. Accessed April 19, 2014. http://www.money.cnn .com/

Jaffe, Eric. "Why are People Rioting over Bigota's Public Transit System?" City Lab. March 20, 2012. Accessed June 13, 2014. http://www.citylab .com

Jaffe, Mark. "Near-record orders spur Vestas wind-turbine production and hiring." *The Denver Post*. December 26, 2013. Accessed March 14, 2014. http://www.denverpost.com/business/ci_24797306/near-record-orders-spur-vestas-wind-turbine-production.

Jenkins, Jesse and others. "Beyond Boom & Bust: Putting Clean Tech on a Path to Subsidy Independence." April 18, 2012. Accessed March 14, 2014. *The Brookings Institution*. http://www.brookings.edu/

Johnson Erik W., Jon Agnone and John D. McCarthy. "Movement organizations, synergistic tactics and environmental public policy." *Social Forces*. 2010. Vol. 88. No. 5. 2267–2292.

Jones, Jeffrey. "In U.S., Most Do Not See Global Warming as Serious Threat." *Gallup*. March 13, 2014. March 20, 2014. http://www.gallup .com

Jorgensen, Tine Herreborg and Jette Egelund Holgaard. "Environmental Reporting: Experiences from Denmark: Working Paper 6." Aalborg University. 2004. Accessed February 19, 2014. http://www.plan.aau .dk/

Kamal-Chaoui, Lamia, and Alexis Robert. "Competitive Cities and Climate Change." OECD Regional Development Working Papers. Paris, France. 2009. Vol 2.

Kiron, David, Nina Kruschwitz, Martin Reeves and Eugene Goh. "The Benefits of Sustainability-Driven Innovation." *MIT Sloan Management Review*. 2013. Vol. 54. No. 2.

Klopott, Freeman. "New York Decision on Fracking Regulations Delayed." *Bloomberg*. January 29, 2014. Accessed April 20, 2014. http://www.bloomberg.com/

Konisky, David M. "Bureaucratic and Public Attitudes toward Environmental Regulation and the Economy." *State & Local Government Review*. 2008. Vol. 40. No. 3. 139–149.

Larsen, Elizabeth F. "NYC approves "Zone Green" text amendment to the zoning resolution." Association of Corporate Council. August 22, 2012.

Leber, Rebecca. "Happy 100th Birthday, Big Oil Tax Breaks." *Climate Progress*. March 1, 2013. Accessed April 11, 2014. http://thinkprogress. org/climate/2013/03/01/1654501/oil-subsidies-century/

Leiserowitz, Anthony A., Edward W. Maibach, Connie Roser-Renouf, Nicholas Smith and Erica Dawson. "Climategate, Public Opinion, and the Loss of Trust." *American Behavioral Scientist*. 2013. Vol. 57. No. 6. 818–837.

Leon, Warren. "CESA Report: The State of State Renewable Portfolio Standards." *Clean Energy States Alliance*. June 28, 2013. Accessed April 28, 2014. http://www.cesa.org/

Levine, Larry. "Philadelphia Gains Approval of Landmark Green Infrastructure Plan, a Model for Smart Water Practices Nationwide." NRDC Switchboard. June 1, 2011. Accessed May 9, 2014. http://switchboard. nrdc.org/

Lindseth, Gard. "The Cities for Climate Protection Campaign (CCPC) and the Framing of Local Climate Policy." *Local Environment*. 2004. Vol. 9. No. 4. 325–336.

Liptak, Adam. "Supreme Court Strikes Down Overall Political Donation Cap." *The New York Times*. April 2, 2014. http://www.nytimes.com

Litman, Todd. "Evaluating Public Transit Benefits and Costs." Victoria Transport Policy Institute. 2006. Accessed May 9, 2014. http://www.nyc.gov/

Living Cities. "New "Green Cities Report" Assesses How Key American Cities are Combating Climate Change." Press Release. May 07, 2009. Washington, DC. http://www.livingcities.org/

Locke, Richard. "Sustainability as Fabric—And Why Smart Managers Will Capitalize First." *MIT Sloan Management Review*. January 2009. 1–8.

Lockwood, Matthew. "The political sustainability of climate policy: The case of the UK Climate Change Act." *Global Environmental Change*. 2013. Vol. 23. 1339–1348.

Loewentheil, Nathaniel. "The Past and Future Politics of U.S. Environmental Reforms." *Yale University, Scholars Strategy Network*. 2013. Accessed March 21, 2014.

Lorenzoni, Irene and Nick F. Pidgeon. "Public views on climate change: European and USA perspectives." *Climatic Change*. 2006. Vol. 77. 73–95.

Lubber, Mindy S. "Short-Term Strategies Don't Work for Wall Street or the Planet." *Harvard Business Review*. September 24, 2008. Accessed April 7, 2014. http://blogs.hbr.org/

Lundin, Barbara Vergetis. "PA investing $60M in water infrastructure." *Fierce Energy*. January 23, 2014. Accessed April 28, 2014. http://www .fierceenergy.com/

Lydenberg, Steve, Jean Rogers, and David Wood. "From Transparency to Performance: Industry-Based Sustainability Reporting on Key Issues." The Hauser Center for Nonprofit Organizations, Harvard University. June 2010. Accessed March 1, 2014. http://www.hks.harvard.edu/ centers/hauser

MacDonald, Paul. "Webberville solar project in Texas means megawatts." *Energy Alternative Sources Magazine*. July/August 2012. http://www .altenerg.com/

Mann, Thomas E. and Rafaela Wakeman. "Growing Gridlock in Congress: An Interactive Graphic." *The Brookings Institution*. November 25, 2013. Accessed March 27, 2014 http://www.brookings.edu/

Maryland Department of the Environment. "States Adopting California's Clean Cars Standards." Accessed April 30, 2014. http://mde.maryland .gov/programs/Air/MobileSources/CleanCars/Pages/states.aspx

Massachusetts Department of Transportation. "GreenDOT Policy Directive." P-10–002. 2010.

Massachusetts Department of Transportation. "GreenDOT." 2014. Accessed April 28, 2014. http://www.massdot.state.ma.us/GreenDOT.aspx

Massachusetts' Businesses for Clean Energy. "Building Energy Efficiency Standards." 2014. Accessed April 28, 2014. http://www.mabizfor cleanenergy.com/

Mayer, Audrey. "Strengths and Weaknesses of Common Sustainability Indices for Multidimensional Systems." *Environment International*. 2008. Vol. 34. 277–291.

Metropolitan Transportation Authority. "Public Transportation for the New York Region." 2013. Accessed June 13, 2014. http://web.mta.info

Moldan, Bedrich, Svatava Janouskova, and Tomas Hak. "How to Understand and Measure Environmental Sustainability: Indicators and Targets." *Ecological Indicators*. 2012. Vol. 17. 4–13.

Mooney, Chris. "Some Like It Hot." *Mother Jones*. May/June 2005. Accessed November 11, 2011. www.motherjones.com

Morris, Jackson and Jordan Stutt. "Energy Efficiency in New York: Midcourse Status Report of '15 by 15.'"Pace Energy and Climate Center, Pace Law School. October 2012.

Morrow, W. Ross, Henry Lee, Kelly Sims Gallagher, and Gustavo Collantes. "Reducing the U.S. Transportation Sector's Oil Consumption and Green House Gas Emissions." Belfer Center. Harvard University. March 2010. Accessed April 30, 2014. http://belfercenter.ksg.harvard.edu/

Moss, Mitchell L. and Carson Qing. "The Dynamic Population of Manhattan." Rudin Center for Transportation Policy and Management. March 2012. Accessed June 13, 2014. http://wagner.nyu.edu.

National Association of State Energy Officials. "NASEO Best Practices Review: Streamlined Renewable Energy Permitting Initiatives." Accessed April 28, 2014. http://www.naseo.org/data/sites/1/documents/publications/NASEO-Best-Practices-Review—Streamlined-RE-Permitting-Initiatives.pdf

National Governors Association. "State Clean Energy Actions: November 2012-June 2013 Update." NGA Paper. October 2013. Washington, D.C.

National Ocean Council. "National Ocean Policy Implementation Plan" April 2013. Accessed on April 25, 2014. http://www.whitehouse.gov

National Renewable Energy Laboratory. "Carbon Taxes: A Review of Experience and Policy Design Considerations." December 2009. Accessed March 11, 2014. http://www.nrel.gov/

National Renewable Energy Laboratory. "Feed-In Tariffs." Last Updated April 26, 2013. http://www.nrel.gov/tech_deployment/state_local_activities/basics_tariffs.html

National Research Council. "Effectiveness and Impact of Corporate Average Fuel Economy (CAFE) Standards." Washington, DC: The National Academies Press. 2002.

National Science Foundation. "Report to the National Science board on the National Science Foundation's Merit Review Process." May 2013. Accessed on April 25, 2014. https://www.nsf.gov/

Natural Resources Defense Council. "Philadelphia, Pennsylvania: A Case Study of how Green Infrastructure is Helping Manage Urban Stormwater Challenges." 2011. http://nrdc.org/

Natural Resources Defense Council. By Alisa Valderrama and Larry Levine. "Financing Stormwater Retrofits in Philadelphia and Beyond." February 2012. http://nrdc.org/

Natural Resources Defense Council. "Sustainable Communities." Accessed
     March 31, 2014. http://www.nrdc.org/sustainable-communities/
New York City Department of City Planning. "Zone Green." Accessed
     May 9, 2014. http://www.nyc.gov/html/gbee/html/codes/zone.shtml
New York City Department of Environmental Protection. "Department
     of Environmental Protection and Department of Buildings Unveil
     New Program to Streamline Approval Process for Upgrading Boilers."
     May 23, 2011. Accessed April 18, 2014. http://www.nyc.gov/
New York City Department of Environmental Protection. "NYC Green
     Infrastructure 2012 Annual Report." 2012.
New York City Department of Environmental Protection. "NYC Green
     Infrastructure Plan." Accessed May 9, 2014. http://www.nyc.gov/
     html / dep / pdf / green _ infrastructure / NYCGreenInfrastructurePlan _
     ExecutiveSummary.pdf
New York City Department of Transportation. "After First 200 Days of Citi
     Bike, NYC DOT Releases New Data Showing that Significant
     Numbers of New Yorkers are Biking, Complementing Transit System."
     Press Release. December 12, 2013. http://www.nyc.gov/
New York City Department of Transportation. "NYC Bike Share Designed
     by New Yorkers." Accessed May 9, 2014. http://www.nyc.gov/html/
     dot/downloads/pdf/bike-share-outreach-report.pdf
New York City Global Partners. "Best Practice: Green Buildings Retrofit
     Program." July 14, 2011. Accessed June 13, 2014. http://www.nyc
     .gov/
New York City Department of Health and Mental Hygiene (NYC
     DOHMH). "Air Pollution and the Health of New Yorkers: The Impact
     of Fine Particles and Ozone." 2011. Accessed May 9, 2014. http://
     www.nyc.gov/
New York City Health Department of Health and Mental Hygiene (NYC
     DOHMH). "New York City Trends in Air Pollution and its Health
     Consequences." September 26, 2013. http://www.nyc.gov/
New York City. "A Stronger, More Resilient New York." 2013. Accessed
     May 9, 2014. http://www.nyc.gov/
New York City. "The New York Community Air Survey: Results from
     Year One Monitoring 2008–2009." 2011. Accessed May 9, 2014.
     http://www.nyc.gov/

New York Power Authority (NYPA). "Governor's Energy Highway Initiative Moves Forward." Accessed April 28, 2014. http://nypa .gov/EnergyHighway/default.htm

New York State Department of Environmental Conservation (NYS DEC). "Wastewater Infrastructure Needs of New York State Report." March 2008. Accessed April 28, 2014. http://www.dec.ny.gov/

New York State Energy Research and Development Authority. "Governor Cuomo Announces NY Green Bank is Open for Business." February 11, 2014. https://www.nyserda.ny.gov/

New York State Energy Research and Development Authority. "Operating Plan for Technology and Market Development Programs (2012–2016)." Second Revision February 15, 2013a. Case 10-M-0457.

New York State Energy Research and Development Authority. "System Benefits Charge in New York: Vision for the Future." September 20, 2010. https://www.nyserda.ny.gov/

New York State Energy Research and Development Authority. "Task Force Announces Update on Progress of N.Y. Energy Highway." April 30, 2013b. https://www.nyserda.ny.gov/

New York State Public Service Commission. "System Benefits Charge." Last updated June 3, 2014. Accessed June 19, 2014. http://www3.dps. ny.gov/

New York State. "Governor Cuomo Launches New York Green Bank Initiative to Transform the State's Clean Energy Economy." September 10, 2013. Accessed April 30, 2014. http://www.governor.ny.gov/

New Zealand. Ministry for the Environment. "International Examples of Emissions Trading" November 16, 2012. Accessed on March 3, 2014. http://www.climatechange.govt.nz/

Newman, Peter. "The Environmental Impact of Cities." *Environment and Urbanization*. 2006. Vol. 18. No. 2. 275–295.

Nisbet, Matthew C. "Communicating Climate Change: Why Frames Matter for Public Engagement." *Environment*. March 2009.

NYS 2100 Commission. "Recommendations to Improve the Strength and Resilience of the Empire State's Infrastructure." Accessed May 1, 2014. http://www.governor.ny.gov/assets/documents/NYS2100.pdf

O'Connor, Claire and Dr. Juliet Christian-Smith. "Implementation of the Agricultural Water Management Planning Act." Natural Resources

Defense Council and the Pacific Institute. *NRDC Issue Paper.* August 2013. Accessed April 28, 2014. http://www.nrdc.org/water/

Office of Management and Budget. Office of the US Government "2013 Draft Report to Congress on the Benefits and Costs of Federal Regulations and Agency Compliance with the Unfunded Mandates Reform Act." 2013a. Washington, D.C. www.whitehouse.gov

Office of Management and Budget. Office of the US Government. "Budget of the United States Government, Fiscal Year 2015: Department of Energy." 2014. Accessed on April 25, 2014. http://www.whitehouse .gov/omb/budget

Office of Management and Budget. Office of the US Government. "Fiscal Year 2013 Budget of the US Government." 2013b. http://www .whitehouse.gov

Office of Science and Technology Policy. Executive Office of the President. "The President's Plan for Science and Innovation: Doubling Funding for Key Science Agencies in the 2010 Budget." 2009. http://www .whitehouse.gov

Office of Science and Technology Policy. Executive Office of the President. "The President's Plan for Science and Innovation: Doubling Funding for Key Science Agencies in the 2011 Budget." 2010. http://www. whitehouse.gov

Office of the Press Secretary. The White House. "President Obama Announces National Fuel Efficiency Policy." May 19, 2009. http:// www.whitehouse.gov/

Oregon Environmental Council. "Low-Carbon Fuels." Accessed April 20, 2014. http://www.oeconline.org/our-work/economy/low-carbon-fuels

Organisation for Economic Co-operation and Development. "OECD Estimates of R&D Expenditure Growth in 2012." January 17, 2014. www.oecd.org

Organisation for Economic Co-operation and Development. "Promoting Sustainable Consumption: Good Practices in OECD Countries." 2008. www.oecd.org

Parenti, Christian. "The Big Green Buy." *The Nation.* July 15, 2010. Accessed April 19, 2014. http://www.thenation.com/

Parris, Thomas M. and Robert W. Kates. "Characterizing and Measuring Sustainable Development." Annual Review of Environment and Resources. 2003. Vol. 28. 559–586.

Patashnik, Eric. "After the Public Interest Prevails: The Political Sustainability of Policy Reform." *Governance: An International Journal of Policy, Administration, and Institutions.* 2003. Vol. 16. No. 2. 203–234.

Pavement to Parks. "About the Pavement to Parks Program." Accessed June 16, 2014. http://pavementtoparks.sfplanning.org

The Pew Charitable Trusts. "U.S. Military Accelerates Deployment of Clean Energy Technologies." January 16, 2014. Accessed June 17, 2014. http://www.pewenvironment.org

The Pew Charitable Trusts. Clean Energy Economy. "Who's Winning the Clean Energy Race?" 2012. http://www.pewenvironment.org

Pew Research Center. "Climate Change: Key Data Points from Pew Research." January 27, 2014. Accessed March 20, 2014. http://www.pewresearch.org

Philadelphia Water Department. "Green Stormwater Infrastructure Program." 2014. Accessed May 9, 2014. http://www.phillywatersheds.org/

Pirog, Robert. "Oil and Natural Gas Industry Tax Issues in the FY2013 Budget Proposal." Congressional Research Service. Report for Congress. March 2, 2012. www.crs.gov

Pollack, Ethan. "Counting Up to Green: Assessing the Green Economy and its Implications for Growth and Equity." *Economic Policy Institute.* October 10, 2012. Accessed February 12, 2014. http://epi.org/

Powell, Lynda. "The Influence of Campaign Contributions on Legislative Policy." *The Forum: A Journal of Applied Research in Contemporary Politics.* October 2013. Vol. 11. Issue 3. 339–355.

Pulia, Michael. "Public Opinion on Environmental Issues: Does It Influence Government Action?" *Res Publica- Journal of Undergraduate Research.* 2008. 6. Issue 1. Article 8.

Quinn, Tracy. "Is California on Track to Meet its 2020 Conservation Goals?" *NRDC Switchboard.* October 11, 2012. http://switchboard.nrdc.org/blogs/

Qureshi, Murad. "Fighting Beijing's Traffic Blues." *China Daily USA.* September 26, 2013. Accessed June 17, 2014. http://usa.chinadaily.com.cn/

Raja, Raymond and Brian Schaffner. "The effects of campaign finance spending bans on electoral outcomes: Evidence from the states about the potential impact of Citizens United v. FEC." *Electoral Studies.* 2014. Vol. 33. 102–114.

Rascoe, Ayesha and Deepa Seetharaman. "U.S. Backs Off Goal of One Million Electric Cars by 2015." January 31, 2013. Accessed March 7, 2014. http://www.reuters.com/

Rayner, Steve. "What Drives Environmental Policy?" *Global Environmental Change.* 2006. Vol. 16. 4–6.

Reed, Stanley. "European Lawmakers Try to Spur Market for Carbon-Emission Credits." *New York Times.* February 6, 2014. Accessed March 2, 2014. http://www.nytimes.com/

Regional Greenhouse Gas Initiative, Inc. (RGGI). "Investment of Proceeds from RGGI CO2 Allowances." February 2011. Accessed April 28, 2014. http://www.rggi.org/

REN21. Renewable Energy Policy Network for the 21st Century. "Renewables 2012 Global Status Report." 2012. Paris: REN21 Secretariat.

Riffkin, Rebecca. "Americans' Outlook for U.S. Environmental Quality Steady." *Gallup.* March 19, 2014. Accessed April 3, 2014. http://www.gallup.com/

Rockefeller Foundation and ARUP. "City Resilience Framework." City Resilience Index. April 2014.

Rockefeller Foundation. "Building Climate Change Resilience." 2009. White Paper. 1–7.

Rosenthal, Elisabeth. "Buses May Aid Climate Battles in Poor Cities." *New York Times.* July 9, 2009. Accessed June 13, 2014. http://www.nytimes.com

Rosenthal, Elisabeth. "Carbon Taxes Make Ireland Even Greener." *New York Times.* December 27, 2012. Accessed March 12, 2014. http://www.nytimes.com

Roth, Bill. "Building Code Revision Launches California Toward Zero Net Energy Buildings." November 11, 2013. http://www.triplepundit.com

S&P Dow Jones Indices and RobeccoSAM. "Results Announced for 2013 Dow Jones Sustainability Indices Review; 24 Sustainability Industry Group Leaders Named." September 12, 2013. Accessed February 28, 2014. www.sustainability-indices.com/

Sarewitz, Daniel. "How science makes environmental controversies worse." *Environmental Science & Policy.* 2004. Vol. 7. 385–403.

Schuman, Cinthia, Lester Salamon, and Giulia Campanaro. "Nonprofit Sector and Government: Clarifying the Relationship." The Aspen

Institute Nonprofit Sector Strategy Group. 2002. http://www
.aspeninstitute.org/sites/default/files/content/docs/NPGOVERN
MENT.PDF

Sciortino, Michael, Seth Nowak, Dan York, and Martin Kushler. "Energy Efficiency Resource Standards: A Progress Report on State Experience." American Council for an Energy Efficient Economy. June 2011. http://aceee.org

Searcy, Cory. "Corporate Sustainability Performance Measurement Systems: A Review and Research Agenda." *Journal of Business Ethics*. 2012. Vol. 107. 239–253.

Securities and Exchange Commission. "SEC Issues Interpretive Guidance on Disclosure Related to Business or Legal Developments Regarding Climate Change." January 27, 2010. Accessed February 19, 2014. http://www.sec.gov/

SFpark. "About." 2014. Accessed May 9, 2014. http://sfpark.org/

SFpark. "San Francisco wins Sustainable Transport Award for SFpark, Pavement to Parks." January 25, 2012. Accessed May 9, 2014. http://sfpark.org/

Shellenberger, Michael and Ted Nordhaus. "The Death of Environmentalism." *The Heartland Institute*. 2005. http://heartland.org

Shenn, Jody. "Deutsche Bank Sells First Homeowner Energy-Efficiency Securities." *Bloomberg News*. March 6, 2014. Accessed March 13, 2014. http://www.bloomberg.com/news/

Sierra Club. "EPA Report Shows Tremendous Benefits of Clean Air Act." March 1, 2011. Accessed June 17, 2014. www.sierraclub.com

Simes, Randy A. "Cincinnati Receives Federal Approval for Innovative Green Infrastructure CSO Fix." June 10, 2013. Urban Cincy. http://www.urbancincy.com/

Simmons, Josephine. "Campaign Financing: Can the US Follow Europe's Example?" Truthout. March 25, 2014. http://truth-out.org/news/item/22660-campaign-financing-can-the-us-follow-europes-example

Singh, Rajesh Kumar, Murty, H.R., Gupta, S.K. and A.K. Dikshit. "An Overview of Sustainability Assessment Methodologies." *Ecological Indicators*. 2012. Vol. 15. 281–299.

Solar Energy Industries Association (SEIA). "Interconnection Standards." Accessed March 25, 2014a. http://www.seia.org/policy/distributed-solar/interconnection-standards

Solar Energy Industries Association (SEIA). "Solar Investment Tax Credit (ITC)." Accessed April 19, 2014b. http://www.seia.org/policy/finance-tax/solar-investment-tax-credit

Sparrow, Bartholomew H. "Who speaks for the people? The President, the Press, and Public Opinion in the United States." *Presidential Studies Quarterly*. 2008. Vol. 3. No. 4. 578–592.

State of New Jersey. Governor's Office of Recovery and Rebuilding. "Resiliency." Accessed April 30, 2014. http://www.state.nj.us/gorr/resiliency/

State of Oregon. "Fact Sheet: Oregon Low Emissions Vehicles." October 3, 2011. Accessed April 28, 2014. Department of Environmental Quality. http://www.deq.state.or.us/

Stavins, Robert and Bradley Whitehead. "Market-Based Environmental Policies." In Thinking Ecologically: The Next Generation of Environmental Policy. Marian R. Chertow and Daniel C. Etsy, eds. Yale University Press. 1997.

Stellberg, Sarah. "Assessment of Energy Efficiency Achievable from Improved Compliance with U.S. Building Energy Codes: 2013 – 2030." Institute for Market Transformation (IMT). February 2013. Accessed April 28, 2014. http://www.imt.org/

Sterman, John. [Interviewed by Michael S. Hopkins]. "A Sober Optimist's Guide to Sustainability." *MIT Sloan Management Review*. January 29, 2009. 1–6.

Steve, Jamie, Severn, Aaron and Raum, Bree. "PTC Fact Sheet for Congress." *American Wind Energy Association*. www.awea.org.

Stewart, Martina, Robert Yoon, Kevin Bohn, Paul Steinhauser, and Peter Hamby. "Super PACs' Money Could Tip Balance of Power in Congress." *CNN*. January 26, 2012. http://www.cnn.com/2012/01/26/politics/super-pac-general/

Stroker, Frank. "Democracy Rules: Why Business Thrives in Democratic Societies." *Cipe Development Blog*. June 27, 2012. http://www.cipe.org/blog/2012/06/27/democracy-rules-why-business-thrives-in-democratic-societies/#.U-ChoVYaods

Succar, Samir and Ralph Cavanagh. "The Promise of the Smart Grid: Goals Policies, and Measurement Must Support Sustainability Benefits." *Natural Resources Defense Council*. October 2012. Accessed March 3, 2014. http://www.nrdc.org/

Sustainable City. "Sustainability Plan/Introduction." Accessed April 18, 2014. http://www.sustainable-city.org/

Svara, James H. "Local Government Action to Promote Sustainability." *International City/County Management Association.* February 1, 2011. Accessed March 28, 2014. http://icma.org/

Svara, James H., Anna Read and Evelina Moulder. "Breaking New Ground: Promoting Environmental and Energy Programs in Local Government." 2011. IBM Center for Business of Government. Conserving Energy and the Environment Series.

Svara, James, Tanya C. Watt and Hee Soun Jang. "How are US Cities doing sustainability? Who is getting on the sustainability train and why?" *Cityscape.* 2013. Vol. 15. No. 1. 9–44.

Swift, Art. "Americans Again Pick Environment Over Economic Growth." *Gallup.* March 20, 2014. Accessed April 3, 2014. http://www.gallup.com/

Székely, Francisco and Marianna Knirsch. "Responsible Leadership and Corporate Social Responsibility: Metrics for Sustainable Performance." *European Management Journal.* 2005. Vol. 23. Issue 6. 628–647.

Tanzil, Dicksen and Beth R. Beloff. "Assessing Impacts: Overview on Sustainability Indicators and Metrics." *Environmental Quality Management.* 2006. Vol. 15. Issue 4. 41–56.

Thomas Reuters. "Thomas Reuters Point Carbon Lowers California Carbon Price Forecast by Two Thirds." September 10, 2013. www.thomasreuters.com

Thompson, Adrienne. "All Eyes on Connecticut: Microgrid Pilot Program Gets Underway." Worldwatch Institute. August 13, 2013. Accessed April 30, 2014. http://blogs.worldwatch.org/

Tomain, Joseph and Sidney Shapiro. "Regulation and Democracy." RedBlog: Penn Program on Regulation. March 24, 2014. http://www.regblog.org/2014/03/24-tomain-shapiro-regulation-democracy.html

Trabish, Herman K. "Solar's Faceoff: Feed In Tariff Versus Net Energy Metering." *The Energy Collective.* January 13, 2014. Accessed March 12, 2014. http://theenergycollective.com/

Transport for London. "Penalties & Enforcement." Accessed June 17, 2014. https://www.tfl.gov.uk/modes/driving/congestion-charge/penalties-and-enforcement

Transportation & Climate Initiative. "Northeast Electric Vehicle Network." Accessed April 30, 2014. http://www.transportationandclimate.org/content/northeast-electric-vehicle-network

Transportation Alternatives. "Fair Tolling: International Examples." 2013. Accessed June 16, 2014. http://transalt.org

TransportPolicy.net. "California: Light –duty: Emissions." Last updated September 12, 2013. Accessed April 28, 2014. http://transportpolicy.net/index.php?title=California:_Light-duty:_Emissions

Tweed, Katherine. "PACE on a Rolle: $43M and Counting." *Green Tech Media*. October 30, 2013. Accessed April 28, 2014. http://www.greentechmedia.com/

Umberger, Allyson. "Distributed Generation: How Localized Energy Production Reduces Vulnerability to Outages and Environmental Damage in the Wake of Climate Change." *Golden Gate University Environmental Law Journal*. 2012. Vol. 6. Issue 1. Symposium Issue: The City As Habitat: A Place for Urban Wildlands. Article 10.

Union of Concerned Scientists. "Existing Cap-and-Trade Programs to Cut Global Warming Emissions." November 9, 2007. Accessed April 28, 2014. http://www.ucsusa.org/

Union of Concerned Scientists. "Fuel Economy Basics." August 23, 2012. Accessed June 17, 2014. http://www.ucsusa.org/

Union of Concerned Scientists. "Production Tax Credit for Renewable Energy." January 31, 2014. Accessed March 14, 2014. http://www.ucsusa.org/

Union of Concerned Scientists. "The IPCC: Who Are They and Why Do Their Climate Reports Matter?" January 29, 2007. Accessed April 2, 2014. http://www.ucsusa.org/

United Kingdom. "The Companies Act 2006 (Strategic Report and Directors' Report) Regulations 2013." 2013. Accessed February 18, 2014. http://www.legislation.gov.uk/

United Nations Development Program and The Global Environment Facility Small Grants Programme. "Environmentally Sustainable Transport and Climate Change." November 2006.

United Nations Environment Programme. "About GEI: What is the 'Green Economy?" Accessed February 12, 2014. http://www.unep.org/greeneconomy/

United Nations Environment Programme. "Enabling conditions: supporting the transition to a global green economy." 2011. http://www.unep.org/

United Nations Environment Programme. "Framework of Global Partnership on Waste Management." Note by the Secretariat. November 2010. http://www.unep.org/

United Nations Environment Programme. "New Global Sustainable Public Procurement Initiative Harnesses Power of Public Spending to Fast-track Green Economy Transition." June 20, 2012. Accessed April 19, 2014. http://www.unep.org/

United Nations Environment Programme. "Reforming Energy Subsidies." 2008. Division of Technology, Industry and Economics. http://www.unep.org/

United Nations Environment Programme, International Labour Organization, International Organization of Employers, International Trade Union Confederation, and Worldwatch Institute. "Green Jobs: Towards Decent Work in a Sustainable, Low-Carbon World." 2008. Accessed February 12, 2014. http://ilo.org/

United Nations Habitat for a Better Urban Future. "New Global Collaboration for Urban Resilience Announced at WUF7." April 11, 2014. Accessed April 25, 2014. http://wuf7.unhabitat.org/

United States Census Bureau. Department of Commerce. "U.S. and World Population Clock." 2014. Accessed April 9, 2014. https://www.census.gov/popclock/

United States Census Bureau. Housing and Household Economic Statistics Division. "Historical Census of Housing Tables." Last revised October 31, 2011. Accessed January 15, 2014. http://www.census.gov/hhes/www/housing/census/historic/owner.html

United States Congress Joint Economic Committee. Prepared by the Majority Staff. "The Pivotal Role of Government Investment in Basic Research." May 2010.

United States Department of Energy. "Austin Energy Wins DOE Wind Power Award." October 25, 2005. http://www.windpoweringamerica.gov/

United States Department of Energy. "California Laws and Incentives for Air Quality/Emissions." Energy Efficiency and Renewable Energy. Last

Updated November 12, 2013. Accessed June 29, 2014. www.afdc
.energy.gov

United States Department of Energy. "Energy Efficiency Trends in Residential and Commercial Buildings." October 2008. Accessed April 28,
2014. http://apps1.eere.energy.gov/

United States Department of Energy. "President's 2015 Budget Proposal
Makes Critical Investments in All-of-the-Above Energy Strategy and
National Security." March 4, 2014. Accessed April 24, 2014. http://
www.energy.gov/

United States Department of Transportation. Federal Transit Administration. "Transit's Role in Environmental Sustainability. Accessed April 18,
2014. http://www.fta.dot.gov/13835_8514.html

United States District Court. Northern District of California. "Case4:10-cv-
03084-CW Document194." August 9, 2012. Accessed April 28, 2014.
http://oag.ca.gov/sites/

United States. Department of Defense and Department of the Interior.
"MoU between The Department of Defense and The Department of
the Interior on Renewable Energy and a Renewable Energy Partnership
Plan." 2012.

United States. Department of Defense. "Quadrennial Defense Review
2014." 2014. http://www.defense.gov/pubs/2014_Quadrennial_Defense_
Review.pdf

United States. Department of Defense. "Strategic Sustainability Performance
Plan: FY 2012." September 2012.

United States. Department of Labor. Bureau of Labor Statistics. "Employment in Green Goods and Services – 2010." News Release. March 22,
2012a. http://www.bls.gov/

United States. Department of Labor. Bureau of Labor Statistics. "Measuring Green Jobs." 2012b. Accessed February 12, 2014. http://www.bls
.gov/

United States. Department of Labor. Bureau of Labor Statistics. "Green
Goods and Services Occupations (GGS-OCC)" October 10, 2012c.
Accessed February 12, 2014. http://www.bls.gov/

United States. Department of Labor. Bureau of Labor Statistics.
"Occupational Employment and Wages in Green Goods and Services
– November 2011: News Release." November 9, 2012d. Accessed
February 12, 2014. http://www.bls.gov/bls/

United States Water Alliance. "United States Water Prize." 2014. Accessed May 9, 2014. http://www.uswateralliance.org/

Unruh, Gregory. "Leading the Sustainability Insurgency." *MIT Sloan Management Review*. 2014.

Urban Green Council. U.S. Green Building Council. "NYC Green Codes Task Force." 2014. Accessed April 16, 2014. http://www.urban greencouncil.org/greencodes

Urban Land Institute. "Mayor Bloomberg Unveils Plan to Create a Stronger, More Resilient New York." June 12, 2013. Accessed April 25, 2014. New York. http://newyork.uli.org/

Urban Sustainability Directors Network. "About Us." 2014. Accessed May 9, 2014. http://usdn.org/

Urbanization Knowledge Partnership. "City Solution: Bus Rapid Transit for Urban Transport." Accessed May 1, 2014. www.urbanknowledge.org

Walker, Leslie Z. "US EPA Grants California Waiver to of Clean Air Act Preemption to Enforce Greenhouse Gas Emission Standards." Abbott & Kindermann LLP. July 8, 2009. http://blog.aklandlaw.com/

Walsh, Jason and Kate Gordon. "Taking Action on Clean Energy and Climate Protection in 2012: Menu of Effective and Feasible Solutions." *Center for American Progress*. April 2012. Accessed March 14, 2014. http://www.americanprogress.org

Wang, Hua and David Bernell. "Environmental Disclosure in China: An Examination of the Green Securities Policy." *The Journal of Environment Development*. 2013. Vol. 22. 339–369.

Washington State Energy Office. "Streamlining Local Government Project Review and Permitting of Renewable Energy Facilities and Infill Development." Department of Commerce Growth Management Services. October 14, 2011. Accessed April 28, 2014. http://www .commerce.wa.gov/

Welna, David. "Congress Is On Pace to be the Least Productive Ever." *National Public Radio*. December 24, 2013. Accessed March 27, 2014. http://www.npr.org

Welton, Shelley. "Regulating Imports Into RGGI: Toward a Legal, Workable Solution." *Columbia Center for Climate Change Law Blog*. August 21, 2013. Accessed April 28, 2014. http://blogs.law.columbia.edu/

Western Climate Initiative, Inc. Accessed April 28, 2014. http://www.wci-inc.org/

White, Adam J. "Infrastructure Policy: Lessons from American History." *The New Atlantis*. 2012. No. 35. 3–31.

White House Council on Environmental Quality. "Federal Leadership in Environmental, Energy and Economic Performance—EXECUTIVE ORDER 13514." 2009. Accessed April 17, 2014. http://www.whitehouse.gov/

Williams, Alex. "That Buzz in Your Ear May Be Green Noise." *The New York Times*. June 15, 2008. http://www.nytimes.com

Wolk, Lois. "Senate Bill 43 Offsite Renewable Energy Self-Generation." California State Senate. Accessed April 28, 2014. http://www.cleanpath.com/sites/default/files/pdfs/news/12.4.12%20SB%2043%20FACT%20SHEET%20FINAL.pdf

World Commission on Environment and Development. "Our Common Future." Oxford: Oxford University Press. United Nations. 1987.

World Economic Forum. Prepared in collaboration with Oliver Wyman. "Infrastructure Investment Policy Blueprint." February 2014. 1–44. www.weforum.org

World Future Council. "Unleashing renewable energy power in developing countries." November 2009. Hamburg, Germany. www.worldfuturecouncil.org

World Health Organization. "Urban Population Growth." 2014. Accessed March 7, 2014. http://www.who.int/

Wray-Lake, Laura, Constance A. Flanagan, and D. Wayne Osgood. "Examining Trends in Adolescent Environmental Attitudes, Beliefs and Behaviors Across Three Decades." *Environmental Behavior*. 2010. Vol. 42. No. 1. 61–85.

WXY Architecture + Urban Design, New York State Energy Research and Development Authority, and Transportation & Climate Initiative. "Creating EV-Ready Towns and Cities: A Guide to Planning and Policy Tools." 2012.

Yeager, David Scott, Samuel B. Larson, Jon A. Krosnick and Trevor Tompson. "Measuring Americans' Issue Priorities a New Version of the Most Important Problem Question Reveals More Concern About Global Warming and the Environment." *Public Opinion Quarterly*. 2011. Vol. 75. No. 1. 125–138.

Yglesias, Matthew. "Beyond Mother Nature." *The New York Times Book Review*. January 28, 2014. http://www.nytimes.com

Yim, Sascha. "Arizona's Net Metering Battle Resolved, With Modest Fee Added for Solar." *Columbia Center for Climate Change Law Blog.* November 27, 2013. Accessed April 29, 2014. http://blogs.law .columbia.edu/

Zborel, Tammy. "Sustainable Connections: Strategies to Support Local Economies." National League of Cities Municipal Action Guide. 2011. Washington, DC.

Zeller, Tom. "Solar Firms Frustrated by Permits." *New York Times.* January 19 2011. Accessed April 14, 2014. http://www.nytimes.com/

Zhang, Fan. "How Fit are Feed-in Tariff Policies? Evidence from the European Wind Market." The World Bank, Europe and Central Asia Region, Office of the Chief Economist. Policy Research Working Paper 6376. February 2013. Accessed April 28, 2014. http://econ .worldbank.org/

Zhu, Charles and Nick Nigro. "Plug-In Electric Vehicles Deployment in the Northeast." *Georgetown Climate Center.* September 2012. Accessed April 28, 2014. http://www.transportationandclimate.org/

# About the Authors

**Steven Cohen** is the executive director and chief operating officer of the Earth Institute, and professor in the practice of public affairs at Columbia University. He is the director of the Master of Science in Sustainability Management Program at Columbia's School of Continuing Education and director of the Master of Public Administration in Environmental Science and Policy Program and the Executive Master of Public Administration's Environmental Policy and Sustainability Management Concentration at the School of International and Public Affairs (SIPA), also at Columbia University. He is also the director of the Research Program on Sustainability Policy and Management. From 2002 to 2006 he also directed the Office of Educational Programs at the Earth Institute. He served as the director of the Executive Master of Public Administration Program at SIPA from 2001 to 2005 and of Columbia's Graduate Program in Public Policy and Administration from 1985 to 1998. From 1987 to 1998, he was associate dean for Faculty at SIPA, and from 1998 to 2001, he was the school's vice dean.

He is a 1970 graduate of James Madison High School in Brooklyn, New York ("Education is the true foundation of civil liberty"). Cohen received his B.A. (1974) in political science from Franklin College of Indiana and his M.A. (1977) and Ph.D. (1979) in political science from the State University of New York in Buffalo. Cohen served as a policy analyst in the U.S. Environmental Protection Agency (EPA) (1977–1978 and 1980–1981) and as a consultant to the EPA (1981–1991, 1992–1997, and 2004–2007).

He is the author of Sustainability Management (2011), Understanding Environmental Policy (2006, 2014), and the first edition of The Effective Public Manager (1988). He has coauthored The Responsible Contract

Manager (2008), four subsequent editions of The Effective Public Manager (1995, 2002, 2008, 2013), Environmental Regulation Through Strategic Planning (1991), Total Quality Management in Government (1993), Tools for Innovators (1998), and Strategic Planning in Environmental Regulation (2005). Dr. Cohen is also a regular contributor to The Huffington Post.

**William Eimicke** is a professor in the practice of international and public Affairs and the founding director of the Picker Center for Executive Education at Columbia University's School of International and Public Affairs, where he has taught numerous courses in public management, policy implementation, and government innovation, as well as run professional training programs in public management. Eimicke served as the deputy fire commissioner for Strategic Planning and Policy from 2007 through the spring of 2010. He led numerous innovations to reduce response time to fires, establish a computerized risk-based inspection program, and provide advanced management training for senior Fire and EMS officers. The FDNY Officers Management Institute (FOMI) was designated as a Top 50 Innovations in American Government for 2008 and 2009 by the Kennedy School of Government.

He received his B.A. (1970) in political science, his M.P.A. (1971), and his Ph.D. (1973), also in political science, from Syracuse University. Eimicke was director of housing for the state of New York (1985–1988); deputy secretary to the governor of New York (1983–1985); deputy commissioner of the New York City Department of Housing, Preservation, and Development (1980–1982)); and assistant director of the New York City Office of Management and Budget (1979–1980). In 1993, he served on Vice President Al Gore's National Performance Review, which sought to "reinvent" the federal government. He has coauthored with Steven Cohen The Responsible Contract Manager (2008), four editions of The Effective Public Manager (1995, 2002, 2008, 2013) and Tools for Innovators (1998). He is also the author of Public Administration in a Democratic Context (1973) and numerous articles on critical public policy and management issues.

**Alison Miller** is deputy executive director of the Earth Institute, Columbia University, where she has worked since 2011. She is also the associate director of the Research Program on Sustainability Policy and Management at the Earth Institute. From 2007–2010, Miller worked as a business development and investor relations associate for an asset management firm, where she worked with institutional clients and consultants. She has previously worked with New York City's Division of Energy Management, providing project management support for energy efficiency projects. Miller has also worked as a consultant to the New York Mayor's Office of Long-Term Planning and Sustainability, where she evaluated and advised on electric vehicle policy. She has co-authored papers and studies on climate policy, sustainability, and management and policy analysis.

Miller received her M.P.A. (2011) in Environmental Science and Policy at Columbia University's School of International and Public Affairs, and her B.A. (2005) in Economics and International Relations from the University of Delaware.

# Index